ROWAN

—— EST 1978 ——

Summerlite
Horizons

A Collection of 15 designs by
Lisa Richardson, Martin Storey,
ARNE & CARLOS, Sasha Kagan
& Georgia Farrell

—— Anemone ——

by Lisa Richardson

Pattern 36
Anleitung 72

Silver Moony

by Martin Storey

Pattern 60
Anleitung 96

Archer

by Lisa Richardson

Pattern 37
Anleitung 73

Kittiwake

by ARNE & CARLOS

Pattern 49
Anleitung 85

Tern

by Georgia Farrell

Pattern 66
Anleitung 102

Stilt

by Martin Storey

Pattern 63
Anleitung 99

—— Avocet ——

by Lisa Richardson

Pattern 43
Anleitung 79

Puffin

by Georgia Farrell

Ruff

by ARNE & CARLOS

Pattern 59
Anleitung 95

—— Cormorant ——

by Sasha Kagan

Pattern 47
Anleitung 83

Blenny

by Martin Storey

Pattern 45
Anleitung 81

Stingray

by Lisa Richardson

Pattern 64
Anleitung 100

Pipefish

by Martin Storey

Pattern 53
Anleitung 89

Redshank

by Martin Storey

Pattern 57
Anleitung 93

Lionfish

by Lisa Richardson

Pattern 51
Anleitung 87

— Summerlite 4ply —

made with egyptian cotton

9802179 100% cotton

Pure White 417	Blossom 444	Ecru 436	Sand Dune 438	Seashell 437	Duck Egg 419
Washed Linen 418	Blushes 420	Still Grey 422	Anchor Grey 446	Green Bay 445	Langoustino 440
Pepper Pot 431	Vintage Claret 443	Periwinkle 424	Buttermilk 421	Aubergine 432	Rooibos 441
Touch of Gold 439	Aqua 433	Pinched Pink 426	High Tide 428	Coral Blush 442	Navy Ink 429

Summerlite DK

made with egyptian cotton

9802191 100% cotton

White
465

Mushroom
454

Pink Powder
472

Linen
460

Plaster
452

Seashell
466

Silvery Blue
468

Pear
463

Favourite Denims
469

Steel
458

Cantaloupe
456

Mocha
451

Khaki
461

Rouge
462

Garden
471

Sailor Blue
470

Black
464

Indigo
450

Lagoon
457

Fuchsia
455

Ocean
459

Summer
453

Coral Blush
467

Anenome

Page 4

YARN
Summerlite 4ply

A	Pepper Pot	431	6	x 50gm
B	Green Bay	445	6	x 50gm
C	Seashell	437	6	x 50gm

CROCHET HOOK
3.00mm (no 11) (US C2/D3) crochet hook

TENSION
22 sts and 12 rows to 10 cm measured over treble patt using 3.00mm (US C2/D3) crochet hook.

FINISHED SIZE
Completed wrap meas 375 cm (147 in) around outer edge and is 86 cm (33¾ in) long.

CROCHET ABBREVIATIONS
ch = chain; **tr** = treble.

WRAP

Using 3.00mm (US C2/D3) crochet hook and yarn A make 11 ch.
Foundation row (RS): 1 tr into 4th ch from hook, 1 tr into each of next 7 ch, turn. 9 sts.
Joining and breaking off colours as required, work in stripe patt and shape wrap as folls:
Row 1: Using yarn B, 3 ch (counts as 1 tr), miss tr at base of 3 ch, (3 tr into next tr, 1 tr into next tr) 4 times, working tr at end of last rep into top of 3 ch at beg of previous row, turn. 17 sts.
Row 2: Using yarn C, 3 ch (counts as 1 tr), miss tr at base of 3 ch, 1 tr into next tr, (3 tr into next tr, 1 tr into each of next 3 tr) 3 times, 3 tr into next tr, 1 tr into next tr, 1 tr into top of 3 ch at beg of previous row, turn. 25 sts.
Row 3: Using yarn A, 3 ch (counts as 1 tr), miss tr at base of 3 ch, 1 tr into each of next 2 tr, (3 tr into next tr, 1 tr into each of next 5 tr) 3 times, 3 tr into next tr, 1 tr into each of next 2 tr, 1 tr into top of 3 ch at beg of previous row, turn. 33 sts.
Row 4: Using yarn B, 3 ch (counts as 1 tr), miss tr at base of 3 ch, 1 tr into each of next 3 tr, (3 tr into next tr, 1 tr into each of next 7 tr) 3 times, 3 tr into next tr, 1 tr into each of next 3 tr, 1 tr into top of 3 ch at beg of previous row, turn. 41 sts.

Row 5: Using yarn C, 3 ch (counts as 1 tr), miss tr at base of 3 ch, 1 tr into each of next 4 tr, (3 tr into next tr, 1 tr into each of next 9 tr) 3 times, 3 tr into next tr, 1 tr into each of next 4 tr, 1 tr into top of 3 ch at beg of previous row, turn. 49 sts.
Row 6: Using yarn A, 3 ch (counts as 1 tr), miss tr at base of 3 ch, 1 tr into each of next 5 tr, (3 tr into next tr, 1 tr into each of next 11 tr) 3 times, 3 tr into next tr, 1 tr into each of next 5 tr, 1 tr into top of 3 ch at beg of previous row, turn. 57 sts.
These 6 rows set stripe patt and shaping.
Now cont in stripe patt throughout, repeating 1 row in each of yarns B, C and A **and at same time** inc 8 sts as before on every row, working 1 st more before first inc at beg of rows and 1 st more after last inc at end of rows and 2 sts more between each set of increases across rows, for a further 95 rows, ending with the foll row:
Next row (WS): Using yarn C, 3 ch (counts as 1 tr), miss tr at base of 3 ch, 1 tr into each of next 100 tr, (3 tr into next tr, 1 tr into each of next 201 tr) 3 times, 3 tr into next tr, 1 tr into each of next 100 tr, 1 tr into top of 3 ch at beg of previous row. 817 sts.
Next row: Using yarn C, 3 ch (counts as 1 tr), miss tr at base of 3 ch, 1 tr into each of next 101 tr, (3 tr into next tr, 1 tr into each of next 203 tr) 3 times, 3 tr into next tr, 1 tr into each of next 101 tr, 1 tr into top of 3 ch at beg of previous row. 825 sts.
Fasten off.

MAKING UP
Press as described on the information page.
See information page for finishing instructions.

Archer •••

Page 8

SIZE

To fit bust

81-86	91-97	102-107	112-117	122-127	cm
32-34	36-38	40-42	44-46	48-50	in

Actual bust measurement of garment

90	101.5	113.5	122	134	cm
35½	40	44¾	48	52¾	in

YARN

Summerlite 4ply

A Seashell 437

2	2	2	2	3	x 50gm

B Touch of Gold 439

2	2	2	2	2	x 50gm

C Green Bay 445

1	2	2	2	2	x 50gm

D Vintage Claret 443

1	2	2	2	2	x 50gm

E Langoustino 440

1	2	2	2	2	x 50gm

CROCHET HOOK

3.00mm (no 11) (US C2/D3) crochet hook

TENSION

27 sts and 16 rows to 10 cm measured over patt using 3.00mm (US C2/D3) crochet hook.

CROCHET ABBREVIATIONS

ch = chain; **dc** = double crochet; **dc2tog** = (insert hook as indicated, yarn over hook and draw a loop through) twice, yarn over hook and draw through all 3 loops on hook; **htr** = half treble; **tr** = treble; **tr2tog** = (yarn over hook and insert hook as indicated, yarn over hook and draw a loop through, yarn over hook and draw through 2 loops on hook) twice, yarn over hook and draw through all 3 loops on hook; **tr3tog** = (yarn over hook and insert hook as indicated, yarn over hook and draw a loop through, yarn over hook and draw through 2 loops on hook) 3 times, yarn over hook and draw through all 4 loops on hook; **sp(s)** = space(s); **ss** = slip stitch; **yoh** = yarn over hook.

STRIPE SEQUENCE

Row 1: Using yarn A.
Row 2: Using yarn B.
Row 3: Using yarn C.
Row 4: Using yarn D.
Row 5: Using yarn E.
These 5 rows form stripe sequence and are repeated.

BACK

Using 3.00mm (US C2/D3) crochet hook and yarn A make 122 [138: 154: 166: 182] ch.
Foundation row (WS): 1 dc into 2nd ch from hook, *1 ch, miss 1 ch, 1 dc into next ch, rep from * to end, turn.
121 [137: 153: 165: 181] sts.
Break off yarn A and join in yarn B.
Joining in and breaking off colours as required, now work in patt as folls:
Row 1 (RS): Using yarn B, 3 ch, 1 tr into next ch sp (counts as 1 tr2tog), *1 ch, tr2tog inserting hook into same ch sp as previous st for first 'leg' and into next ch sp for second 'leg', rep from * until second 'leg' of tr2tog has been worked into last ch sp, 1 ch, tr2tog inserting hook into same ch sp as previous st for first 'leg' and into last dc for second 'leg', turn.
Row 2: Using yarn C, 1 ch (does NOT count as st), 1 dc into first st, *1 dc into next ch sp, 1 ch, miss next st, rep from * to last ch sp, 1 dc into last ch sp, 1 dc into last st, turn.
Row 3: Using yarn D, 3 ch (counts as 1 tr), tr2tog inserting hook into first st for first 'leg' and into next ch sp for second 'leg', *1 ch, tr2tog inserting hook into same ch sp as previous st for first 'leg' and into next ch sp for second 'leg', rep from * ending with second 'leg' of last tr2tog into last st, 1 tr into same st, turn.
Row 4: Using yarn E, 1 ch (does NOT count as st), 1 dc into first st, *1 ch, miss next st, 1 dc into next ch sp, rep from * working last dc into top of 3 ch at beg of previous row, turn.
These 4 rows form patt and set rows 2 to 5 of stripe sequence.
Beg with row 1 of stripe sequence and keeping stripe sequence correct throughout, cont in patt as folls:
Work 6 [6: 10: 10: 14] rows, ending with row 2 of patt and RS facing for next row.
Shape side seams
Next row (RS): 3 ch, miss first 2 sts, 1 tr into next ch sp (counts

as 1 tr2tog) − 1 st decreased, patt to end working second 'leg' of last tr2tog into last st − 1 st decreased, turn. 119 [135: 151: 163: 179] sts.

Next row: 1 ch (does NOT count as st), 1 dc into first st, ★1 dc into next ch sp, 1 ch, miss next st, rep from ★ to last ch sp, 1 dc into last ch sp, 1 dc into top of 3 ch at beg of previous row, turn.

Rep last 2 rows 3 times more. 113 [129: 145: 157: 173] sts.

Beg with row 3 of patt, work straight for 12 rows, ending with row 2 of patt and RS facing for next row.

Next row (RS): 4 ch (counts as 1 tr and 1 ch) − 1 st increased, tr2tog working first 'leg' into st at base of 4 ch and second 'leg' into next ch sp, patt until second 'leg' of last tr2tog has been worked into last st, 1 ch, 1 tr into same st − 1 st increased, turn. 115 [131: 147: 159: 175] sts.

Next row: 1 ch (does NOT count as st), 1 dc into first st, ★1 dc into next ch sp, 1 ch, miss next st, rep from ★ to last ch sp, 1 dc into last ch sp, 1 dc into 3rd of 4 ch at beg of previous row, turn.

Rep last 2 rows 3 times more. 121 [137: 153: 165: 181] sts.

Beg with row 3 of patt, work straight for 9 rows, ending with row 3 of patt and **WS** facing for next row, and after 1 row using yarn C [C: B: B: A].

(Back should meas approx 30 [30: 32.5: 32.5: 35] cm.)

Shape armholes

Keeping stripe sequence correct, cont as folls:

Next row (WS): Ss into each of first 9 [9: 13: 13: 17] sts − 9 [9: 13: 13: 17] sts decreased, 1 ch (does NOT count as st), 1 dc into next st, 1 dc into next ch sp, ★1 ch, miss next st, 1 dc into next ch sp, rep from ★ to last 10 [10: 14: 14: 18] sts, 1 dc into next st and turn, leaving last 9 [9: 13: 13: 17] sts unworked − 9 [9: 9: 13: 17] sts decreased. 103 [119: 127: 139: 147] sts.

Sizes 91-97 cm, 102-107 cm, 112-117 cm and 122-127 cm only

Next row (RS): 3 ch, miss first 2 sts, 1 tr into next ch sp (counts as 1 tr2tog) − 1 st decreased, patt to end working second 'leg' of last tr2tog into last st − 1 st decreased, turn. − [117: 125: 137: 145] sts.

Next row: 1 ch (does NOT count as st), dc2tog into first st and first ch sp − 1 st decreased, ★1 ch, miss next st, 1 dc into next st, rep from ★ to last 3 sts, 1 ch, miss next st, dc2tog into last ch sp and top of 3 ch at beg of previous row − 1 st decreased, turn. − [115: 123: 135: 143] sts.

Next row: 3 ch, miss st at base of 3 ch, 1 tr into first ch sp (counts as 1 tr2tog) − 1 st decreased, tr2tog working first 'leg' into same ch sp as previous st and second 'leg' into next ch sp, patt until second 'leg' of tr2tog has been worked into last ch sp, tr2tog working first 'leg' into same ch sp as previous st and second 'leg' into last st − 1 st decreased, turn. − [113: 121: 133: 141] sts.

Next row: 1 ch (does NOT count as st), dc2tog into first 2 sts − 1 st decreased, 1 dc into next next ch sp, ★1 ch, miss next st, 1 dc into next ch sp, rep from ★ to last 2 sts, dc2tog into last 2 sts − 1 st decreased, turn. − [111: 119: 131: 139] sts.

Rep last 4 rows once more. − [103: 111: 123: 131] sts.

All sizes

Next row: 3 ch, miss first 2 sts, 1 tr into next ch sp (counts as 1 tr2tog) − 1 st decreased, patt to end working second 'leg' of last tr2tog into last st − 1 st decreased, turn. 101 [101: 109: 121: 129] sts.

Next row: 1 ch (does NOT count as st), 1 dc into first st, ★1 dc into next ch sp, 1 ch, miss next st, rep from ★ to last ch sp, 1 dc into

last ch sp, 1 dc into top of 3 ch at beg of previous row, turn.

Rep last 2 rows 6 [2: 2: 4: 4] times more, ending with RS facing for next row. 89 [97: 105: 113: 121] sts.

Beg with row 3 of patt, cont straight in patt until armhole meas 21 [22.5: 24: 25.5: 27] cm, ending with RS facing for next row.

Fasten off.

Place markers 5 [6.5: 7.5: 9: 10] cm in from each side edge along top edge to denote back neck. (Back neck should meas approx 23 [23: 24: 24: 25] cm.)

FRONT

Left side section

Using 3.00mm (US C2/D3) crochet hook and yarn A make 5 ch.

Foundation row (RS): 1 tr into 5th ch from hook (counts as 1 tr, 1 ch and 1 tr), turn. 3 sts.

Joining in and breaking off colours as required, work in patt and shape side section as folls:

Row 1 (WS): Using yarn B, 1 ch (does NOT count as st), 1 dc into first st, 1 ch − 1 st increased, 1 dc into ch sp, 1 ch, 1 dc into 3rd of 4 ch at beg of previous row − 1 st increased, turn. 5 sts.

Row 2: Using yarn C, 4 ch (counts as 1 tr and 1 ch) − 2 sts increased, tr2tog working first 'leg' into st at base of 4 ch and second 'leg' into first ch sp, 1 ch, tr2tog working first 'leg' into same ch sp as previous st and second 'leg' into next ch sp, 1 ch, tr2tog working first 'leg' into same ch sp as previous st and second 'leg' into last st, 1 ch, 1 tr into last st − 2 sts increased, turn. 9 sts.

Row 3: Using yarn D, 1 ch (does NOT count as st), 1 dc into first st, 1 ch − 1 st increased, (1 dc into next ch sp, 1 ch, miss next st) 3 times, 1 dc into last ch sp, 1 ch, 1 dc into 3rd of 4 ch at beg of previous row − 1 st increased, turn. 11 sts.

Row 4: Using yarn E, 4 ch (counts as 1 tr and 1 ch) − 2 sts increased, tr2tog working first 'leg' into st at base of 4 ch and second 'leg' into first ch sp, (1 ch, tr2tog working first 'leg' into same ch sp as previous st and second 'leg' into next ch sp) 4 times, 1 ch, tr2tog working first 'leg' into same ch sp as previous st and second 'leg' into last st, 1 ch, 1 tr into last st − 2 sts increased, turn. 15 sts.

Row 5: Using yarn A, 1 ch (does NOT count as st), 1 dc into first st, 1 ch − 1 st increased, (1 dc into next ch sp, 1 ch, miss next st) 6 times, 1 dc into last ch sp, 1 ch, 1 dc into 3rd of 4 ch at beg of previous row − 1 st increased, turn. 17 sts.

Last 2 rows set patt and stripe sequence, with 2 sts increased at each end of every RS row and 1 st increased at each end of every WS row.

Beg with row 2 of stripe sequence and keeping stripe sequence correct as set, cont as folls:

Row 6 (RS): 4 ch (counts as 1 tr and 1 ch) − 2 sts increased, tr2tog working first 'leg' into st at base of 4 ch and second 'leg' into first ch sp, ★1 ch, tr2tog working first 'leg' into same ch sp as previous st and second 'leg' into next ch sp, rep from ★ until second 'leg' of tr2tog has been worked into last ch sp, 1 ch, tr2tog working first 'leg' into same ch sp as previous st and second 'leg' into last st, 1 ch, 1 tr into last st − 2 sts increased, turn.

Row 7: 1 ch (does NOT count as st), 1 dc into first st, 1 ch − 1 st increased, 1 dc into first ch sp, ★1 ch, miss next st, 1 dc into next ch sp, rep from ★ until dc has been worked into last ch sp, 1 ch, 1 dc into 3rd of 4 ch at beg of previous row − 1 st increased, turn.

Rep rows 6 and 7, 8 [10: 11: 13: 14] times more, then rep row 6 again, ending after 1 row using yarn E [D: A: E: B] and with **WS** facing for next row. 75 [87: 93: 105: 111] sts.

Fasten off.

Right side section

Work as given for left side section but do NOT fasten off at end of last row.

Join side sections

Next row (WS): Using yarn A [E: B: A: C], work next row of right side section as folls: 1 ch (does NOT count as st), 1 dc into first st, (1 dc into next ch sp, 1 ch, miss next st) 36 [42: 45: 51: 54] times, 1 dc into last ch sp, 1 ch, 1 dc into 3rd of 4 ch at beg of previous row, 1 ch (mark this ch with a coloured thread), then, with **WS** facing, work across last row of left side section as folls: 1 dc into first st, 1 ch, (1 dc into next ch sp, 1 ch, miss next st) 36 [42: 45: 51: 54] times, 1 dc into last ch sp, 1 dc into 3rd of 4 ch at beg of previous row, turn. 153 [177: 189: 213: 225] sts.

Beg with row 2 [1: 3: 2: 4] of stripe sequence and keeping stripe sequence correct throughout, now shape sides and centre front as folls:

Next row (RS): 4 ch (counts as 1 tr and 1 ch), tr2tog working first 'leg' into st at base of 4 ch and second 'leg' into first ch sp, (1 ch, tr2tog working first 'leg' into same ch sp as previous st and second 'leg' into next ch sp) 36 [42: 45: 51: 54] times, 1 ch, tr3tog working first 'leg' into same ch sp as previous st, second 'leg' into marked ch at centre front between two side sections, and third 'leg' into next ch sp, (1 ch, tr2tog working first 'leg into same ch sp as previous st and second 'leg' into next ch sp) 36 [42: 45: 51: 54] times, 1 ch, tr2tog working first 'leg' into same ch sp as previous st and second 'leg' into last st, 1 ch, 1 tr into last st, turn.

Next row: 1 ch (does NOT count as st), 2 dc into first st, 1 ch, 1 dc into first ch sp, (1 ch, miss next st, 1 dc into next ch sp) 35 [41: 44: 50: 53] times, 1 ch, miss next st, dc2tog into next 2 ch sps, 1 ch, miss next tr3tog at centre front, dc2tog into next 2 ch sps, (1 ch, miss next st, 1 dc into next ch sp) 35 [41: 44: 50: 53] times, 1 ch, miss last tr2tog, 1 dc into last ch sp, 1 ch, 2 dc into 3rd of 4 ch at beg of previous row, turn.

Last 2 rows set patt and shaping at sides and centre front.

Rep last 2 rows until front matches back AT SIDE SEAM EDGE to beg of armhole shaping, ending with RS facing for next row.

Place a marker at each end of last row to denote beg of armhole shaping.

Place a third marker in ch sp between the two 'dc2tog' of last row to denote centre front.

Shape armholes

Row 1 (RS): 3 ch, miss first 2 sts, tr2tog working first 'leg' into first ch sp and second 'leg' into next ch sp (counts as 1 tr3tog) − 4 sts decreased, *1 ch, tr2tog working first 'leg' into same ch sp as previous st and second 'leg' into next ch sp*, rep from * to * until second 'leg' of tr2tog has been worked into ch sp **before** marked ch sp at centre front, 1 ch, tr3tog working first 'leg' into same ch sp as previous st, second 'leg' into marked ch sp at centre front and third 'leg' into next ch sp, move centre front marker to tr3tog just worked, rep from * to * until second 'leg' of tr2tog has been worked into last-but-one ch sp, 1 ch, tr3tog working first 'leg' into same ch sp, second 'leg' into next ch sp and third 'leg' into last st − 4 sts

decreased, turn. 145 [169: 181: 205: 217] sts.

Row 2: 1 ch (does NOT count as st), 2 dc into first st, 1 ch, 1 dc into first ch sp, *1 ch, miss next st, 1 dc into next ch sp*, rep from * to * until dc has been worked into third ch sp **BEFORE** marked tr3tog at centre front, 1 ch, miss next st, dc2tog into next 2 ch sps, 1 ch, move centre front marker to ch sp just worked, miss next tr3tog at centre front, dc2tog into next 2 ch sps, rep from * to * until dc has been worked into last ch sp, 1 ch, 2 dc into last st, turn.

Rep last 2 rows 1 [3: 3: 4: 4] times more, ending with RS facing for next row. 137 [145: 157: 173: 185] sts.

Next row (RS): 3 ch (counts as 1 tr), tr2tog working first 'leg' into st at base of 3 ch and second 'leg' into first ch sp − 1 st decreased, *1 ch, tr2tog working first 'leg' into same ch sp as previous st and second 'leg' into next ch sp*, rep from * to * until second 'leg' of tr2tog has been worked into ch sp **BEFORE** marked ch sp at centre front, 1 ch, tr3tog working first 'leg' into same ch sp as previous st, second 'leg' into marked ch sp at centre front and third 'leg' into next ch sp, move centre front marker to tr3tog just worked, rep from * to * until second leg of tr2tog has been worked into last ch sp, 1 ch, tr2tog working first 'leg' into same ch sp as previous st and second 'leg' into last st, 1 tr into last st − 1 st decreased, turn. 135 [143: 155: 171: 183] sts.

Next row: 1 ch (does NOT count as st), (1 dc, 1 ch, 1 dc) into first st, *1 ch, miss next st, 1 dc into next ch sp*, rep from * to * until dc has been worked into third ch sp **BEFORE** marked tr3tog at centre front, 1 ch, miss next st, dc2tog into next 2 ch sps, 1 ch, move centre front marker to ch sp just worked, miss next tr3tog at centre front, dc2tog into next 2 ch sps, rep from * to * until dc has been worked into last ch sp, 1 ch, miss last tr2tog, (1 dc, 1 ch, 1 dc) into top of 3 ch at beg of previous row, turn.

Next row: 3 ch, 1 tr into first ch sp (counts as 1 tr2tog) − 1 st decreased, *1 ch, tr2tog working first 'leg' into same ch sp as previous st and second 'leg' into next ch sp*, rep from * to * until second 'leg' of tr2tog has been worked into ch sp **BEFORE** marked ch sp at centre front, 1 ch, tr3tog working first 'leg' into same ch sp as previous st, second 'leg' into marked ch sp at centre front and third 'leg' into next ch sp, move centre front marker to tr3tog just worked, rep from * to * until second 'leg' of tr2tog has been worked into last ch sp, 1 ch, tr2tog working first 'leg' into same ch sp as previous st and second 'leg' into last st − 1 st decreased, turn. 133 [141: 153: 169: 181] sts.

Next row: 1 ch (does NOT count as st), 2 dc into first st, 1 ch, 1 dc into first ch sp, *1 ch, miss next st, 1 dc into next ch sp*, rep from * to * until dc has been worked into third ch sp **BEFORE** marked tr3tog at centre front, 1 ch, miss next tr2tog, dc2tog into next 2 ch sps, 1 ch, move centre front marker to ch sp just worked, miss next tr3tog at centre front, dc2tog into next 2 ch sps, rep from * to * until dc has been worked into last ch sp, 1 ch, 2 dc into last st and turn, leaving 3 ch at beg of previous row unworked.

Rep last 4 rows 3 [2: 2: 3: 3] times more, ending with RS facing for next row. 121 [133: 145: 157: 169] sts.

Armhole shaping is now complete.

Cont in patt and stripe sequence, shaping centre front and sides as folls:

Next row (RS): 4 ch (counts as 1 tr and 1 ch), tr2tog working first 'leg' into st at base of 4 ch and second 'leg' into first ch sp, *1 ch, tr2tog working first 'leg' into same ch sp as previous st and second 'leg' into next ch sp*, rep from * to * until second 'leg' of tr2tog has been worked into ch sp **BEFORE** marked ch sp at centre front, 1 ch, tr3tog working first 'leg' into same ch sp, second 'leg' into marked ch sp at centre front and third 'leg' into next ch sp, move centre front marker to tr3tog just worked, rep from * to * until second 'leg' of tr2tog has been worked into last ch sp, 1 ch, tr2tog working first 'leg' into same ch sp as previous st and second 'leg' into last st, 1 ch, 1 tr into last st, turn.

Next row: 1 ch (does NOT count as st), 2 dc into first st, 1 ch, 1 dc into first ch sp, *1 ch, miss next st, 1 dc into next ch sp*, rep from * to * until dc has been worked into third ch sp **BEFORE** marked tr3tog at centre front, 1 ch, miss next st, dc2tog into next 2 ch sps, 1 ch, move centre front marker to ch sp just worked, miss next tr3tog at centre front, dc2tog into next 2 ch sps, rep from * to * until dc has been worked into last ch sp, 1 ch, 2 dc into 3rd of 4 ch at beg of previous row, turn.

These 2 rows set patt and shaping at centre front and sides.

Keeping stripe sequence correct, rep these 2 rows until armhole edge meas 19 [20.5: 22: 23.5: 25] cm, ending with RS facing for next row.

Divide for neck

Next row (RS): 4 ch (counts as 1 tr and 1 ch), tr2tog working first 'leg' into st at base of 4 ch and second 'leg' into first ch sp, (1 ch, tr2tog working first 'leg' into same ch sp as previous st and second 'leg' into next ch sp) 4 [6: 8: 10: 12] times, 1 ch, yoh, insert hook into same ch sp as previous st and draw a loop through, yoh and draw through 2 loops, yoh, insert hook into next ch sp and draw a loop through, yoh and draw through 2 loops, (yoh) twice, insert hook into next ch sp and draw a loop through, (yoh and draw through 2 loops) twice, yoh and draw through all 4 loops on hook, turn. 13 [17: 21: 25: 29] sts.

Work each side of neck separately.

Next row (WS): 1 ch (does NOT count as st), 1 dc into first st, 1 dc into first ch sp, (1 ch, miss next st, 1 dc into next ch sp) 5 [7: 9: 11: 13] times, 1 dc into 3rd of 4 ch at beg of previous row, turn.

Next row: 4 ch (counts as 1 tr and 1 ch), tr2tog working first 'leg' into st at base of 4 ch and second 'leg' into first ch sp, (1 ch, tr2tog working first 'leg' into same ch sp as previous st and second 'leg' into next ch sp) 4 [6: 8: 10: 12] times, 1 ch, tr2tog working first 'leg' into same ch sp as previous st and second 'leg' into last st, turn.

Next row: 1 ch (does NOT count as st), 1 dc into first st, 1 dc into first ch sp, (1 ch, miss next st, 1 dc into next ch sp) 2 [4: 6: 8: 10] times, 1 ch, miss next st, dc2tog into next 2 ch sps and turn, leaving rem 3 sts unworked. 8 [12: 16: 20: 24] sts.

Size 81-86 cm only

Next row (RS): 1 ch (does NOT count as st), miss first st, insert hook into first ch sp and draw a loop through, yoh, insert hook into next ch sp and draw a loop through, yoh and draw through all 4 loops on hook, 1 ch, yoh, insert hook into same ch sp as previous st and draw a loop through, yoh, insert hook into next ch sp and draw a loop through, yoh and draw through 2 loops, yoh and draw through all 4 loops on hook, 1 ch, tr2tog working first 'leg' into same ch sp as previous st and second 'leg' into last st. 5 sts.

Sizes 91-97 cm, 102-107 cm, 112-117 cm and 122-127 cm only

Next row (RS): 1 ch (does NOT count as st), miss first st, insert hook into first ch sp and draw a loop through, yoh, insert hook into next ch sp and draw a loop through, yoh and draw through all 4 loops on hook, 1 ch, yoh, insert hook into same ch sp as previous st and draw a loop through, yoh, insert hook into next ch sp and draw a loop through, yoh and draw through 2 loops, yoh and draw through all 4 loops on hook, (1 ch, tr2tog working first 'leg' into same ch sp as previous st and second 'leg' into next ch sp) − [2: 4: 6: 8] times, 1 ch, tr2tog working first 'leg' into same ch sp as previous st and second 'leg' into last st, turn. − [9: 13: 17: 21] sts.

Next row: 1 ch (does NOT count as st), 1 dc into first st, 1 dc into first ch sp, (1 ch, miss next st, 1 dc into next ch sp) − [1: 3: 5: 7] times, 1 ch, miss next st, dc2tog into next 2 ch sps and turn, leaving rem st unworked. − [6: 10: 14: 18] sts.

Size 91-97 cm only

Next row (RS): 1 ch (does NOT count as st), miss first st, insert hook into first ch sp and draw a loop through, yoh, insert hook into next ch sp and draw a loop through, yoh and draw through all 4 loops on hook, 1 ch, yoh, insert hook into same ch sp as previous st and draw a loop through, yoh, insert hook into last st and draw a loop through, yoh and draw through 2 loops, yoh and draw through all 4 loops on hook. 3 sts.

Size 102-107 cm only

Next row (RS): 1 ch (does NOT count as st), miss first st, dc2tog into first 2 ch sps, 1 ch, insert hook into same ch sp as previous st and draw a loop through, yoh, insert hook into next ch sp and draw a loop through, yoh and draw through all 4 loops on hook, 1 ch, yoh, insert hook into same ch sp as previous st and draw a loop through, yoh, insert hook into next ch sp and draw a loop through, yoh and draw through all 5 loops on hook, 1 ch, yoh, insert hook into same ch sp as previous st and draw a loop through, yoh, insert hook into last st and draw a loop through, yoh and draw through 2 loops, yoh and draw through all 4 loops on hook. 7 sts.

Size 112-117 cm only

Next row (RS): 1 ch (does NOT count as st), miss first st, dc2tog into first 2 ch sps, 1 ch, insert hook into same ch sp as previous st and draw a loop through, yoh, insert hook into next ch sp and draw a loop through, yoh and draw through all 4 loops on hook, 1 ch, yoh, insert hook into same ch sp as previous st and draw a loop through, yoh, insert hook into next ch sp and draw a loop through, yoh and draw through all 5 loops on hook, 1 ch, yoh, insert hook into same ch sp as previous st and draw a loop through, yoh, insert hook into next ch sp and draw a loop through, yoh and draw through 2 loops, yoh and draw through all 4 loops on hook, 1 ch, tr2tog working first 'leg' into same ch sp as previous st and second 'leg' into next ch sp, 1 ch, yoh, insert hook into same ch sp as previous st and draw a loop through, yoh, insert hook into next ch sp and draw a loop through, yoh and draw through 2 loops, (yoh) twice, insert hook into last st and draw a loop through, (yoh and draw through 2 loops) twice, yoh and draw through all 3 loops on hook. 11 sts.

Size 122-127 cm only

Next row (RS): 1 ch (does NOT count as st), miss first st, dc2tog into first 2 ch sps, 1 ch, dc2tog into same ch sp as previous st and next ch sp, 1 ch, insert hook into same ch sp as previous st and draw a loop through, yoh, insert hook into next ch sp and draw a loop through, yoh and draw through all 4 loops on hook, 1 ch, yoh, insert hook into same ch sp as previous st and draw a loop through, yoh, insert hook into next ch sp and draw a loop through, yoh and draw through all 5 loops on hook, 1 ch, yoh, insert hook into same ch sp as previous st and draw a loop through, yoh, insert hook into next ch sp and draw a loop through, yoh and draw through 2 loops, yoh and draw through all 4 loops on hook, (1 ch, tr2tog working first 'leg' into same ch sp as previous st and second 'leg' into next ch sp) twice, 1 ch, tr2tog working first 'leg' into same ch sp as previous st and second 'leg' into last st, turn. 15 sts.

Next row: 1 ch (does NOT count as st), 1 dc into first st, 1 dc into first ch sp, (1 ch, miss next st, 1 dc into next ch sp) 4 times, 1 ch, miss next st, dc2tog into next 2 ch sps and turn, leaving rem st unworked. 12 sts.

Next row: 1 ch (does NOT count as st), miss first st, dc2tog into first 2 ch sps, 1 ch, dc2tog into same ch sp as previous st and next ch sp, 1 ch, insert hook into same ch sp as previous st and draw a loop through, yoh, insert hook into next ch sp and draw a loop through, yoh and draw through all 4 loops on hook, 1 ch, yoh, insert hook into same ch sp as previous st and draw a loop through, yoh, insert hook into next ch sp and draw a loop through, yoh and draw through 2 loops, yoh and draw through all 4 loops on hook, 1 ch, tr2tog working first 'leg' into same ch sp as previous st and second 'leg' into last st. 9 sts.

All sizes
Fasten off.

With RS facing, miss next 45 [47: 49: 51: 53] ch sps, rejoin appropriate colour of stripe sequence into next ch sp, 4 ch (does NOT count as st), tr2tog working first 'leg' into next ch sp and second 'leg' into foll ch sp, (1 ch, tr2tog working first 'leg' into same ch sp as previous st and second 'leg' into next ch sp) 4 [6: 8: 10: 12] times, 1 ch, tr2tog working first 'leg' into same ch sp as previous st and second 'leg' into last st, 1 ch, 1 tr into last st, turn. 13 [17: 21: 25: 29] sts.

Next row (WS): 1 ch (does NOT count as st), 1 dc into first st, 1 dc into first ch sp, (1 ch, miss next st, 1 dc into next ch sp) 5 [7: 9: 11: 13] times, 1 dc into last st and turn, leaving 4 ch at beg of previous row unworked.

Next row: 3 ch, miss first 2 sts, 1 tr into next ch sp (counts as 1 tr2tog), (1 ch, tr2tog working first 'leg' into same ch sp as previous st and second 'leg' into next ch sp) 4 [6: 8: 10: 12] times, 1 ch, tr2tog working first 'leg' into same ch sp as previous st and second 'leg' into last st, 1 ch, 1 tr into last st, turn.

Next row: Ss across and into first tr2tog, 1 ch (does NOT count as st), dc2tog into next 2 ch sps, (1 ch, miss next st, 1 dc into next ch sp) 3 [5: 7: 9: 11] times, 1 dc into last st and turn, leaving 3 ch at beg of previous row unworked. 8 [12: 16: 20: 24] sts.

Size 81–86 cm only
Next row (RS): 3 ch, miss first 2 sts, 1 tr into first ch sp (counts as 1 tr2tog), 1 ch, yoh, insert hook into same ch sp as previous st and draw a loop through, yoh and draw through 2 loops, yoh, insert hook into next ch sp, yoh and draw a loop through, yoh and draw through all 4 loops on hook, 1 ch, yoh, insert hook into same ch sp as previous st and draw a loop through, insert hook into next ch sp and draw a loop through, yoh and draw through all 4 loops on hook. 5 sts.

Sizes 91–97 cm, 102–107 cm, 112–117 cm and 122–127 cm only
Next row (RS): 3 ch, miss first 2 sts, 1 tr into first ch sp (counts as 1 tr2tog), (1 ch, tr2tog working first 'leg' into same ch sp as previous st and second 'leg' into next ch sp) – [2: 4: 6: 8] times, 1 ch, yoh, insert hook into same ch sp as previous st and draw a loop through, yoh and draw through 2 loops, yoh, insert hook into next ch sp, yoh and draw a loop through, yoh and draw through all 4 loops on hook, 1 ch, yoh, insert hook into same ch sp as previous st and draw a loop through, insert hook into next ch sp and draw a loop through, yoh and draw through all 4 loops on hook and turn, leaving rem st unworked. – [9: 13: 17: 21 sts].

Next row: 1 ch (does NOT count as st), miss first st, dc2tog into first 2 ch sps, (1 ch, miss next st, 1 dc into next ch sp) – [2: 4: 6: 8] times, 1 dc into last st, turn. – [6: 10: 14: 18] sts.

Size 91–97 cm only
Next row (RS): 3 ch (does NOT count as st), miss first 2 sts, 1 htr into first ch sp, 1 ch, yoh, insert hook into same ch sp as previous st and draw a loop through, insert hook into next ch sp and draw a loop through, yoh and draw through all 4 loops on hook, leave rem st unworked. 3 sts.

Size 102–107 cm only
Next row (RS): 3 ch (does NOT count as st), miss first 2 sts, 1 htr into first ch sp, 1 ch, yoh, insert hook into same ch sp as previous st and draw a loop through, yoh, insert hook into next ch sp and draw a loop through, yoh and draw through all 5 loops on hook, 1 ch, yoh, insert hook into same ch sp as previous st and draw a loop through, insert hook into next ch sp and draw a loop through, yoh and draw through all 4 loops on hook, 1 ch, dc2tog into same ch sp as previous st and next ch sp, leaving rem st unworked. 7 sts.

Size 112–117 cm only
Next row (RS): 4 ch (does NOT count as st), miss first 2 sts, 1 tr into first ch sp, 1 ch, tr2tog working first 'leg' into same ch sp as previous st and second 'leg' into next ch sp, 1 ch, yoh, insert hook into same ch sp as previous st and draw a loop through, yoh and draw through 2 loops, yoh, insert hook into next ch sp and draw a loop through, yoh and draw through all 4 loops on hook, 1 ch, yoh, insert hook into same ch sp as previous st and draw a loop through, yoh, insert hook into next ch sp and draw a loop through, yoh and draw through all 5 loops on hook, 1 ch, yoh, insert hook into same ch sp as previous st and draw a loop through, insert hook into next ch sp and draw a loop through, yoh and draw through all 4 loops on hook, 1 ch, dc2tog into same ch sp as previous st and next ch sp, leaving rem st unworked. 11 sts.

Size 122–127 cm only
Next row (RS): 3 ch, miss first 2 sts, 1 tr into next ch sp (counts as 1 tr2tog), (1 ch, tr2tog working first 'leg' into same ch sp as previous st and second 'leg' into next ch sp) twice, 1 ch, yoh, insert hook into same ch sp as previous st and draw a loop through, yoh and draw through 2 loops, yoh, insert hook into next ch sp and draw a loop through, yoh and draw through all 4 loops on hook, 1 ch, yoh, insert hook into same ch sp as previous st and draw a loop through, yoh, insert hook into next ch sp and draw a loop through, yoh and draw through all 5 loops on hook, 1 ch, yoh, insert hook into same ch sp as previous st and draw a loop through, insert hook into next ch sp and draw a loop through, yoh and draw through all 4 loops on

41

hook, (1 ch, dc2tog into next 2 ch sps) twice and turn, leaving rem st unworked. 15 sts.

Next row: 1 ch (does NOT count as st), miss first st, dc2tog into first 2 ch sps, (1 ch, miss next st, 1 dc into next ch sp) 5 times, 1 dc into last st, turn. 12 sts.

Next row: 3 ch, miss first 2 sts, 1 tr into next ch sp (counts as 1 tr2tog), 1 ch, yoh, insert hook into same ch sp as previous st and draw a loop through, yoh and draw through 2 loops, yoh, insert hook into next ch sp and draw a loop through, yoh and draw through all 4 loops on hook, 1 ch, yoh, insert hook into same ch sp as previous st and draw a loop through, insert hook into next ch sp and draw a loop through, yoh and draw through all 4 loops on hook, (1 ch, dc2tog into next 2 ch sps) twice and leave rem st unworked. 9 sts.

All sizes
Fasten off.

MAKING UP
Press as described on the information page.
Join both shoulder seams.
Neck edging
With RS facing and using 3.00mm (US C2/D3) crochet hook and

yarn A, attach yarn at left shoulder seam, 1 ch (does NOT count as st), then work in dc evenly around entire neck edge, ss to first dc, do NOT turn.

Next round (RS): 1 ch (does NOT count as st), then working from LEFT TO RIGHT instead of right to left, work 1 dc into each dc of previous round, ss to first dc.

Fasten off.★★
Join side seams.
Armhole edgings (both alike)
With RS facing and using 3.00mm (US C2/D3) crochet hook and yarn A, attach yarn at top of side seam, 1 ch (does NOT count as st), then work in dc evenly around entire armhole edge, ss to first dc, do NOT turn.

Complete as given for neck edging.
Lower edging
With RS facing and using 3.00mm (US C2/D3) crochet hook and yarn A, attach yarn at base of left side seam, 1 ch (does NOT count as st), then work 1 dc into each st across entire lower edge, ss to first dc, do NOT turn.

Complete as given for neck edging.
See information page for finishing instructions.

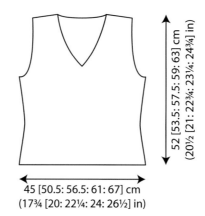

52 [53.5: 57.5: 59: 63] cm
(20½ [21: 22¾: 23¼: 24¾] in)

45 [50.5: 56.5: 61: 67] cm
(17¾ [20: 22¼: 24: 26½] in)

Avocet ••

Page 16

SIZE

To fit bust

81-86	91-97	102-107	112-117	122-127	cm
32-34	36-38	40-42	44-46	48-50	in

Actual bust measurement of garment

94	106	117	128	139	cm
37	41¾	46	50½	54¾	in

YARN

Summerlite DK

A Khaki 461

10	11	13	14	15	x 50gm

B Linen 460

1	1	1	1	1	x 50gm

NEEDLES

1 pair 3¼mm (no 10) (US 3) needles
1 pair 3¾mm (no 9) (US 5) needles

CROCHET HOOK

3.00mm (no 11) (US C2/D3) crochet hook

TENSION

22 sts and 30 rows to 10 cm measured over st st using 3¾mm (US 5) needles.

BACK

Using 3¼mm (US 3) needles and yarn A cast on 110 [124: 136: 148: 160] sts.
Row 1 (RS): K0 [0: 1: 0: 1], P2 [1: 2: 1: 2], ★K2, P2, rep from ★ to last 0 [3: 1: 3: 1] sts, K0 [2: 1: 2: 1], P0 [1: 0: 1: 0].
Row 2: P0 [0: 1: 0: 1], K2 [1: 2: 1: 2], ★P2, K2, rep from ★ to last 0 [3: 1: 3: 1] sts, P0 [2: 1: 2: 1], K0 [1: 0: 1: 0].
These 2 rows form rib.
Work in rib for a further 27 rows, ending with **WS** facing for next row.
Row 30 (WS): Work 2tog, (rib 52 [59: 65: 71: 77], work 2tog) twice. 107 [121: 133: 145: 157] sts.
Change to 3¾mm (US 5) needles.
Beg with a K row, now work in st st throughout as folls:
Cont straight until back meas 20 [20.5: 21: 21.5: 22] cm, ending with RS facing for next row.

Next row (RS): K2, sl 1, K1, psso, K to last 4 sts, K2tog, K2.
Working all side seam decreases as set by last row, dec 1 st at each end of 10th and foll 10th row, then on 3 foll 8th rows. 95 [109: 121: 133: 145] sts.
Work 15 rows, ending with RS facing for next row.
Next row (RS): K3, M1, K to last 3 sts, M1, K1.
Working all side seam increases as set by last row, inc 1 st at each end of 10th and foll 10th row, then on foll 12th row. 103 [117: 129: 141: 153] sts.
Work 13 rows, ending with RS facing for next row.
Shape armholes
Cast off 4 [5: 6: 7: 8] sts at beg of next 2 rows. 95 [107: 117: 127: 137] sts.
Next row (RS): K2, sl 1, K1, psso, K to last 4 sts, K2tog, K2.
Next row: P2, P2tog, P to last 4 sts, P2tog tbl, P2.
Working all armhole decreases as set by last 2 rows, dec 1 st at each end of next 3 [7: 9: 9: 9] rows, then on foll 5 [5: 5: 6: 7] alt rows. 75 [79: 85: 93: 101] sts.
Cont straight until armhole meas 20 [21.5: 23: 24.5: 26] cm, ending with RS facing for next row.
Shape shoulders
Cast off 5 [6: 6: 7: 8] sts at beg of next 6 rows, then 6 [5: 7: 8: 8] sts at beg of foll 2 rows. 33 [33: 35: 35: 37] sts.
Back neckband
Change to 3¼mm (US 3) needles.
Next row (RS): K1, ★P1, K1, rep from ★ to end.
Next row: P1, ★K1, P1, rep from ★ to end.
Cast off in rib.

FRONT

Using 3¼mm (US 3) needles and yarn A cast on 108 [122: 134: 146: 158] sts.
Row 1 (RS): K0 [0: 1: 0: 1], P2 [1: 2: 1: 2], (K2, P2) 11 [13: 14: 16: 17] times, (K2tog, yfwd, yrn, sl 1, K1, psso) 4 times, (P2, K2) 11 [13: 14: 16: 17] times, P2 [1: 2: 1: 2], K0 [0: 1: 0: 1].
Row 2: P0 [0: 1: 0: 1], K2 [1: 2: 1: 2], (P2, K2) 11 [13: 14: 16: 17] times, (P1, P into front and back of yfwd, yrn of previous row, P1) 4 times, (K2, P2) 11 [13: 14: 16: 17] times, K2 [1: 2: 1: 2], P0 [0: 1: 0: 1].
These 2 rows form patt - centre eyelet panel of 16 sts with rib at each side.
Work in patt for a further 28 rows, dec 1 st at each end of last row

and ending with RS facing for next row. 106 [120: 132: 144: 156] sts.
Change to 3¾mm (US 5) needles.
Now work in patt as folls:
Row 1 (RS): K45 [52: 58: 64: 70], (K2tog, yfwd, yrn, sl 1, K1, psso) 4 times, K45 [52: 58: 64: 70].
Row 2: P45 [52: 58: 64: 70], (P1, P into front and back of yfwd, yrn of previous row, P1) 4 times, P45 [52: 58: 64: 70].
These 2 rows form patt – centre eyelet panel of 16 sts with st st at each side.
Cont in patt until front meas 20 [20.5: 21: 21.5: 22] cm, ending with RS facing for next row.
Keeping patt correct and working all side seam decreases in same way as back side seam decreases, dec 1 st at each end of next and 2 foll 10th rows, then on 3 foll 8th rows. 94 [108: 120: 132: 144] sts.
Work 15 rows, ending with RS facing for next row.
Working all side seam increases in same way as back side seam increases, inc 1 st at each end of next and 2 foll 10th rows.
100 [114: 126: 138: 150] sts.
Work 11 rows, ending with RS facing for next row.
Divide for front neck
Next row (RS): K3, M1, K37 [44: 50: 56: 62], K2tog, patt 8 sts, cast on 1 st and turn, leaving rem sts on a holder.
Work each side of neck separately and cont on these 51 [58: 64: 70: 76] sts for first side of neck as folls:
Next row: K1, patt 8 sts, P to end.
Next row: K to last 9 sts, patt 8 sts, K1.
Next row: K1, patt 8 sts, P to end.
Next row (RS): K to last 11 sts, K2tog, patt 8 sts, K1.
These 4 rows set neck decreases 9 sts in from end of dec row with a K st at neck edge on every row.
Rep last 4 rows twice more, then first of these 4 rows again, ending with RS facing for next row. 48 [55: 61: 67: 73] sts.
Shape armhole
Keeping patt correct, cast off 4 [5: 6: 7: 8] sts at beg of next row. 44 [50: 55: 60: 65] sts.
Work 1 row.
Working armhole decreases in same way as back armhole decreases, dec 1 st at armhole edge of next 5 [9: 11: 11: 11] rows, then on foll 5 [5: 5: 6: 7] alt rows **and at same time** dec 1 st inside neck edge as before on next and 3 [4: 5: 5: 6] foll 4th rows, working all neck decreases 9 sts in from neck edge as before. 30 [31: 33: 37: 40] sts.
Work 1 [1: 3: 3: 5] rows, ending with RS facing for next row.
Dec 1 st at neck edge **only** on next and 5 [2: 1: 0: 0] foll 4th rows, then on 2 [4: 5: 6: 6] foll 6th rows. 22 [24: 26: 30: 33] sts.
Cont straight until front matches back to beg of shoulder shaping, ending with RS facing for next row.
Shape shoulder
Cast off 5 [6: 6: 7: 8] sts at beg of next and foll 2 alt rows.
Work 1 row.
Cast off rem 7 [6: 8: 9: 9] sts.
With RS facing, rejoin yarn to sts on holder, cast on 1 st, patt 8 sts, sl 1, K1, psso, K37 [44: 50: 56: 62], M1, K3. 51 [58: 64: 70: 76] sts.
Complete to match first side, reversing shapings, working neck decreases as 'sl 1, K1, psso' instead of 'K2tog' 9 sts in from beg of neck dec rows.

SLEEVES
Using 3¼mm (US 3) needles and yarn A cast on 54 [54: 58: 58: 58] sts.
Row 1 (RS): K2, *P2, K2, rep from * to end.
Row 2: P2, *K2, P2, rep from * to end.
These 2 rows form rib.
Work in rib for a further 16 rows, dec [inc: dec: dec: inc] 1 st at end of last row and ending with RS facing for next row. 53 [55: 57: 57: 59] sts.
Change to 3¾mm (US 5) needles.
Beg with a K row, work in st st throughout as folls:
Working all sleeve increases in same way as side seam increases, inc 1 st at each end of 9th [9th: 9th: 7th: 7th] and every foll 10th [8th: 8th: 6th: 6th] row to 75 [67: 85: 73: 83] sts, then on every foll – [10th: –: 8th: 8th] row until there are – [79: –: 89: 93] sts.
Cont straight until sleeve meas 46 [46: 47: 47: 47] cm, ending with RS facing for next row.
Shape top
Cast off 4 [5: 6: 7: 8] sts at beg of next 2 rows. 67 [69: 73: 75: 77] sts.
Working all sleeve top decreases in same way as armhole decreases, dec 1 st at each end of next 3 rows, then on foll 2 alt rows, then on 3 [4: 5: 6: 7] foll 4th rows. 51 [51: 53: 53: 53] sts.
Work 1 row.
Dec 1 st at each end of next and every foll alt row until 31 sts rem, then on foll 7 rows, ending with RS facing for next row.
Cast off rem 17 sts.

MAKING UP
Press as described on the information page.

Using 3.00mm (US C2/D3) crochet hook and yarn B, make 4 lengths of chain, each one long enough to thread through eyelet holes from cast-on edge of front to top of shoulders. Thread through eyelet holes and secure on WS.

Matching inside edges of front neck to top of back neckband, join shoulder seams using back stitch, or mattress stitch if preferred.
See information page for finishing instructions, setting in sleeves using the set-in method.

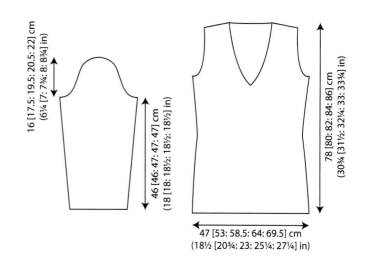

Blenny ●●●

Page 25

SIZE
To fit bust

81-86	91-97	102-107	112-117	122-127	cm
32-34	36-38	40-42	44-46	48-50	in

Actual bust measurement of garment

91	102	112	122	132	cm
35¾	40¼	44	48	52	in

YARN
Summerlite 4ply
A Still Grey 422

6	7	7	8	9	x 50gm

B Touch of Gold 439

1	1	1	1	1	x 50gm

C Anchor Grey 446

1	1	1	1	1	x 50gm

NEEDLES
1 pair 2¼mm (no 13) (US 1) needles
1 pair 3mm (no 11) (US 2/3) needles

TENSION
28 sts and 36 rows to 10 cm measured over st st, 26 sts and 40 rows to 10 cm measured over slip st patt, and 25 sts and 40 rows to 10 cm measured over moss st, all using 3mm (US 2/3) needles.

SPECIAL ABBREVIATIONS
sl 1 wyib = on RS rows, slip one st purlwise with yarn in back (WS) of work; **sl 1 wyif** = on WS rows, slip one st purlwise with yarn in front (WS) of work.

BACK
Using 2¼mm (US 1) needles and yarn A cast on 126 [142: 158: 170: 186] sts.
Row 1 (RS): K2, *P2, K2, rep from * to end.
Row 2: P2, *K2, P2, rep from * to end.
These 2 rows form rib.
Cont in rib until back meas 6 cm, inc [inc: dec: inc: dec] 1 st at end of last row and ending with RS facing for next row. 127 [143: 157: 171: 185] sts.
Change to 3mm (US 2/3) needles.

Beg with a K row, work in st st until back meas 33.5 [34: 34.5: 35: 35.5] cm, ending with RS facing for next row.
Shape raglan armholes
Cast off 4 [5: 6: 7: 8] sts at beg of next row. 123 [138: 151: 164: 177] sts.
Next row (WS): Cast off 4 [5: 6: 7: 8] sts, P until there are 6 [7: 4: 6: 6] sts on right needle, P2tog, (P13 [11: 13: 11: 12], P2tog) 7 [9: 9: 11: 11] times, P6 [7: 4: 6: 7]. 111 [123: 135: 145: 157] sts.
Joining and breaking off colours as required, now work in slip st patt and shape raglan armholes as folls:
Row 1 (RS): Using yarn B, K2, sl 1, K1, psso, K3 [1: 3: 0: 2], *sl 1 wyib – see special abbreviation, K3, rep from * to last 8 [6: 8: 5: 7] sts, sl 1 wyib, K3 [1: 3: 0: 2], K2tog, K2. 109 [121: 133: 143: 155] sts.
Row 2: Using yarn B, P6 [4: 6: 3: 5], *sl 1 wyif – see special abbreviation, P3, rep from * to last 7 [5: 7: 4: 6] sts, sl 1 wyif, P6 [4: 6: 3: 5].
Row 3: Using yarn A, knit.
Row 4: Using yarn A, purl.
Row 5: Using yarn C, K2, sl 1, K1, psso, K0 [2: 0: 1: 3], *sl 1 wyib, K3, rep from * to last 5 [7: 5: 6: 8] sts, sl 1 wyib, K0 [2: 0: 1: 3], K2tog, K2. 107 [119: 131: 141: 153] sts.
Row 6: Using yarn C, P3 [5: 3: 4: 6], *sl 1 wyif, P3, rep from * to last 4 [6: 4: 5: 7] sts, sl 1 wyif, P3 [5: 3: 4: 6].
Row 7: Using yarn C, K3 [5: 3: 4: 6], *sl 1 wyib, K3, rep from * to last 4 [6: 4: 5: 7] sts, sl 1 wyib, K3 [5: 3: 4: 6].
Row 8: As row 6.
Row 9: Using yarn A, K2, sl 1, K1, psso, K to last 4 sts, K2tog, K2. 105 [117: 129: 139: 151] sts.
Row 10: Using yarn A, purl.
These 10 rows set slip st patt and raglan armhole shaping.
Keeping patt correct and working all raglan armhole decreases as set by last 10 rows, cont in patt for a further 13 rows, dec 1 st at raglan armhole edges of 3rd [3rd: 3rd: 3rd: next] and 2 [2: 2: 0: 0] foll 4th rows, then on foll 0 [0: 1: 5: 6] alt rows, ending with row 3 of slip st patt and **WS** facing for next row. 99 [111: 121: 127: 137] sts.
Break off yarn B and yarn C and cont in yarn A **only** throughout.
Next row (WS): P11 [12: 14: 14: 10], P2tog, (P23 [26: 28: 30: 21], P2tog) 3 [3: 3: 3: 5] times, P11 [13: 15: 15: 10]. 95 [107: 117: 123: 131] sts.
Now work in moss st as folls:
Row 1 (RS): K2, sl 1, K1, psso, P1, *K1, P1, rep from * to last 4 sts, K2tog, K2. 93 [105: 115: 121: 129] sts.

Row 2: P4, K1, ★P1, K1, rep from ★ to last 4 sts, P4.

These 2 rows set moss st.

Keeping moss st correct throughout, dec 1 st at raglan armhole edges of 3rd [3rd: next: next: next] and 3 [0: 0: 0: 0] foll 4th rows, then on foll 20 [29: 33: 36: 39] alt rows.

Work 1 row, ending with RS facing for next row.

Leave rem 45 [45: 47: 47: 49] sts on a holder.

FRONT

Work as given for back until 65 [65: 71: 71: 77] sts rem in raglan armhole shaping.

Work 1 row, ending with RS facing for next row.

Shape front neck

Next row (RS): K2, sl 1, K1, psso, patt 14 [14: 17: 17: 20] sts and turn, leaving rem sts on a holder. 17 [17: 20: 20: 23] sts.

Work each side of neck separately.

Dec 1 st at neck edge of next 6 rows, then on foll 2 alt rows, then on 0 [0: 1: 1: 2] foll 4th rows **and at same time** dec 1 st at raglan armhole edge of 2nd and foll 4 [4: 6: 6: 8] alt rows. 4 sts.

Next row (WS): P4.

Next row: K2, sl 1, K1, psso.

Next row: P3.

Next row: K1, sl 1, K1, psso.

Next row: P2.

Next row: K2tog and fasten off.

With RS facing, slip centre 29 sts onto a holder, rejoin yarn and patt to last 4 sts, K2tog, K2.

Complete to match first side, reversing shapings.

SLEEVES

Using 2¼mm (US 1) needles and yarn A cast on 66 [70: 74: 74: 78] sts.

Work in rib as given for back for 6 cm, inc [inc: dec: dec: dec] 1 st at end of last row and ending with RS facing for next row. 67 [71: 73: 73: 77] sts.

Change to 3mm (US 2/3) needles.

Beg with a K row, work in st st for 6 [6: 4: 4: 4] rows, ending with RS facing for next row.

Next row (RS): K3, M1, K to last 3 sts, M1, K3.

Working all sleeve increases as set by last row, inc 1 st at each end of 6th [6th: 4th: 4th: 4th] and every foll 6th [6th: 4th: 4th: 4th] row to 87 [99: 83: 101: 111] sts, then on every foll 8th [-: 6th: 6th: 6th] row until there are 93 [-: 105: 111: 117] sts.

Cont straight until sleeve meas 33 [33: 34: 34: 34] cm, ending with RS facing for next row.

Shape raglan

Cast off 4 [5: 6: 7: 8] sts at beg of next row. 89 [94: 99: 104: 109] sts.

Next row (WS): Cast off 4 [5: 6: 7: 8] sts, P until there are 6 [6: 5: 7: 7] sts on right needle, P2tog, (P12 [13: 14: 14: 15], P2tog) 5 times, P7 [6: 6: 8: 7]. 79 [83: 87: 91: 95] sts.

Joining and breaking off colours as required, now work in slip st patt and shape raglan as folls:

Row 1 (RS): Using yarn B, K2, sl 1, K1, psso, K3 [1: 3: 1: 3], ★sl 1 wyib, K3, rep from ★ to last 8 [6: 8: 6: 8] sts, sl 1 wyib, K3 [1: 3: 1: 3], K2tog, K2. 77 [81: 85: 89: 93] sts.

Row 2: Using yarn B, P6 [4: 6: 4: 6], ★sl 1 wyif, P3, rep from ★ to last 7 [5: 7: 5: 7] sts, sl 1 wyif, P6 [4: 6: 4: 6].

Row 3: Using yarn A, knit.

Row 4: Using yarn A, purl.

Row 5: Using yarn C, K2, sl 1, K1, psso, K0 [2: 0: 2: 0], ★sl 1 wyib, K3, rep from ★ to last 5 [7: 5: 7: 5] sts, sl 1 wyib, K0 [2: 0: 2: 0], K2tog, K2. 75 [79: 83: 87: 91] sts.

Row 6: Using yarn C, P3 [5: 3: 5: 3], ★sl 1 wyif, P3, rep from ★ to last 4 [6: 4: 6: 4] sts, sl 1 wyif, P3 [5: 3: 5: 3].

Row 7: Using yarn C, K3 [5: 3: 5: 3], ★sl 1 wyib, K3, rep from ★ to last 4 [6: 4: 6: 4] sts, sl 1 wyib, K3 [5: 3: 5: 3].

Row 8: As row 6.

Row 9: Using yarn A, K2, sl 1, K1, psso, K to last 4 sts, K2tog, K2. 73 [77: 81: 85: 89] sts.

Row 10: Using yarn A, purl.

These 10 rows set slip st patt and raglan shaping.

Keeping patt correct and working all raglan decreases as set by last 10 rows, cont in patt for a further 13 rows, dec 1 st at raglan edges of 3rd and 2 foll 4th rows, ending with row 3 of slip st patt and **WS** facing for next row. 67 [71: 75: 79: 83] sts.

Break off yarn B and yarn C and cont in yarn A **only** throughout.

Next row (WS): P16 [17: 18: 19: 20], P2tog, P31 [33: 35: 37: 39], P2tog, P16 [17: 18: 19: 20]. 65 [69: 73: 77: 81] sts.

Now work in moss st as folls:

Row 1 (RS): K2, sl 1, K1, psso, P1, ★K1, P1, rep from ★ to last 4 sts, K2tog, K2. 63 [67: 71: 75: 79] sts.

Row 2: P4, K1, ★P1, K1, rep from ★ to last 4 sts, P4.

These 2 rows set moss st.

Keeping moss st correct throughout, dec 1 st at raglan edges of 3rd and 3 [4: 5: 6: 7] foll 4th rows, then on foll 18 [19: 20: 21: 22] alt rows. 19 sts.

Work 1 row, ending with RS facing for next row.

Left sleeve only

Next row (RS): K2, sl 1, K1, psso, patt to last 4 sts, K2tog, K2. 17 sts.

Next row: Cast off 5 sts, patt to last 3 sts, P3. 12 sts.

Next row: K2, sl 1, K1, psso, patt to end. 11 sts.

Next row: Cast off 6 sts, patt to last 3 sts, P3.

Right sleeve only

Next row (RS): Cast off 6 sts, patt to last 4 sts, K2tog, K2. 12 sts.

Next row: P3, patt to end.

Rep last 2 rows once more.

Both sleeves

Cast off rem 5 sts.

MAKING UP

Press as described on the information page.

Join both front and right back raglan seams using back stitch, or mattress stitch if preferred.

Neckband

With RS facing, using 2¼mm (US 1) needles and yarn A, pick up and knit 17 sts from top of left sleeve, and 12 [12: 15: 15: 18] sts down left side of front neck, K across 29 sts on front holder as folls: K4, M1, (K10, M1) twice, K5, pick up and knit 12 [12: 15: 15: 18] sts up right side of front neck, 17 sts from top of right sleeve, then K across 45 [45: 47: 47: 49] sts on back holder as folls: K4 [4: 3: 3: 4], M1, (K9 [9: 10: 10: 10], M1) 4 times, K5 [5: 4: 4: 5]. 140 [140: 148: 148: 156] sts.

Beg with a P row, work in st st for 9 rows, ending with RS facing

for next row.
Using a 3mm (US 2/3) needle, cast off knitwise.

See information page for finishing instructions.

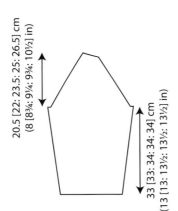

20.5 [22: 23.5: 25: 26.5] cm
(8 [8¾: 9¼: 9¾: 10½] in)

33 [33: 34: 34: 34] cm
(13 [13: 13½: 13½: 13½] in)

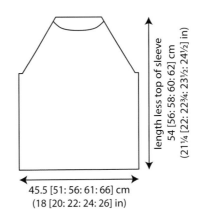

length less top of sleeve
54 [56: 58: 60: 62] cm
(21¼ [22: 22¾: 23½: 24½] in)

45.5 [51: 56: 61: 66] cm
(18 [20: 22: 24: 26] in)

Cormorant ••

Page 22

YARN

Summerlite 4ply

A	Duck Egg 419	3	x 50gm
B	Langoustino 440	2	x 50gm
C	Vintage Claret 443	2	x 50gm
D	Blossom 444	1	x 50gm
E	Rooibos 441	1	x 50gm
F	Pinched Pink 426	2	x 50gm
G	Blushes 420	1	x 50gm

NEEDLES

1 pair 4mm (no 8) (US 6) needles

CROCHET HOOK

2.50mm (no 12) (US B1/C2) crochet hook

TENSION

28 sts and 25 rows to 10 cm measured over patterned st st using 4mm (US 6) needles.

FINISHED SIZE

Completed scarf is 56 cm (22 in) wide and approx 234 cm (92 in) long (including borders and tassels).

SCARF

Using 4mm (US 6) needles and yarn A cast on 151 sts, leaving a length of yarn at least 15 cm long at end of cast-on sts.
Next row (WS): Purl.
Joining in and breaking off colours as required, and stranding yarn not in use across WS to end of each row, work in patt as folls:
Row 1 (RS): Using yarn A K1, *using yarn B K1, using yarn A K1, rep from * to end.
Row 2: Using yarn B P1, *using yarn A P1, using yarn B P1, rep from * to end.
Rows 3 and 4: As rows 1 and 2.
Row 5: Using yarn A K1, *using yarn C K1, using yarn A K1, rep from * to end.
Row 6: Using yarn C P1, *using yarn A P1, using yarn C P1, rep from * to end.
Row 7: Using yarn B K1, *using yarn C K1, using yarn B K1, rep from * to end.
Row 8: Using yarn C P1, *using yarn B P1, using yarn C P1, rep from * to end.
Row 9: As row 7.
Row 10: Using yarn C P1, *using yarn D P1, using yarn C P1, rep from * to end.
Row 11: Using yarn D K1, *using yarn C K1, using yarn D K1,

rep from ★ to end.
Row 12: As row 10.
Row 13: Using yarn D K1, ★using yarn E K1, using yarn D K1, rep from ★ to end.
Row 14: Using yarn E P1, ★using yarn D P1, using yarn E P1, rep from ★ to end.
Row 15: Using yarn F K1, ★using yarn E K1, using yarn F K1, rep from ★ to end.
Row 16: Using yarn E P1, ★using yarn F P1, using yarn E P1, rep from ★ to end.
Row 17: Using yarn F K1, ★using yarn C K1, using yarn F K1, rep from ★ to end.
Row 18: Using yarn C P1, ★using yarn A P1, using yarn C P1, rep from ★ to end.
Row 19: Using yarn A K1, ★using yarn C K1, using yarn A K1, rep from ★ to end.
Row 20: Using yarn F P1, ★using yarn A P1, using yarn F P1, rep from ★ to end.
Row 21: Using yarn A K1, ★using yarn F K1, using yarn A K1, rep from ★ to end.
Row 22: As row 20.
Row 23: Using yarn A K1, ★using yarn E K1, using yarn A K1, rep from ★ to end.
Row 24: Using yarn E P1, ★using yarn A P1, using yarn E P1, rep from ★ to end.
Row 25: Using yarn B K1, ★using yarn E K1, using yarn B K1, rep from ★ to end.
Row 26: Using yarn E P1, ★using yarn B P1, using yarn E P1, rep from ★ to end.
Row 27: As row 25.
Row 28: Using yarn C P1, ★using yarn B P1, using yarn C P1, rep from ★ to end.
Row 29: Using yarn B K1, ★using yarn C K1, using yarn B K1, rep from ★ to end.
Row 30: Using yarn C P1, ★using yarn E P1, using yarn C P1, rep from ★ to end.
Row 31: Using yarn E K1, ★using yarn C K1, using yarn E K1, rep from ★ to end.
Row 32: Using yarn C P1, ★using yarn A P1, using yarn C P1, rep from ★ to end.
Row 33: Using yarn A K1, ★using yarn C K1, using yarn A K1, rep from ★ to end.
Row 34: Using yarn F P1, ★using yarn G P1, using yarn F P1, rep from ★ to end.
Row 35: Using yarn G K1, ★using yarn F K1, using yarn G K1, rep from ★ to end.
Rows 36 to 39: As rows 34 and 35 twice.
Row 40: Using yarn C P1, ★using yarn G P1, using yarn C P1, rep from ★ to end.
Row 41: Using yarn G K1, ★using yarn C K1, using yarn G K1, rep from ★ to end.
Row 42: Using yarn C P1, ★using yarn F P1, using yarn C P1, rep from ★ to end.
Row 43: Using yarn F K1, ★using yarn C K1, using yarn F K1, rep from ★ to end.
Row 44: Using yarn C P1, ★using yarn B P1, using yarn C P1, rep

from ★ to end.
Row 45: Using yarn B K1, ★using yarn C K1, using yarn B K1, rep from ★ to end.
Row 46: As row 44.
Row 47: Using yarn B K1, ★using yarn A K1, using yarn B K1, rep from ★ to end.
Row 48: Using yarn A P1, ★using yarn B P1, using yarn A P1, rep from ★ to end.
Rows 49 and 50: As rows 47 and 48.
Row 51: As row 47.
Row 52: As row 26.
Row 53: As row 25.
Row 54: As row 26.
Rows 55 and 56: As rows 15 and 16.
Row 57: Using yarn F K1, ★using yarn D K1, using yarn F K1, rep from ★ to end.
Row 58: Using yarn D P1, ★using yarn F P1, using yarn D P1, rep from ★ to end.
Rows 59 and 60: As rows 57 and 58.
These 60 rows form patt.
Rep these 60 rows 8 times more, then rep rows 1 to 4 again, ending with RS facing for next row.
Using yarn A, cast off.

MAKING UP
Press as described on the information page.

Border
With RS facing and using 2.50mm (US B1/C2) crochet hook and yarn A, join yarn to first st on cast-on edge, 1 ch (does NOT count as a st), 2 dc into same st, work 147 dc evenly along cast-on edge to last st, 3 dc into last st, work in dc evenly along first long row-end edge of scarf to cast-off edge (**ensuring there is a multiple of 3 dc along this row-end edge**), 3 dc into first st along cast-off edge, work 147 dc evenly along cast-off edge to last st, 3 dc into last st, work in dc evenly along second long row-end edge of scarf to cast-on edge (**ensuring there is a multiple of 3 dc along this row-end edge**), 1 dc into same st as first 2 dc, ss to first dc.
Next round (RS): 3 ch, ss into dc at base of 3 ch (picot made), ★ss into each of next 3 dc, 3 ch, ss into same st as last ss, rep from ★ to last 2 sts, ss into each of last 2 sts, ss into st at base of first picot. Fasten off.

Tassels
Cut 3 x 15 cm lengths of yarn A for each tassel. Fold a group of 3 lengths of yarn in half, insert crochet hook through first picot at corner of one short edge of scarf, pull yarn lengths through and thread ends of yarn through this loop. Pull tight to secure tassel. Repeat until a tassel has been made in each picot along both short edges of scarf. Trim tassels to 6 cm long.

See information page for finishing instructions.

Kittiwake ••

Page 10

SIZE

To fit bust

81-86	91-97	102-107	112-117	122-127	cm
32-34	36-38	40-42	44-46	48-50	in

Actual bust measurement of garment

87.5	99.5	109	119.5	129	cm
34½	39¼	43	47	50¾	in

YARN

Summerlite 4ply

A Navy Ink 429

2	2	2	2	3	x 50gm

B Pure White 417

2	2	2	3	3	x 50gm

C Aqua 433

2	2	2	2	3	x 50gm

D Periwinkle 424

2	2	2	2	3	x 50gm

E Touch of Gold 439

2	2	2	2	2	x 50gm

NEEDLES

1 pair 2¼mm (no 13) (US 1) needles
1 pair 3mm (no 11) (US 2/3) needles

TENSION

34 sts and 40 rows to 10 cm measured over patt, when slightly stretched, using 3mm (US 2/3) needles.

STRIPE SEQUENCE

Rows 1 to 10: Using yarn B.
Rows 11 to 20: Using yarn C.
Rows 21 to 30: Using yarn D.
Rows 31 to 40: Using yarn E.
These 40 rows form stripe sequence and are repeated.

BACK

Using 2¼mm (US 1) needles and yarn A cast on 118 [134: 146: 162: 174] sts.
Row 1 (RS): K2, *P2, K2, rep from * to end.
Row 2: P2, *K2, P2, rep from * end.

These 2 rows form rib.
Work in rib until back meas 10 cm, ending with **WS** facing for next row.
Sizes 81-86 cm, 91-97 cm and 112-117 cm only
Next row (WS): Rib 4 [2: -: 1: -], M1, *rib 5, M1, rep from * to last 4 [2: -: 1: -] sts, rib 4 [2: -: 1: -]. 141 [161: -: 195: -] sts.
Sizes 102-107 cm and 122-127 cm sizes only
Next row (WS): Rib 1, M1, (rib 5, M1) – [-: 2: -: 0] times, *rib 4, M1, (rib 5, M1) 3 times, rep from * to last 2 sts, rib 2. – [-: 177: -: 211] sts.
All sizes
Break off yarn A.
Change to 3mm (US 2/3) needles.
Beg with row 1 of stripe sequence and joining and breaking off colours as required, work in patt as folls:
Row 1 (RS): Using yarn B, P1 [0: 0: 0: 0], K2 [1: 1: 2: 2], *P2, K2, rep from * to last 2 [0: 0: 1: 1] sts, P2 [0: 0: 1: 1].
Row 2: Using yarn B, K1 [0: 0: 0: 0], P2 [1: 1: 2: 2], *K2, P2, rep from * to last 2 [0: 0: 1: 1] sts, K2 [0: 0: 1: 1].
These 2 rows form patt.
Keeping stripe sequence correct, cont straight in patt for 16 rows, ending with RS facing for next row.
Inc 1 st at each end of next and 3 foll 18th rows, taking inc sts into patt. 149 [169: 185: 203: 219] sts.
Cont straight until back meas approx 32.5 [33: 33.5: 34: 34.5] cm, ending with row 10 [12: 14: 16: 18] of stripe sequence and RS facing for next row.
Shape armholes
Keeping patt and stripe sequence correct, cast off 4 [6: 7: 8: 9] sts at beg of next 2 rows. 141 [157: 171: 187: 201] sts.
Dec 1 st at each end of next 5 [9: 11: 15: 15] rows, then on foll 7 [7: 7: 6: 7] alt rows, then on foll 4th row. 115 [123: 133: 143: 155] sts.
Cont straight until armhole meas 19.5 [21: 22.5: 24: 25.5] cm, ending with RS facing for next row.
Shape back neck
Next row (RS): Patt 30 [34: 37: 42: 47] sts and turn, leaving rem sts on a holder.
Work each side of neck separately.
Dec 1 st at neck edge of next row. 29 [33: 36: 41: 46] sts.
Shape shoulder
Cast off 6 [7: 8: 9: 10] sts at beg of next and foll alt row **and at same**

time dec 1 st at neck edge of next 3 rows. 14 [16: 17: 20: 23] sts.
Work 1 row, ending with RS facing for next row.
Cast off 6 [7: 8: 9: 11] sts at beg and dec 1 st at end of next row.
Work 1 row.
Cast off rem 7 [8: 8: 10: 11] sts.
With RS facing, slip centre 55 [55: 59: 59: 61] sts onto a holder, rejoin appropriate yarn and patt to end.
Complete to match first side, reversing shapings.

FRONT

Work as given for back until 42 [42: 46: 46: 50] rows less have been worked than on back to beg of shoulder shaping, ending with RS facing for next row.

Shape front neck

Next row (RS): Patt 44 [48: 52: 57: 63] sts and turn, leaving rem sts on a holder.
Work each side of neck separately.
Keeping patt and stripe sequence correct, dec 1 st at neck edge of next 10 rows, then on foll 6 alt rows, then on 3 [3: 4: 4: 5] foll 4th rows. 25 [29: 32: 37: 42] sts.
Work 7 rows, ending with RS facing for next row.

Shape shoulder

Cast off 6 [7: 8: 9: 10] sts at beg of next and foll 2 [2: 2: 2: 1] alt rows, then − [−: −: −: 11] sts at beg of foll − [−: −: −: 1] alt row.
Work 1 row.
Cast off rem 7 [8: 8: 10: 11] sts.
With RS facing, slip centre 27 [27: 29: 29: 29] sts onto a holder, rejoin appropriate yarn and patt to end.
Complete to match first side, reversing shapings.

SLEEVES

Using 2¼mm (US 1) needles and yarn A cast on 78 [82: 90: 94: 102] sts.
Work in rib as given for back until sleeve meas 5 cm, ending with **WS** facing for next row.

Sizes 81-86 cm, 91-97 cm, 102-107 cm and 112-117 cm only
Next row (WS): Rib 3 [2: 3: 2: -], M1, ★(rib 4, M1) 1 [2: 1: 1: -] times, (rib 5, M1) 1 [1: 2: 1: -] times, rep from ★ to last 3 [2: 3: 2: -] sts, rib 3 [2: 3: 2: -]. 95 [101: 109: 115: -] sts.

Size 122-127 cm only
Next row (WS): Rib 1, M1, ★rib 5, M1, rep from ★ to last st, rib 1. 123 sts.

All sizes
Break off yarn A.
Change to 3mm (US 2/3) needles.
Beg with **row 21** of stripe sequence and joining and breaking off colours as required, work in patt as folls:

Row 1 (RS): Using yarn D, P2 [1: 1: 0: 0], K2, ★P2, K2, rep from ★ to last 3 [2: 2: 1: 1] sts, P2 [2: 2: 1: 1], K1 [0: 0: 0: 0].
Row 2: K2 [1: 1: 0: 0], P2, ★K2, P2, rep from ★ to last 3 [2: 2: 1: 1] sts, K2 [2: 2: 1: 1], P1 [0: 0: 0: 0].
These 2 rows form patt.
Keeping stripe sequence correct, inc 1 st at each end of next and foll 6 [7: 4: 5: 2] alt rows, then on 3 [3: 5: 5: 7] foll 4th rows, taking inc sts into patt. 115 [123: 129: 137: 143] sts.
Work 3 rows, ending with row 10 [12: 14: 16: 18] of stripe sequence

and RS facing for next row. (Sleeve should meas approx 12.5 [13: 13.5: 14: 14.5] cm.)

Shape top

Keeping patt and stripe sequence correct, cast off 4 [6: 7: 8: 9] sts at beg of next 2 rows. 107 [111: 115: 121: 125] sts.
Dec 1 st at each end of next 13 rows, then on foll 5 alt rows, then on 3 [4: 5: 5: 6] foll 4th rows. 65 [67: 69: 75: 77] sts.
Work 1 row.
Dec 1 st at each end of next and every foll alt row until 49 sts rem, then on foll 11 rows, ending with RS facing for next row.
Cast off rem 27 sts.

MAKING UP

Do NOT press.
Join right shoulder seam using back stitch, or mattress stitch if preferred.

Neckband

With RS facing and using 2¼mm (US 1) needles and yarn A, pick up and knit 35 [35: 39: 39: 42] sts down left side of front neck, K across 27 [27: 29: 29: 29] sts on front holder as folls: K2 [2: 1: 1: 1], K2tog, (K3 [3: 4: 4: 4], K2tog) 4 times, K3 [3: 2: 2: 2], pick up and knit 35 [35: 39: 39: 42] sts up right side of front neck, and 6 sts down right side of back neck, K across 55 [55: 59: 59: 61] sts on back holder as folls: K2 [2: 3: 3: 4], K2tog, (K4 [4: 3: 3: 3], K2tog) 8 [8: 10: 10: 10] times, K3 [3: 4: 4: 5], then pick up and knit 6 sts up left side of back neck. 150 [150: 162: 162: 170] sts.
Beg with row 2, work in rib as given for back for 11 rows, ending with RS facing for next row.
Cast off in rib.
See information page for finishing instructions, setting in sleeves using the set-in method.

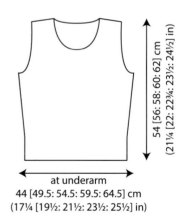

at underarm
44 [49.5: 54.5: 59.5: 64.5] cm
(17¼ [19½: 21½: 23½: 25½] in)

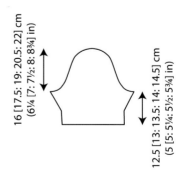

Lionfish •••

Page 32

SIZE
To fit bust

81-86	91-97	102-107	112-117	122-127	cm
32-34	36-38	40-42	44-46	48-50	in

Actual bust measurement of garment

100	111	121	131	141	cm
39¼	43¾	47¾	51½	55½	in

YARN
Summerlite 4ply
A Still Grey 422

7	8	9	9	10	x 50gm

B Touch of Gold 439

3	3	3	3	4	x 50gm

NEEDLES
2¾mm (no 12) (US 2) circular needle at least 120 cm long
3mm (no 11) (US 2/3) circular needle at least 120 cm long
Set of 4 double-pointed 2¾mm (no 12) (US 2) needles
Set of 4 double-pointed 3mm (no 11) (US 2/3) needles

TENSION
28 sts and 36 rows to 10 cm measured over st st using 3mm (US 2/3) needles.

STRIPE SEQUENCE
Rounds 1 to 10: Using yarn A.
Round 11: Using yarn B.
Round 12: Using yarn A.
Round 13: Using yarn B.
Rounds 14 to 19: As rows 12 and 13, 3 times.
Rounds 20 to 29: Using yarn A.
Round 30: Using yarn B.
Round 31: Using yarn A.
Round 32: Using yarn B.
Rounds 33 to 38: As rows 31 and 32, 3 times.
These 38 rounds form stripe sequence and are repeated.

BODY (knitted in one piece to armholes)
Using 2¾mm (US 2) circular needle and yarn A cast on 280 [312: 340: 368: 396] sts.

Taking care not to twist cast-on edge, work in rounds as folls:
Round 1 (RS): Knit.
This round forms st st.
Place marker between first and last sts of round just knitted to denote beg and end of rounds – this marker denotes centre back point.
Cont in st st throughout as folls:
Work a further 5 rounds.
Change to 3mm (US 2/3) circular needle.
Beg with round 1 and joining in and breaking off colours as required, work in stripe sequence until body meas approx 45 cm (allowing cast-on edge to roll), ending with round 5 of stripe sequence.
Divide for armholes
Next round: K65 [73: 80: 87: 94] and slip these sts onto a holder (for left back), K10 and slip these 10 sts onto another holder (for left underarm), K130 [146: 160: 174: 188] and slip these sts onto another holder (for front), K next 10 sts and slip these sts onto another holder (for right underarm), K65 [73: 80: 87: 94] and slip these sts onto another holder (for right back).
Break yarn.

SLEEVES
Using set of 4 double-pointed 2¾mm (US 2) needles and yarn A cast on 56 [58: 60: 60: 62] sts.
Taking care not to twist cast-on edge, work in rounds as folls:
Round 1 (RS): Knit.
This round forms st st.
Place marker on first st of round just knitted to denote beg and end of rounds – this marker "sits" along sleeve "seam".
Cont in st st throughout as folls:
Work a further 4 rounds.
Round 6 (RS): K2 [3: 4: 4: 5], M1, *K3, M1, rep from * to last 3 [4: 5: 5: 6] sts, K3 [4: 5: 5: 6]. 74 [76: 78: 78: 80] sts.
Change to set of 4 double-pointed 3mm (US 2/3) needles.
Beg with round 1 and joining in and breaking off colours as required, work in stripe sequence for 10 [8: 8: 6: 6] rounds.
Next round (RS): K1, M1, K to last st, M1, K1. 76 [78: 80: 80: 82] sts.
Working all sleeve increases as set by last round and keeping stripe sequence correct throughout, cont as folls:
Inc 1 st at each end of 10th [8th: 8th: 6th: 6th] and 4 [1: 11: 6: 14]

foll 10th [8th: 8th: 6th: 6th] rounds, then on 7 [12: 4: 12: 6] foll 12th [10th: 10th: 8th: 8th] rounds. 100 [106: 112: 118: 124] sts. Cont straight until sleeve meas approx 45 cm (allowing cast-on edge to roll), ending with round 5 of stripe sequence.

Next round: K5 and slip these sts onto a holder (for underarm), K to last 5 sts, K rem 5 sts and slip these 5 sts onto same holder as first 5 sts (so there are 10 sts on underarm holder).

Break yarn and leave rem 90 [96: 102: 108: 114] sts on another holder.

YOKE

With RS facing, using 3mm (US 2/3) circular needle and yarn A, work across all sts from holders as folls: K across 65 [73: 80: 87: 94] sts on left back holder, 90 [96: 102: 108: 114] sts on left sleeve holder, 130 [146: 160: 174: 188] sts on front holder, 90 [96: 102: 108: 114] sts on right sleeve holder, and 65 [73: 80: 87: 94] sts on right back holder. 440 [484: 524: 564: 604] sts.

Place marker between first and last sts of round just knitted to denote beg and end of rounds – this marker denotes centre back point.

Beg with round 8 of stripe sequence and working in st st throughout, cont as folls:

Work 1 round.

Next round: K26 [21: 19: 22: 26], K2tog, *K53 [38: 42: 45: 48], K2tog, rep from * to last 27 [21: 19: 23: 26] sts, K27 [21: 19: 23: 26]. 432 [472: 512: 552: 592] sts.

Work 9 [9: 11: 11: 11] rounds, ending with round 18 [18: 20: 20: 20] of stripe sequence.

(**Note:** As number of sts decreases, change from circular needle to set of 4 double-pointed needles).

Sizes 81–86 cm, 102–107 cm and 112–117 cm only

Next round: K5 [-: 1: 8: -], K2tog, *K10 [-: 11: 11:-], K2tog, rep from * to last 5 [-: 2: 9: -] sts, K5 [-: 2: 9: -]. 396 [-: 472: 510: -] sts.

Sizes 91–97 cm and 122–127 cm only

Next round: K- [3: -: -: 5], K2tog, *K11, K2tog, K- [10: -: -: 12], K2tog, rep from * to last – [17: -: -: 18] sts, K11, K2tog, K- [4: -: -: 5]. – [434: -: -: 548] sts.

All sizes

Work 9 [9: 11: 11: 11] rounds, ending with round 28 [28: 32: 32: 32] of stripe sequence.

Sizes 81–86 cm and 112–117 cm only

Next round: K11 [-: -: 6: -], K2tog, *K10 [-: -: 9: -], K2tog, rep from * to last 11 [-: -: 7: -] sts, K11 [-: -: 7: -]. 364 [-: -: 464: -] sts.

Sizes 91–97 cm, 102–107 cm and 122–127 cm only

Next round: K- [9: 9: -: 5], K2tog, *K- [11: 9: -: 9], K2tog, K- [10: 8: -: 8], K2tog, rep from * to last – [23: 20: -: 16] sts, K- [11: 9: -: 9], K2tog, K- [10: 9: -: 5]. – [400: 428: -: 496] sts.

All sizes

Work 9 [9: 11: 11: 11] rounds, ending with round 38 [38: 6: 6: 6] of stripe sequence.

Sizes 81–86 cm, 91–97 cm, 102–107 cm and 112–117 cm only

Next round: K3 [5: 5: 6: -], K2tog, *K9 [10: 6: 6: -], K10 [11: 7: 7: -], K2tog, rep from * to last 14 [18: 13: 14: -] sts, K9 [10: 6: 6: -], K2tog, K3 [6: 5: 6: -]. 332 [368: 378: 410: -] sts.

Size 122–127 cm only

Next round: K8, K2tog, *K7, K2tog, rep from * to last 9 sts, K9. 442 sts.

All sizes

Work 9 [9: 9: 11: 11] rounds, ending with round 10 [10: 16: 18: 18] of stripe sequence.

Sizes 81–86 cm, 91–97 cm, and 102–107 cm only

Next round: K7 [8: 3: -: -], K2tog, *K7 [8: 8: -: -], K2tog, rep from * to last 8 [8: 3: -: -] sts, K8 [8: 3: -: -]. 296 [332: 340: -: -] sts.

Sizes 112–117 cm and 122–127 cm only

Next round: K- [-: -: 9: 5], K2tog, *K8, K2tog, K- [-: -: 7: 9], K2tog, rep from * to last – [-: -: 19: 15] sts, K8, K2tog, K- [-: -: 9: 5]. – [-: -: 368: 400] sts.

All sizes

Work 9 [9: 9: 11: 11] rounds, ending with round 20 [20: 26: 30: 30] of stripe sequence.

Sizes 81–86 cm, 91–97 cm, and 122–127 cm only

Next round: K7 [1: -: -: 3], K2tog, *K6, K2tog, rep from * to last 7 [1: -: -: 3] sts, K7 [1: -: -: 3]. 260 [290: -: -: 350] sts.

Sizes 102–107 cm and 112–117 cm only

Next round: K- [-: 8: 7: -], K2tog, *K5, K2tog, K6, K2tog, rep from * to last – [-: 15: 14: -] sts, K5, K2tog, K- [-: 8: 7: -]. – [-: 296: 320: -] sts.

All sizes

Work 9 [9: 9: 11: 11] rounds, ending with round 30 [30: 36: 4: 4] of stripe sequence.

Next round: K5 [4: 7: 6: 2], K2tog, *K6 [6: 6: 4: 5], K2tog, rep from * to last 5 [4: 7: 6: 3] sts, K5 [4: 7: 6: 3]. 228 [254: 260: 268: 300] sts. Work 7 [9: 9: 9: 11] rounds, ending with round 38 [2: 8: 14: 16] of stripe sequence.

Sizes 81–86 cm, 91–97 cm, 102–107 cm and 122–127 cm only

Next round: K4 [2: 5: -: 2], K2tog, *K5 [6: 6: -: 4], K2tog, rep from * to last 5 [2: 5: -: 2] sts, K5 [2: 5: -: 2]. 196 [222: 228: -: 250] sts.

Size 112–117 cm only

Next round: K2, K2tog, *K5, K2tog, K6, K2tog, rep from * to last 9 sts, K5, K2tog, K2. 232 sts.

All sizes

Work 7 [9: 9: 9: 11] rounds, ending with round 8 [12: 18: 24: 28] of stripe sequence.

Next round: K2 [5: 2: 4: 1], K2tog, *K5 [4: 4: 4: 3], K2tog, rep from * to last 3 [5: 2: 4: 2] sts, K3 [5: 2: 4: 2]. 168 [186: 190: 194: 200] sts. Work 7 [9: 9: 9: 11] rounds, ending with round 16 [22: 28: 34: 2] of stripe sequence.

Sizes 81–86 cm and 102–107 cm only

Next round: K2 [-: 1: -: -], K2tog, *K5 [-: 3: -: -], K2tog, rep from * to last 3 [-: 2: -: -] sts, K3 [-: 2: -: -]. 144 [-: 152: -: -] sts.

Size 91–97 cm only

Next round: K2, K2tog, *K2, K2tog, (K3, K2tog) 6 times, rep from * to last 12 sts, K2, K2tog, K3, K2tog, K3. 148 sts.

Sizes 112–117 cm and 122–127 cm only

Next round: K- [-: -: 4: 2], K2tog, *K2, K2tog, K3, K2tog, rep from * to last – [-: -: 8: 7] sts, K2, K2tog, K- [-: -: 4: 3]. – [-: -: 152: 156] sts.

All sizes

Break yarn B and cont using yarn A only.

Neckband

Change to set of 4 double-pointed 2¾mm (US 2) needles.

Work in st st for 6 rows.

Cast off using a 3mm (US 2/3) needle.

MAKING UP

Press as described on the information page.

Join underarm seams by grafting together sets of 10 sts on underarm holders.

See information page for finishing instructions.

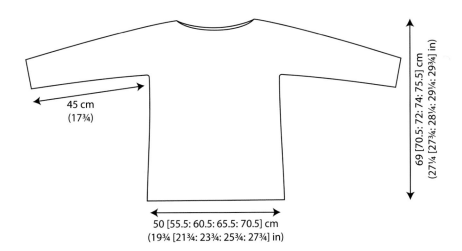

45 cm
(17¾)

69 [70.5: 72: 74: 75.5] cm
(27¼ [27¾: 28¼: 29¼: 29¾] in)

50 [55.5: 60.5: 65.5: 70.5] cm
(19¾ [21¾: 23¾: 25¾: 27¾] in)

Pipefish •••

Page 28

SIZE

To fit bust

| 81-86 | 91-97 | 102-107 | 112-117 | 122-127 | cm |
| 32-34 | 36-38 | 40-42 | 44-46 | 48-50 | in |

Actual bust measurement of garment

| 90 | 101.5 | 111.5 | 121.5 | 131.5 | cm |
| 35½ | 40 | 44 | 47¾ | 51¾ | in |

YARN

Summerlite 4ply

A Still Grey 422

| 4 | 5 | 5 | 6 | 6 | x 50gm |

B Sand Dune 438

| 1 | 1 | 1 | 1 | 1 | x 50gm |

C Anchor Grey 446

| 1 | 1 | 1 | 1 | 1 | x 50gm |

D Duck Egg 419

| 1 | 1 | 1 | 1 | 1 | x 50gm |

NEEDLES

1 pair 3mm (no 11) (US 2/3) needles

3mm (no 11) (US 2/3) circular needle at least 100 [100: 100: 120: 120] cm long

TENSION

28 sts and 36 rows to 10 cm measured over st st, 27 sts and 50 rows to 10 cm measured over border patt, both using 3mm (US 2/3) needles.

SPECIAL ABBREVIATION

sl 1 wyif = slip one st purlwise with yarn in front (RS) of work.

BACK

Using 3mm (US 2/3) needles and yarn A cast on 121 [137: 151: 163: 177] sts.

Joining and breaking off colours as required, work in border patt as folls:

Row 1 (RS): Using yarn A, K1, *sl 1 wyif – see special abbreviation, K1, rep from * to end.

Row 2: Using yarn A, purl.

Rows 3 and 4: Using yarn B, as rows 1 and 2.

Rows 5 and 6: Using yarn C, as rows 1 and 2.

Rows 7 and 8: Using yarn D, as rows 1 and 2.

These 8 rows form border patt.

Work in border patt for a further 21 rows, ending with row 5 of border patt and **WS** facing for next row.

Row 30 (WS): Using yarn C, P12 [12: 15: 9: 10], M1, (P24 [28: 30: 24: 26], M1) 4 [4: 4: 6: 6] times, P13 [13: 16: 10: 11].
126 [142: 156: 170: 184].

Break off yarn C.

Beg with a K row, cont in st st using yarn A **only** throughout as folls:
Cont straight until back meas 27 [27.5: 28: 28.5: 29] cm, ending with RS facing for next row.

Shape armholes

Cast off 6 [7: 8: 9: 10] sts at beg of next 2 rows. 114 [128: 140: 152: 164] sts.

Dec 1 st at each end of next 7 [11: 13: 15: 15] rows, then on foll 4 [4: 4: 4: 5] alt rows. 92 [98: 106: 114: 124] sts.

Cont straight until armhole meas 19 [20.5: 22: 23.5: 25] cm, ending with RS facing for next row.

Shape shoulders

Cast off 4 [4: 5: 6: 6] sts at beg of next 2 rows, then 4 [4: 5: 6: 7] sts at beg of foll 2 rows. 76 [82: 86: 90: 98] sts.

Shape back neck

Next row (RS): Cast off 4 [5: 5: 6: 7] sts, K until there are 11 [13: 14: 15: 17] sts on right needle and turn, leaving rem sts on a holder.
Work each side of neck separately.

Dec 1 at neck edge of next 3 rows **and at same time** cast off 4 [5: 5: 6: 7] sts at beg of 2nd row.
Cast off rem 4 [5: 6: 6: 7] sts.

With RS facing, slip centre 46 [46: 48: 48: 50] sts onto a holder, rejoin yarn and K to end.
Complete to match first side, reversing shapings.

LEFT FRONT

Using 3mm (US 2/3) needles and yarn A cast on 53 [61: 67: 75: 81] sts.
Joining and breaking off colours as required, work in border patt as given for back for 29 rows, ending with row 5 of border patt and **WS** facing for next row.

Next row (WS): Using yarn C, P13 [15: 10: 19: 13], M1, (P27 [31: 23: 37: 27], M1) 1 [1: 2: 1: 2] times, P13 [15: 11: 19: 14]. 55 [63: 70: 77: 84] sts.

Break off yarn C.

Beg with a K row, cont in st st using yarn A **only** throughout as folls:
Cont straight until left front matches back to beg of armhole shaping, ending with RS facing for next row.

Shape armhole and front slope

Cast off 6 [7: 8: 9: 10] sts at beg and dec 1 st at end of next row.
48 [55: 61: 67: 73] sts.

Work 1 row.

Dec 1 st at armhole edge of next 7 [11: 13: 15: 15] rows, then on foll 4 [4: 4: 4: 5] alt rows **and at same time** dec 1 st at front slope edge on next [next: next: 3rd: 3rd] and foll 4 [1: 0: 0: 0] alt rows, then on 1 [4: 5: 5: 5] foll 4th rows. 31 [34: 38: 42: 47] sts.

Dec 1 st at front slope edge **only** on 2nd [4th: 4th: 4th: 2nd] and 10 [10: 11: 10: 10] foll 4th rows, then on − [−: −: 1: 2] foll − [−: −: 6th: 6th] rows. 20 [23: 26: 30: 34] sts.

Cont straight until left front matches back to beg of shoulder shaping, ending with RS facing for next row.

Shape shoulder

Cast off 4 [4: 5: 6: 6] sts at beg of next and foll 3 [1: 3: 3: 0] alt rows, then − [5: −: −: 7] sts at beg of foll − [2: −: −: 3] alt rows.
Work 1 row.
Cast off rem 4 [5: 6: 6: 7] sts.

RIGHT FRONT

Work as given for left front, reversing shapings.

SLEEVES

Using 3mm (US 2/3) needles and yarn A cast on 71 [77: 83: 89: 97] sts.
Joining and breaking off colours as required, work in border patt as given for back for 29 rows, ending with row 5 of border patt and **WS** facing for next row.

Next row (WS): Using yarn C, P11 [12: 13: 14: 16], M1, (P24 [26: 28: 30: 32], M1) twice, P12 [13: 14: 15: 17]. 74 [80: 86: 92: 100] sts.
Break off yarn C.

Beg with a K row, cont in st st using yarn A **only** throughout as folls:
Inc 1 st at each end of 3rd [3rd: 5th: 5th: 5th] and every foll 4th row to 90 [96: 96: 102: 104] sts, then on every foll − [−: 6th: 6th: 6th] row until there are − [−: 100: 106: 112] sts.

Work 3 [3: 5: 5: 5] rows, ending with RS facing for next row. (Sleeve should meas approx 15 [15: 16: 16: 16] cm.)

Shape top

Cast off 6 [7: 8: 9: 10] sts at beg of next 2 rows. 78 [82: 84: 88: 92] sts.
Dec 1 st at each end of next 3 rows, then on foll 5 alt rows, then on 3 [4: 5: 6: 7] foll 4th rows. 56 [58: 58: 60: 62] sts.
Work 1 row.
Dec 1 st at each end of next and every foll alt row until 36 sts rem, then on foll 7 rows, ending with RS facing for next row.
Cast off rem 22 sts.

MAKING UP

Press as described on the information page.
Join both shoulder seams using back stitch, or mattress stitch if preferred.

Front and back neckband

With RS facing, using 3mm (US 2/3) circular needle and yarn A, beg and ending at front cast-on edges, pick up and knit 73 [74: 76: 77: 78] sts up right front opening edge to beg of front slope shaping, 60 [64: 68: 72: 76] sts up right front slope to right shoulder seam, and 3 sts down right side of back neck, K across 46 [46: 48: 48: 50] sts on back holder dec 1 st at centre, pick up and knit 3 sts up left side of back neck, 60 [64: 68: 72: 76] sts down left front slope to beg of front slope shaping, then 73 [74: 76: 77: 78] sts down left front opening edge.
317 [327: 341: 351: 363] sts.

Joining and breaking off colours as required and beg with **row 2**, work in border patt as given for back for 29 rows, ending with row 6 of patt and RS facing for next row.

Using yarn C, cast off knitwise.

See information page for finishing instructions, setting in sleeves using the set-in method.

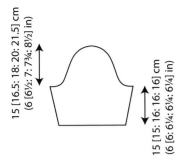

15 [16.5: 18: 20: 21.5] cm
(6 [6½: 7: 7¾: 8½] in)

15 [15: 16: 16: 16] cm
(6 [6: 6¼: 6¼: 6¼] in)

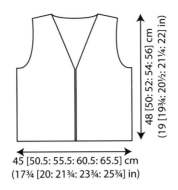

48 [50: 52: 54: 56] cm
(19 [19¾: 20½: 21¼: 22] in)

45 [50.5: 55.5: 60.5: 65.5] cm
(17¾ [20: 21¾: 23¾: 25¾] in)

Puffin •••

Page 18

SIZE

To fit bust

| 81-86 | 91-97 | 102-107 | 112-117 | 122-127 | cm |
| 32-34 | 36-38 | 40-42 | 44-46 | 48-50 | in |

Actual bust measurement of garment

| 103 | 113 | 123 | 133 | 143 | cm |
| 40½ | 44½ | 48½ | 52¼ | 56¼ | in |

YARN

Summerlite DK

A Coral Blush 467

| 1 | 1 | 2 | 2 | 2 | x 50gm |

B Favourite Denims 469

| 1 | 1 | 1 | 2 | 2 | x 50gm |

C Summer 453

| 1 | 1 | 1 | 2 | 2 | x 50gm |

D Silvery Blue 468

| 1 | 1 | 1 | 2 | 2 | x 50gm |

E Pink Powder 472

| 1 | 1 | 1 | 2 | 2 | x 50gm |

F Khaki 461

| 1 | 1 | 1 | 1 | 2 | x 50gm |

G White 465

| 1 | 1 | 1 | 1 | 1 | x 50gm |

H Black 464

| 2 | 3 | 3 | 3 | 4 | x 50gm |

NEEDLES

1 pair 3¼mm (no 10) (US 3) needles
1 pair 3¾mm (no 9) (US 5) needles

TENSION

20 sts and 38 rows to 10 cm measured over patt using 3¾mm (US 5) needles.

BACK

Using 3¼mm (US 3) needles and yarn H cast on 103 [113: 123: 133: 143] sts.

Row 1 (RS): K1, *P1, K1, rep from * to end.

Row 2: P1, *K1, P1, rep from * to end.

These 2 rows form rib.

Work in rib for a further 14 rows, ending with RS facing for next row.

Break off yarn H.

Change to 3¾mm (US 5) needles.

Joining and breaking off colours as required, now work in patt as folls:

Row 1 (RS): Using yarn A, knit.

Row 2: Using yarn A, purl.

Rows 3 and 4: Using yarn B, knit.

Row 5: Using yarn A, K2, *yfwd, K2tog, rep from * to last st, K1.

Row 6: Using yarn A, knit.

Row 7: Using yarn B, purl.

Row 8: Using yarn B, knit.

Rows 9 to 16: As rows 1 to 8, using yarn C instead of yarn A and yarn D instead of yarn B.

Rows 17 to 24: As rows 1 to 8, using yarn E instead of yarn A and yarn F instead of yarn B.

Rows 25 to 32: As rows 1 to 8, using yarn G instead of yarn A and yarn H instead of yarn B.

These 32 rows form patt.

Cont in patt until back meas 44 [46: 48: 50: 52] cm, ending with RS facing for next row.

Shape shoulders

Keeping patt correct, cast off 3 [3: 4: 4: 5] sts at beg of next 4 rows, then 3 [4: 4: 5: 5] sts at beg of foll 2 rows. 85 [93: 99: 107: 113] sts.

Shape back neck

Next row (RS): Cast off 3 [4: 4: 5: 5] sts, patt until there are 23 [26: 28: 31: 33] sts on right needle and turn, leaving rem sts on a holder. Work each side of neck separately.

Dec 1 st at neck edge of next 4 rows, then on foll 2 alt rows **and at same time** cast off 3 [4: 4: 5: 5] sts at beg of 2nd and foll 2 [3: 2: 3: 2] alt rows, then 4 [–: 5: –: 6] sts at beg of foll 1 [–: 1: –: 1] alt row. Work 1 row.

Cast off rem 4 [4: 5: 5: 6] sts.

With RS facing, slip centre 33 [33: 35: 35: 37] sts onto a holder, rejoin appropriate yarn and patt to end.

Complete to match first side, reversing shapings.

FRONT

Work as given for back until 12 [12: 16: 16: 20] rows less have been worked than on back to beg of shoulder shaping, ending with RS facing for next row.

Shape front neck

Next row (RS): Patt 38 [43: 48: 53: 58] sts and turn, leaving rem sts on a holder.

Work each side of neck separately.

Keeping patt correct, dec 1 st at neck edge of next 6 rows, then on foll 2 [2: 3: 3: 3] alt rows, then on 0 [0: 0: 0: 1] foll 4th row. 30 [35: 39: 44: 48] sts.

Work 1 [1: 3: 3: 3] rows, ending with RS facing for next row.

Shape shoulder

Cast off 3 [3: 4: 4: 5] sts at beg and dec 1 st at end of next row. 26 [31: 34: 39: 42] sts.

Work 1 row.

Cast off 3 [3: 4: 4: 5] sts at beg of next and foll 5 [0: 5: 0: 5] alt rows, then 4 [4: 5: 5: 6] sts at beg of foll 1 [6: 1: 6: 1] alt rows.

Work 1 row.

Cast off rem 4 [4: 5: 5: 6] sts.

With RS facing, slip centre 27 sts onto a holder, rejoin appropriate yarn and patt to end.

Complete to match first side, reversing shapings.

SLEEVES

Using 3¼mm (US 3) needles and yarn H cast on 73 [79: 85: 91: 97] sts.

Work in rib as given for back for 16 rows, ending with RS facing for next row.

Break off yarn H.

Change to 3¾mm (US 5) needles.

Joining and breaking off colours as required, work in patt as given for back until sleeve meas 15 [15: 16: 16: 16] cm, ending with RS facing for next row.

Cast off using same yarn as previous row.

MAKING UP

Press as described on the information page.

Join right shoulder seam using back stitch, or mattress stitch if preferred.

Neckband

With RS facing and using 3¼mm (US 3) needles and yarn H, pick up and knit 21 [21: 24: 24: 27] sts down left side of front neck, K across 27 sts on front holder, pick up and knit 21 [21: 24: 24: 27] sts up right side of front neck, and 8 sts down right side of back neck, K across 33 [33: 35: 35: 37] sts on back holder inc 1 st at centre, then pick up and knit 8 sts up left side of back neck. 119 [119: 127: 127: 135] sts.

Beg with row 2, work in rib as given for back for 9 rows, ending with RS facing for next row.

Cast off in rib.

Join left shoulder and neckband seam. Mark points along side seam edges 18.5 [20: 21.5: 23: 24.5] cm either side of shoulder seams (to denote base of armhole openings).

See information page for finishing instructions, setting in sleeves using the straight cast-off method.

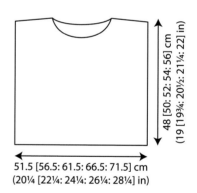

51.5 [56.5: 61.5: 66.5: 71.5] cm
(20¼ [22¼: 24¼: 26¼: 28¼] in)

48 [50: 52: 54: 56] cm
(19 [19¾: 20½: 21¼: 22] in)

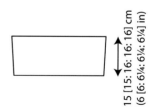

15 [15: 16: 16: 16] cm
(6 [6: 6¼: 6¼: 6¼] in)

Redshank •••

Page 30

SIZE

To fit bust

81-86	91-97	102-107	112-117	122-127	cm
32-34	36-38	40-42	44-46	48-50	in

Actual bust measurement of garment

141	152	162	172	182	cm
55½	59¾	63¾	67¾	71¾	in

YARN

Summerlite 4ply

A Seashell 437

5	6	6	7	7	x 50gm

B Still Grey 422

5	6	6	7	7	x 50gm

C Anchor Grey 446

3	3	3	4	4	x 50gm

NEEDLES

1 pair 2¾mm (no 12) (US 2) needles
1 pair 3¼mm (no 10) (US 3) needles
3¼mm (no 10) (US 3) circular needle at least 120 cm long

TENSION

34 sts and 68 rows to 10 cm measured over slip moss st patt using 3¼mm (US 3) needles.
32 sts and 44 rows to 10 cm measured over rib patt using 2¾mm (US 2) needles.

SPECIAL ABBREVIATIONS

yb = bring yarn to back (WS) of work; **yft** = take yarn to front (RS) of work.

STRIPE SEQUENCE A

Rows 1 and 2: Using yarn A.
Rows 3 and 4: Using yarn B.
Rows 5 to 12: As rows 1 to 4 twice.
Rows 13 and 14: Using yarn A.
Rows 15 and 16: Using yarn C.
Rows 17 to 24: As rows 13 to 16 twice.
These 24 rows form stripe sequence A and are repeated.

STRIPE SEQUENCE B

Rows 1 and 2: Using yarn A.
Rows 3 and 4: Using yarn B.
Rows 5 to 24: As rows 1 to 4, 5 times.
Rows 25 and 26: Using yarn A.
Rows 27 and 28: Using yarn C.
Rows 29 to 48: As rows 25 to 28, 5 times.
These 48 rows form stripe sequence B and are repeated.

BACK

Using 2¾mm (US 2) needles and yarn B cast on 237 [257: 273: 293: 309] sts.
Row 1 (RS): *P2, K2, rep from * to last st, P1.
Row 2: *K2, P2, rep from * to last st, K1.
These 2 rows form rib patt.
Cont in rib patt until back meas 10 cm, inc 1 [1: 1: 0: 0] st at each end of last row and ending with RS facing for next row.
239 [259: 275: 293: 309] sts.
Change to 3¼mm (US 3) needles.
Joining and breaking off colours as required, work in slip moss st patt and stripe sequence A as folls:
Row 1 (RS): Using yarn A, K1, *sl 1 purlwise, K1, rep from * to end.
Row 2: Using yarn A, K1, *yb – see special abbreviation, sl 1 purlwise, yft – see special abbreviation, K1, rep from * to end.
Row 3: Using yarn B, K2, *sl 1 purlwise, K1, rep from * to last st, K1.
Row 4: Using yarn B, K2, *yb, sl 1 purlwise, yft, K1, rep from * to last st, K1.
These 4 rows form slip moss st patt and set first 4 rows of stripe sequence A.
Beg with row 5 of stripe sequence A, cont straight in patt for a further 80 rows, ending with row 4 of patt, row 12 of stripe sequence A and RS facing for next row.
Shape underarms
Changing to 3¼mm (US 3) circular needle when there are too many sts to fit on straight needles and keeping stripe sequence A correct, inc 1 st at each end of next and 5 [6: 7: 8: 8] foll 6th rows, then on 10 [12: 13: 12: 12] foll 4th rows, then on foll 10 [9: 11: 11: 9] alt rows, then on foll 9 [7: 5: 5: 9] rows, taking inc sts into patt and ending with RS facing for next row. 309 [329: 349: 367: 387] sts.

Cast on 4 sts at beg of next 8 rows. 341 [361: 381: 399: 419] sts.
Place a marker at each end of last row to denote end of underarm shaping.

Cont straight in patt for 24 [14: 2: 0: 0] rows, ending with row 24 of stripe sequence A and RS facing for next row.

Beg with row 1, now work in stripe sequence B throughout as folls:
Cont straight in patt for 42 [56: 70: 74: 76] rows, ending with row 42 [8: 22: 26: 28] of stripe sequence B and RS facing for next row.
Place a marker at each end of last row to denote start of overarm shaping.

Shape overarms
Keeping patt and stripe sequence B correct, cast off 4 sts at beg of next 12 [16: 20: 20: 20] rows. 293 [297: 301: 319: 339] sts.★★
Dec 1 st at each end of next 57 [53: 47: 45: 45] rows, then on foll 21 [17: 15: 18: 20] alt rows, then on foll 11 [19: 25: 31: 37] rows, ending with row 20 [34: 48: 14: 26] of stripe sequence B and RS facing for next row. 115 [119: 127: 131: 135] sts.

Shape back neck and shoulders
Next row (RS): Work 2 tog, patt 29 [31: 33: 35: 35] sts and turn, leaving rem sts on a holder. 30 [32: 34: 36: 36] sts.
Work each side of neck separately.
Dec 1 st at neck edge of next 4 [4: 3: 1: 1] rows, then on foll 1 [0: 0: 0: 0] alt row **and at same time** dec 1 st at overarm edge of next 6 [4: 3: 1: 1] rows. 19 [24: 28: 34: 34] sts.

Sizes 81-86 cm and 91-97 cm only
Next row (WS): Patt to last 2 sts, work 2tog. 18 [23: –: –: –] sts.

All sizes
Cast off 4 sts at beg of next and foll 2 [3: 4: 5: 5] alt rows **and at same time** dec 1 st at neck edge of next 1 [1: 1: 3: 3] rows, then on foll 1 [2: 3: 3: 3] alt rows.
Work 1 row.
Cast off rem 4 sts.
With RS facing, rejoin appropriate yarn and cast off centre 53 [53: 57: 57: 61] sts, patt to last 2 sts, work 2 tog. 30 [32: 34: 36: 36] sts.
Complete to match first side, reversing shapings.

FRONT
Work as given for back to ★★.
Dec 1 st at each end of next 57 [53: 47: 45: 45] rows, then on foll 12 [12: 10: 16: 18] alt rows. 155 [167: 187: 197: 213] sts.
Work 1 row, ending with row 40 [6: 14: 28: 34] of stripe sequence B and RS facing for next row.

Shape front neck and shoulders
Next row (RS): Work 2 tog, patt 57 [63: 72: 77: 84] sts and turn, leaving rem sts on a holder. 58 [64: 73: 78: 85] sts.
Work each side of neck separately.
Dec 1 st at overarm edge of 2nd and foll 7 [3: 3: 0: 0] alt rows, then on foll 18 [25: 26: 32: 38] rows **and at same time** dec 1 st at neck edge of next 6 rows, then on foll 5 alt rows, then on 3 foll 4th rows, then on 1 [0: 1: 1: 2] foll 6th rows, ending with **WS** [RS: **WS**: **WS**: **WS**] facing for next row. 17 [21: 28: 30: 30] sts.

Size 81-86 cm only
Next row (WS): Patt to last 2 sts, work 2tog. 16 sts.
Cast off 4 sts at beg of next and foll 2 alt rows. 4 sts.

Size 91-97 cm only
Cast off 4 sts at beg of next and foll 3 alt rows **and at same time**

dec 1 st at neck edge of next row. 4 sts.

Size 102-107 cm only
Dec 1 st at overarm edge **only** of next 3 rows. 25 sts.
Cast off 4 sts at beg of next and foll 4 alt rows **and at same time** dec 1 st at neck edge of 3rd row. 4 sts.

Sizes 112-117 cm and 122-127 cm only
Next row (WS): Patt to last 2 sts, work 2tog. 29 sts.
Cast off 4 sts at beg of next and foll 5 alt rows **and at same time** dec 1 st at neck edge of 5th row. 4 sts.

All sizes
Work 1 row.
Cast off rem 4 sts.
With RS facing, rejoin appropriate yarn and cast off centre 37 [37: 39: 39: 41] sts, patt to last 2 sts, work 2 tog. 58 [64: 73: 78: 85] sts.
Complete to match first side, reversing shapings.

MAKING UP
Press as described on the information page.
Join right shoulder and overarm seam using back stitch, or mattress stitch if preferred.

Neckband
With RS facing, using 2¾mm (US 2) needles and yarn B, pick up and knit 21 [21: 23: 23: 26] sts down left side of front neck, 35 [35: 36: 36: 38] sts from front, 21 [21: 23: 23: 26] sts up right side of front neck, 7 sts down right side of back neck, 50 [50: 53: 53: 57] sts from back, and 7 sts up left side of back neck. 141 [141: 149: 149: 161] sts.
Beg with row 2, work in rib patt as given for back for 2.5 cm, ending with RS facing for next row.
Cast off in rib patt.
Join left shoulder, overarm seam and neckband seam.

Cuffs (both alike)
With RS facing, using 2¾mm (US 2) needles and yarn B, pick up and knit 61 [65: 69: 69: 73] sts along row-end edge of cuff between markers.
Beg with row 2, work in rib patt as given for back for 10 cm, ending with RS facing for next row.
Cast off in rib patt.
Join side, underarm and sleeve seams.

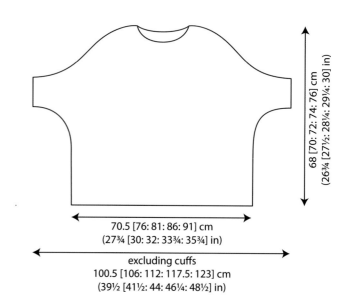

68 [70: 72: 74: 76] cm
(26¾ [27½: 28¼: 29¼: 30] in)

70.5 [76: 81: 86: 91] cm
(27¾ [30: 32: 33¾: 35¾] in)

excluding cuffs
100.5 [106: 112: 117.5: 123] cm
(39½ [41½: 44: 46¼: 48½] in)

Ruff •

Page 20

YARN

Summerlite DK

A	White 465	2	x 50gm
B	Garden 471	1	x 50gm
C	Lagoon 457	2	x 50gm
D	Summer 453	1	x 50gm
E	Rouge 462	2	x 50gm
F	Cantaloupe 456	1	x 50gm
G	Fuchsia 455	2	x 50gm
H	Indigo 450	1	x 50gm

NEEDLES
3¾mm (no 9) (US 5) circular needle at least 120 cm long

TENSION
22 sts and 40 rows to 10 cm measured over garter st using 3¾mm (US 5) needles.

FINISHED SIZE
Completed scarf is 29.5 cm (11½ in) wide and 180 cm (70¾ in) long (excluding fringing).

SCARF
Using 3¾mm (US 5) circular needle and yarn A cast on 396 sts, leaving a length of yarn at least 15 cm long at end of cast-on sts.
Work backwards and forwards in rows as folls:
Row 1 (RS): Using yarn A, knit.
Break off yarn A, leaving a 15 cm length of yarn (for fringing).
Rejoin yarn A with a 15 cm length of yarn at beg of next row (for fringing).
Row 2: Using yarn A, knit.
Break off yarn A, leaving a 15 cm length of yarn.
Join in yarn B with a 15 cm length of yarn at beg of next row.
Row 3: Using yarn B, knit.
Break off yarn B, leaving a 15 cm length of yarn.
Rejoin yarn B with a 15 cm length of yarn at beg of next row.
Row 4: Using yarn B, knit.
Joining in yarn at the beg and breaking off yarn at the end of each row leaving 15 cm lengths of yarn for fringing, cont in garter st stripes as folls:
Rows 5 to 8: Using yarn C, knit.

Rows 9 and 10: Using yarn D, knit.
Rows 11 to 14: Using yarn E, knit.
Rows 15 and 16: Using yarn F, knit.
Rows 17 and 18: Using yarn A, knit.
Rows 19 to 22: Using yarn G, knit.
Rows 23 and 24: Using yarn A, knit.
Rows 25 to 28: Using yarn H, knit.
Rows 29 to 32: Using yarn F, knit.
Rows 33 to 36: Using yarn H, knit.
Rows 37 and 38: Using yarn A, knit.
Rows 39 to 42: Using yarn G, knit.
Rows 43 and 44: Using yarn A, knit.
Rows 45 and 46: Using yarn F, knit.
Rows 47 to 50: Using yarn E, knit.
Rows 51 and 52: Using yarn D, knit.
Rows 53 to 56: Using yarn C, knit.
Rows 57 and 58: Using yarn B, knit.
Rows 59 to 116: As rows 1 to 58.
Row 117: Using yarn A, knit.
Leaving a 15 cm length of yarn at beg and end of row, cast off (on **WS**).

MAKING UP
Do NOT press.
To make fringing, knot yarn ends together in groups of 4 at each end of scarf and trim ends to lengths of 10 cm.
See information page for finishing instructions.

Silver Moony •••

Page 6

SIZE

To fit bust

81-86	91-97	102-107	112-117	122-127	cm
32-34	36-38	40-42	44-46	48-50	in

Actual bust measurement of garment

88	99	110	121	132	cm
34¾	39	43¼	47¾	52	in

YARN

Summerlite DK

A Linen 460

8	9	10	11	12	x 50gm

B Indigo 450

1	1	1	1	1	x 50gm

C Black 464

1	1	1	1	1	x 50gm

D Cantaloupe 456

1	1	1	1	1	x 50gm

E Rouge 462

1	1	1	1	1	x 50gm

F Khaki 461

1	1	1	1	1	x 50gm

NEEDLES

1 pair 3¼mm (no 10) (US 3) needles
1 pair 3¾mm (no 9) (US 5) needles

BUTTONS – 8 x 9427224190 (metal shank) from Groves. Please see information page for contact details.

TENSION

22 sts and 37 rows to 10 cm measured over patt using 3¾mm (US 5) needles.

SPECIAL ABBREVIATIONS

sl 1 wyib = on WS rows, slip one st purlwise with yarn in back (RS) of work; **sl 1 wyif** = on RS rows, slip one st purlwise with yarn in front (RS) of work.

STRIPE SEQUENCE

Rows 1 and 2: Using yarn A.
Rows 3 and 4: Using yarn B.
Rows 5 to 8: Using yarn A.
Rows 9 and 10: Using yarn C.
Rows 11 to 14: Using yarn A.
Rows 15 and 16: Using yarn D.
Rows 17 to 20: Using yarn A.
Rows 21 and 22: Using yarn E.
Rows 23 to 26: Using yarn A.
Rows 27 and 28: Using yarn F.
Rows 29 and 30: Using yarn A.
These 30 rows form stripe sequence and are repeated.

BACK

Using 3¼mm (US 3) needles and yarn A cast on 101 [113: 125: 137: 149] sts.
Work in g st for 6 rows, ending with RS facing for next row.
Change to 3¾mm (US 5) needles.
Joining and breaking off colours as required, work in patt and stripe sequence as folls:
Row 1 (RS): Using yarn A, knit.
Row 2: Using yarn A, purl.
Row 3: Using yarn B, P2, *sl 1 wyif – see special abbreviation, P1, rep from * to last st, P1.
Row 4: Using yarn B, K1, *sl 1 wyib – see special abbreviation, K1, rep from * to end.
Row 5: Using yarn A, knit.
Row 6: Using yarn A, purl.
These 6 rows form patt and set first 6 rows of stripe sequence.
Beg with row 7 of stripe sequence, cont in patt for a further 8 [8: 10: 10: 12] rows, ending with RS facing for next row.
Keeping patt and stripe sequence correct, dec 1 st at each end of next and 3 foll 10th rows, then on 2 foll 8th rows. 89 [101: 113: 125: 137] sts.
Work 17 rows, ending with RS facing for next row.
Inc 1 st at each end of next and 2 foll 12th rows, then on foll 14th row, taking inc sts into patt. 97 [109: 121: 133: 145] sts.
Work 15 rows, ending with row 12 [12: 14: 14: 16] of stripe sequence and RS facing for next row. (Back should meas approx 37 [37: 37.5: 37.5: 38.5] cm.)
Shape armholes
Keeping patt and stripe sequence correct, cast off 3 [4: 5: 6: 7] sts at

beg of next 2 rows. 91 [101: 111: 121: 131] sts.

Dec 1 st at each end of next 3 [7: 9: 9: 11] rows, then on foll 5 [4: 4: 5: 5] alt rows, then on foll 4th row. 73 [77: 83: 91: 97] sts.

Cont straight until armhole meas 19.5 [21: 22.5: 24: 25.5] cm, ending with RS facing for next row.

Shape back neck

Next row (RS): Patt 24 [26: 28: 32: 34] sts and turn, leaving rem sts on a holder.

Work each side of neck separately.

Dec 1 st at neck edge of next row. 23 [25: 27: 31: 33] sts.

Shape shoulder

Cast off 5 [5: 6: 7: 7] sts at beg of next and foll 2 alt rows **and at same time** dec 1 st at neck edge of next 3 rows, then on foll alt row.

Work 1 row.

Cast off rem 4 [6: 5: 6: 8] sts.

With RS facing, rejoin appropriate yarn and cast off centre 25 [25: 27: 27: 29] sts, patt to end.

Complete to match first side, reversing shapings.

LEFT FRONT

Using 3¼mm (US 3) needles and yarn A cast on 48 [54: 60: 66: 72] sts.

Work in g st for 6 rows, ending with RS facing for next row.

Change to 3¾mm (US 5) needles.

Joining and breaking off colours as required, work in patt and stripe sequence as folls:

Row 1 (RS): Using yarn A, knit.

Row 2: Using yarn A, purl.

Row 3: Using yarn B, P2, *sl 1 wyif, P1, rep from * to end.

Row 4: Using yarn B, K2, *sl 1 wyib, K1, rep from * to end.

Row 5: Using yarn A, knit.

Row 6: Using yarn A, purl.

These 6 rows form patt and set first 6 rows of stripe sequence.

Beg with row 7 of stripe sequence, cont in patt for a further 8 [8: 10: 10: 12] rows, ending with RS facing for next row.

Keeping patt and stripe sequence correct, dec 1 st at beg of next and 3 foll 10th rows, then on 2 foll 8th rows. 42 [48: 54: 60: 66] sts.

Work 17 rows, ending with RS facing for next row.

Inc 1 st at beg of next and 2 foll 12th rows, then on foll 14th row, taking inc sts into patt. 46 [52: 58: 64: 70] sts.

Work 15 rows, ending with row 12 [12: 14: 14: 16] of stripe sequence and RS facing for next row. (Left front should meas approx 37 [37: 37.5: 37.5: 38.5] cm.)

Shape armhole

Keeping patt and stripe sequence correct, cast off 3 [4: 5: 6: 7] sts at beg of next row. 43 [48: 53: 58: 63] sts.

Work 1 row.

Dec 1 st at armhole edge of next 3 [7: 9: 9: 11] rows, then on foll 5 [4: 4: 5: 5] alt rows, then on foll 4th row. 34 [36: 39: 43: 46] sts.

Cont straight until 24 [24: 28: 28: 32] rows less have been worked than on back to beg of shoulder shaping, ending with RS facing for next row.

Shape front neck

Next row (RS): Patt 29 [31: 34: 38: 41] sts, cast off rem 5 sts.

Break off yarn.

With **WS** facing, rejoin yarn and cont as folls:

Dec 1 st at neck edge of next 6 rows, then on foll 2 alt rows, then on 2 [2: 3: 3: 4] foll 4th rows. 19 [21: 23: 27: 29] sts.

Work 5 rows, ending with RS facing for next row.

Shape shoulder

Cast off 5 [5: 6: 7: 7] sts at beg of next and foll 2 alt rows.

Work 1 row.

Cast off rem 4 [6: 5: 6: 8] sts.

RIGHT FRONT

Using 3¼mm (US 3) needles and yarn A cast on 48 [54: 60: 66: 72] sts.

Work in g st for 6 rows, ending with RS facing for next row.

Change to 3¾mm (US 5) needles.

Joining and breaking off colours as required, work in patt and stripe sequence as folls:

Row 1 (RS): Using yarn A, knit.

Row 2: Using yarn A, purl.

Row 3: Using yarn B, *P1, sl 1 wyif, rep from * to last 2 sts, P2.

Row 4: Using yarn B, *K1, sl 1 wyib, rep from * to last 2 sts, K2.

Row 5: Using yarn A, knit.

Row 6: Using yarn A, purl.

These 6 rows form patt and set first 6 rows of stripe sequence.

Complete to match left front, reversing shapings and working first row of neck shaping as folls:

Shape front neck

Next row (RS): Cast off 5 sts, patt to end. 29 [31: 34: 38: 41] sts.

SLEEVES

Using 3¼mm (US 3) needles and yarn A cast on 51 [53: 55: 55: 57] sts.

Work in g st for 6 rows, ending with RS facing for next row.

Change to 3¾mm (US 5) needles.

Joining and breaking off colours as required and beg with row 1 of stripe sequence, now work in patt as given for back, inc 1 st at each end of 13th [13th: 11th: 9th: 9th] and every foll 12th [12th: 10th: 8th: 8th] row to 59 [75: 63: 67: 77] sts, then on every foll 14th [14th: 12th: 10th: 10th] row until there are 73 [77: 81: 87: 91] sts, taking inc sts into patt.

Cont straight until sleeve meas approx 45 [45: 46: 46: 46.5] cm, ending with row 12 [12: 14: 14: 16] of stripe sequence and RS facing for next row.

Shape top

Keeping patt and stripe sequence correct, cast off 3 [4: 5: 6: 7] sts at beg of next 2 rows. 67 [69: 71: 75: 77] sts.

Dec 1 st at each end of next 3 rows, then on foll 3 alt rows, then on 8 [9: 11: 12: 14] foll 4th rows. 39 [39: 37: 39: 37] sts.

Work 1 row.

Dec 1 st at each end of next and every foll alt row until 27 sts rem, then on foll 5 rows, ending with RS facing for next row.

Cast off rem 17 sts.

MAKING UP

Press as described on the information page.

Join both shoulder seams using back stitch, or mattress stitch if preferred.

Button band

With RS facing, using 3¼mm (US 3) needles and yarn A, pick up and knit 114 [114: 121: 121: 128] sts evenly down left front opening edge, from top of neck shaping to cast-on edge.

Work in g st for 8 rows, ending with **WS** facing for next row.

Cast off knitwise (on **WS**).

Buttonhole band

With RS facing, using 3¼mm (US 3) needles and yarn A, pick up and knit 114 [114: 121: 121: 128] sts evenly up right front opening edge, from cast-on edge to top of neck shaping.

Work in g st for 3 rows, ending with RS facing for next row.

Row 4 (RS): K5, *yfwd, K2tog (to make a buttonhole), K13 [13: 14: 14: 15], rep from * 6 times more, yfwd, K2tog (to make 8th buttonhole), K2.

Work in g st for a further 4 rows, ending with **WS** facing for next row.

Cast off knitwise (on **WS**).

Neckband

With RS facing, using 3¼mm (US 3) needles and yarn A, pick up and knit 5 sts across top of buttonhole band, 28 [28: 31: 31: 34] sts up right side of front neck, 6 sts down right side of back neck, 25 [25: 27: 27: 29] sts across centre back neck, 6 sts up left side of back neck, 28 [28: 31: 31: 34] sts down left side of front neck, then 5 sts across top of button band. 103 [103: 111: 111: 119] sts.

Beg with a P row, work in st st for 7 rows, ending with RS facing for next row.

Using a 3¾mm (US 5) needle, cast off knitwise.

See information page for finishing instructions, setting in sleeves using the set-in method.

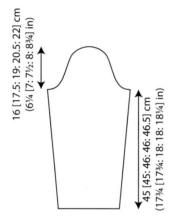

16 [17.5: 19: 20.5: 22] cm (6¼ [7: 7½: 8: 8¾] in)

45 [45: 46: 46: 46.5] cm (17¾ [17¾: 18: 18: 18¼] in)

58.5 [60: 62: 63.5: 66] cm (23 [23½: 24½: 25: 26] in)

44 [49.5: 55: 60.5: 66] cm (17¼ [19½: 21¾: 23¾: 26] in)

Stilt ••

Page 14

YARN

Summerlite 4ply

A	Seashell 437	6	x 50gm
B	Periwinkle 424	4	x 50gm
C	Navy Ink 429	3	x 50gm

NEEDLES

1 pair 2¾mm (no 12) (US 2) needles
1 pair 3¼mm (no 10) (US 3) needles

TENSION

34 sts and 68 rows to 10 cm measured over patt using 3¼mm (US 3) needles.

FINISHED SIZE

Completed scarf is 45 cm (17¾ in) wide and approx 210 cm (82¾ in) long.

SPECIAL ABBREVIATIONS

yb = bring yarn to back (WS) of work; **yft** = take yarn to front (RS) of work.

STRIPE SEQUENCE A

Rows 1 and 2: Using yarn A.
Rows 3 and 4: Using yarn B.
Rows 5 to 12: As rows 1 to 4 twice.
Rows 13 and 14: Using yarn A.
Rows 15 and 16: Using yarn C.
Rows 17 to 24: As rows 13 to 16 twice.
These 24 rows form stripe sequence A and are repeated.

STRIPE SEQUENCE B

Rows 1 and 2: Using yarn A.
Rows 3 and 4: Using yarn B.
Rows 5 to 24: As rows 1 to 4, 5 times.
Rows 25 and 26: Using yarn A.
Rows 27 and 28: Using yarn C.
Rows 29 to 48: As rows 25 to 28, 5 times.
These 48 rows form stripe sequence B and are repeated.

SCARF

Using 2¾mm (US 2) needles and yarn A cast on 126 sts.
Work in g st for 5 rows, ending with **WS** facing for next row.
Row 6 (WS): K5, M1, ★K4, M1, K5, M1, rep from ★ to last 4 sts, K4. 153 sts.
Change to 3¼mm (US 3) needles.
Joining in and breaking off colours as required, work in patt and stripe sequence A as folls:
Row 1 (RS): Using yarn A, K1, ★sl 1 purlwise, K1, rep from ★ to end.
Row 2: Using yarn A, K1, ★yb – see special abbreviation, sl 1 purlwise, yft – see special abbreviation, K1, rep from ★ to end.
Row 3: Using yarn B, K2, ★sl 1 purlwise, K1, rep from ★ to last st, K1.
Row 4: Using yarn B, K2, ★yb, sl 1 purlwise, yft, K1, rep from ★ to last st, K1.
These 4 rows form patt and set first 4 rows of stripe sequence A.
Cont in patt throughout as folls:
Beg with row 5 of stripe sequence A, work a further 284 rows, ending with row 24 of stripe sequence A and RS facing for next row.
Beg with row 1, now work in stripe sequence B, repeating the 48 row repeat 17 times, then rows 1 to 24 again, ending with RS facing for next row (840 rows of stripe sequence B worked in total).
Beg with row 13, now work in stripe sequence A for 288 rows, ending with row 12 of stripe sequence A and RS facing for next row.
Break off yarn B and yarn C and cont in yarn A only.
Change to 2¾mm (US 2) needles.
Next row (RS): K4, K2tog, ★K3, K2tog, K4, K2tog, rep from ★ to last 4 sts, K4. 126 sts.
Work in g st for 6 rows, ending with **WS** facing for next row.
Cast off knitwise (on **WS**).

MAKING UP

Press as described on the information page.
See information page for finishing instructions.

Stingray ••

Page 26

SIZE
To fit bust

| 81-86 | 91-97 | 102-107 | 112-117 | 122-127 | cm |
| 32-34 | 36-38 | 40-42 | 44-46 | 48-50 | in |

Actual bust measurement of garment

| 94.5 | 105.5 | 116.5 | 127.5 | 138 | cm |
| 37¼ | 41½ | 45¾ | 50¼ | 54¼ | in |

YARN
Summerlite DK

A Linen 460

| 9 | 10 | 11 | 12 | 13 | x 50gm |

B Rouge 462

| 1 | 1 | 1 | 1 | 1 | x 50gm |

C Mocha 451

| 1 | 1 | 1 | 1 | 1 | x 50gm |

D Plaster 452

| 1 | 1 | 1 | 1 | 1 | x 50gm |

NEEDLES
1 pair 3¼mm (no 10) (US 3) needles
1 pair 3¾mm (no 9) (US 5) needles

TENSION
22 sts and 30 rows to 10 cm measured over st st using 3¾mm (US 5) needles.

STRIPE SEQUENCE FOR CUFFS
Rows 1 and 2: Using yarn B.
Rows 3 and 4: Using yarn C.
Rows 5 and 6: Using yarn D.
Rows 7 and 8: Using yarn A.
Rows 9 and 10: Using yarn D.
Rows 11 and 12: Using yarn C.
Rows 13 and 14: Using yarn B.
Rows 15 and 16: Using yarn C.
Rows 17 and 18: Using yarn D.
Rows 19 and 20: Using yarn A.
Rows 21 and 22: Using yarn D.
Rows 23 and 24: Using yarn C.
Rows 25 and 26: Using yarn B.
Rows 27 and 28: Using yarn C.

Rows 29 and 30: Using yarn D.
These 30 rows form stripe sequence for cuffs.

STRIPE SEQUENCE FOR NECKBAND
Rows 1 and 2: Using yarn D.
Rows 3 and 4: Using yarn C.
Rows 5 and 6: Using yarn B.
Rows 7 and 8: Using yarn C.
Rows 9 and 10: Using yarn D.
Rows 11 and 12: Using yarn A.
Rows 13 to 36: As rows 1 to 12 twice.
Rows 37 to 40: As rows 1 to 4.
Row 41: Using yarn B.
These 41 rows form stripe sequence for neckband.

BACK
Using 3¼mm (US 3) needles and yarn A cast on 104 [116: 128: 140: 152] sts.
Row 1 (RS): K2, *P1, K2, rep from * to end.
Row 2: P2, *K1, P2, rep from * end.
These 2 rows form rib.
Work in rib for a further 2 rows, ending with RS facing for next row.
Change to 3¾mm (US 5) needles.
Beg with a K row, now work in st st throughout as folls:
Cont straight until back meas 35 [35.5: 36: 36.5: 37] cm, ending with RS facing for next row.
Shape armholes
Cast off 4 [5: 6: 7: 8] sts at beg of next 2 rows. 96 [106: 116: 126: 136] sts.
Next row (RS): K2, K2tog, K to last 4 sts, sl 1, K1, psso, K2.
Next row: P2, P2tog tbl, P to last 4 sts, P2tog, P2.
Working all armhole decreases as set by last 2 rows, dec 1 st at each end of next 5 [7: 7: 9: 9] rows, then on foll 5 [5: 6: 6: 7] alt rows. 72 [78: 86: 92: 100] sts.
Cont straight until armhole meas 21 [22.5: 24: 25.5: 27] cm, ending with RS facing for next row.
Shape shoulders and back neck
Next row (RS): Cast off 4 [5: 6: 7: 7] sts, K until there are 18 [20: 22: 24: 27] sts on right needle and turn, leaving rem sts on a holder. Work each side of neck separately.

Working all back neck decreases in same way as armhole decreases, dec 1 st at neck edge of next 4 rows **and at same time** cast off 4 [5: 6: 7: 7] sts at beg of 2nd row, then 5 [5: 5: 6: 7: 8] sts at beg of foll alt row.

Work 1 row.

Cast off rem 5 [6: 6: 6: 8] sts.

With RS facing, slip centre 28 [28: 30: 30: 32] sts onto a holder, rejoin yarn and K to end.

Complete to match first side, reversing shapings.

FRONT

Work as given for back until 16 [16: 18: 18: 20] rows less have been worked than on back to beg of shoulder shaping, ending with RS facing for next row.

Shape front neck

Next row (RS): K25 [28: 32: 35: 39] and turn, leaving rem sts on a holder.

Work each side of neck separately.

Working front neck decreases in same way as armhole decreases, dec 1 st at neck edge of next 4 rows, then on foll 3 [3: 4: 4: 5] alt rows. 18 [21: 24: 27: 30] sts.

Work 5 rows, ending with RS facing for next row.

Shape shoulder

Cast off 4 [5: 6: 7: 7] sts at beg of next and foll alt row, then 5 [5: 6: 7: 8] sts at beg of foll alt row.

Work 1 row.

Cast off rem 5 [6: 6: 6: 8] sts.

With RS facing, slip centre 22 sts onto a holder, rejoin yarn and K to end.

Complete to match first side, reversing shapings.

SLEEVES

Using 3¼mm (US 3) needles and yarn B cast on 42 [42: 46: 46: 50] sts.

Row 1 (RS): K1 [1: 0: 0: 2], *P1, K2, rep from * to last 2 [2: 1: 1: 0] sts, P1 [1: 1: 1: 0], K1 [1: 0: 0: 0].

Row 2: P1 [1: 0: 0: 2], *K1, P2, rep from * to last 2 [2: 1: 1: 0] sts, K1 [1: 1: 1: 0], P1 [1: 0: 0: 0].

These 2 rows form rib.

Beg with **row 3** of stripe sequence for cuffs and joining in and breaking off colours as required, cont in rib, inc 1 st at each end of 3rd and 5 foll 4th rows, then on foll 2 alt rows, taking inc sts into rib. 58 [58: 62: 62: 66] sts.

Work 1 row, ending with row 30 of stripe sequence and RS facing for next row.

Change to 3¾mm (US 5) needles.

Join yarn A and beg with a K row, now work in st st and yarn A throughout as folls:

Work 12 [8: 8: 6: 6] rows, ending with RS facing for next row.

Next row (RS): K3, M1, K to last 3 sts, M1, K3.

Working all sleeve increases as set by last row, inc 1 st at each end of 12th [8th: 8th: 6th: 6th] and every foll 12th [8th: 8th: 8th: 8th] row to 74 [72: 72: 88: 92] sts, then on every foll – [10th: 10th: –: –] row until there are – [80: 84: –: –] sts.

Cont straight until sleeve meas 46 [46: 47: 47: 47] cm, ending with RS facing for next row.

Shape top

Cast off 4 [5: 6: 7: 8] sts at beg of next 2 rows. 66 [70: 72: 74: 76] sts. Working all sleeve top decreases in same way as armhole decreases, dec 1 st at each end of next 5 rows, then on foll 4 alt rows, then on 5 [5: 6: 7: 8] foll 4th rows. 38 [42: 42: 42: 42] sts.

Work 1 row.

Dec 1 st at each end of next and every foll alt row until 24 sts rem, then on foll 3 rows, ending with RS facing for next row.

Cast off rem 18 sts.

MAKING UP

Press as described on the information page.

Join right shoulder seam using back stitch, or mattress stitch if preferred.

Neckband

With RS facing and using 3¼mm (US 3) needles and yarn D, pick up and knit 21 [21: 23: 23: 25] sts down left side of front neck, K across 22 sts on front holder, pick up and knit 21 [21: 23: 23: 25] sts up right side of front neck, and 6 sts down right side of back neck, K across 28 [28: 30: 30: 32] sts on back holder, then pick up and knit 6 sts up left side of back neck. 104 [104: 110: 110: 116] sts.

Beg with **row 2** of stripe sequence for neckband and row 2 of rib, joining in and breaking off colours as required, work in rib as given for back for 40 rows, ending with row 41 of stripe sequence and **WS** facing for next row.

Using yarn B, cast off in rib (on **WS**).

See information page for finishing instructions, setting in sleeves using the set-in method.

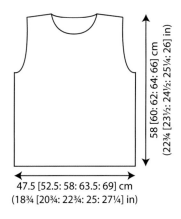

47.5 [52.5: 58: 63.5: 69] cm
(18¾ [20¾: 22¾: 25: 27¼] in)

58 [60: 62: 64: 66] cm
(22¾ [23½: 24½: 25¼: 26] in)

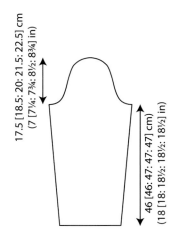

17.5 [18.5: 20: 21.5: 22.5] cm
(7 [7¼: 7¾: 8½: 8¾] in)

46 [46: 47: 47: 47] cm
(18 [18: 18½: 18½: 18½] in)

Tern •••

Page 12

SIZE

To fit bust

81-86	91-97	102-107	112-117	122-127	cm
32-34	36-38	40-42	44-46	48-50	in

Actual bust measurement of garment

93.5	103.5	113.5	123.5	133.5	cm
36¾	40¾	44¾	48½	52½	in

YARN

Summerlite 4ply

A Seashell 437

5	6	6	7	8	x 50gm

B Anchor Grey 446

1	1	1	1	1	x 50gm

NEEDLES

1 pair 2¼mm (no 13) (US 1) needles
1 pair 3mm (no 11) (US 2/3) needles

TENSION

28 sts and 36 rows to 10 cm measured over st st using 3mm (US 2/3) needles.

BACK

Using 2¼mm (US 1) needles and yarn A cast on 131 [145: 159: 173: 187] sts.

Work in g st for 10 rows, ending with RS facing for next row.

Change to 3mm (US 2/3) needles.

Beg with a K row, now work in st st for 4 rows, ending with RS facing for next row.

Joining and breaking off colours as required and using the **intarsia** technique as described on the information page when working from chart, work colour stripes and chevrons as folls:

Row 1 (RS): Using yarn B K82 [89: 97: 104: 112], work 11 sts as row 1 of body chart, using yarn B K38 [45: 51: 58: 64].

Row 2: Using yarn B P38 [45: 51: 58: 64], work 11 sts as row 2 of body chart, using yarn B P82 [89: 97: 104: 112].

These 2 rows set placement of body chart.

Working appropriate rows of body chart as set, cont in st st, working colour stripes as folls:

Rows 3 and 4: Using yarn B.

Rows 5 to 8: Using yarn A.

Rows 9 to 12: Using yarn B.

Rows 13 to 16: Using yarn A.

Rows 17 to 20: Using yarn B.

Rows 21 to 26: Using yarn A.

These 26 rows complete colour stripes and chevrons.

Break off yarn B and cont in st st, beg with a K row, using yarn A **only** as folls:

★★Cont straight until back meas 24 [24.5: 25: 25.5: 26] cm, ending with RS facing for next row.

Shape armholes

Cast off 4 [5: 6: 7: 8] sts at beg of next 2 rows. 123 [135: 147: 159: 171] sts.

Dec 1 st at each end of next 9 [11: 13: 15: 17] rows, then on foll 3 alt rows, then on foll 4th row. 97 [105: 113: 121: 129] sts.

Cont straight until armhole meas 18 [19.5: 21: 22.5: 24] cm, ending with RS facing for next row.

Shape shoulders and back neck

Next row (RS): Cast off 4 [5: 5: 6: 7] sts, K until there are 22 [25: 28: 31: 33] sts on right needle and turn, leaving rem sts on a holder. Work each side of neck separately.

Dec 1 st at neck edge of next 4 rows, then on foll alt row **and at same time** cast off 4 [5: 5: 6: 7] sts at beg of 2nd row, 4 [5: 6: 6: 7] sts at beg of foll alt row, then 4 [5: 6: 7: 7] sts at beg of foll alt row. Work 1 row.

Cast off rem 5 [5: 6: 7: 7] sts.

With RS facing, slip centre 45 [45: 47: 47: 49] sts onto a holder, rejoin yarn and K to end.

Complete to match first side, reversing shapings.

FRONT

Using 2¼mm (US 1) needles and yarn A cast on 131 [145: 159: 173: 187] sts.

Work in g st for 10 rows, ending with RS facing for next row.

Change to 3mm (US 2/3) needles.

Beg with a K row, now work in st st for 4 rows, ending with RS facing for next row.

Joining and breaking off colours as required and using the **intarsia** technique as described on the information page when working from chart, work colour stripes and chevrons as folls:

Row 1 (RS): Using yarn B K38 [45: 51: 58: 64], work 11 sts as row

1 of body chart, using yarn B K82 [89: 97: 104: 112].

Row 2: Using yarn B P82 [89: 97: 104: 112], work 11 sts as row 2 of body chart, using yarn B P38 [45: 51: 58: 64].

These 2 rows set placement of body chart.

Working appropriate rows of body chart as set, cont in st st, working colour stripes as folls:

Rows 3 and 4: Using yarn B.

Rows 5 to 8: Using yarn A.

Rows 9 to 12: Using yarn B.

Rows 13 to 16: Using yarn A.

Rows 17 to 20: Using yarn B.

Rows 21 to 26: Using yarn A.

These 26 rows complete colour stripes and chevrons.

Break off yarn B and cont in st st, beg with a K row, using yarn A **only** as folls:

Work as given for back from ★★ until 20 [20: 22: 22: 24] rows less have been worked than on back to beg of shoulder shaping, ending with RS facing for next row.

Shape front neck

Next row (RS): K32 [36: 40: 44: 48] and turn, leaving rem sts on a holder.

Work each side of neck separately.

Dec 1 st at neck edge of next 8 rows, then on foll 2 [2: 3: 3: 4] alt rows, then on foll 4th row. 21 [25: 28: 32: 35] sts.

Work 3 rows, ending with RS facing for next row.

Shape shoulder

Cast off 4 [5: 5: 6: 7] sts at beg of next and foll 3 [3: 1: 2: 3] alt rows, then − [-: 6: 7: -] sts at beg of foll − [-: 2: 1: -] alt rows.

Work 1 row.

Cast off rem 5 [5: 6: 7: 7] sts.

With RS facing, slip centre 33 sts onto a holder, rejoin yarn and K to end.

Complete to match first side, reversing shapings.

SLEEVES

Using 2¼mm (US 1) needles and yarn A cast on 53 [55: 57: 59: 61] sts.

Work in g st for 10 rows, ending with RS facing for next row.

Change to 3mm (US 2/3) needles.

Beg with a K row, now work in st st for 4 rows, ending with RS facing for next row.

Joining and breaking off colours as required and using the **intarsia** technique as described on the information page when working from chart, work colour stripe and chevron as folls:

Row 1 (RS): Using yarn B inc in first st, K20 [21: 22: 23: 24], work 11 sts as row 1 of sleeve chart, using yarn B K20 [21: 22: 23: 24], inc in last st. 55 [57: 59: 61: 63] sts.

Row 2: Using yarn B P22 [23: 24: 25: 26], work 11 sts as row 2 of sleeve chart, using yarn B P22 [23: 24: 25: 26].

Row 3: Using yarn B K22 [23: 24: 25: 26], work 11 sts as row 3 of sleeve chart, using yarn B K22 [23: 24: 25: 26].

Row 4: Using yarn B P22 [23: 24: 25: 26], work 11 sts as row 4 of sleeve chart, using yarn B P22 [23: 24: 25: 26].

Row 5: Using yarn A (inc in first st) 0 [1: 1: 1: 1] time, K22 [22: 23: 24: 25], work 11 sts as row 5 of sleeve chart, using yarn A K22 [22: 23: 24: 25], (inc in last st) 0 [1: 1: 1: 1] time. 55 [59: 61: 63: 65] sts.

Row 6: Using yarn A P22 [24: 25: 26: 27], work 11 sts as row 6 of sleeve chart, using yarn A P22 [24: 25: 26: 27].

Row 7: Using yarn A (inc in first st) 1 [0: 0: 0: 0] time, K21 [24: 25: 26: 27], work 11 sts as row 7 of sleeve chart, using yarn A K21 [24: 25: 26: 27], (inc in last st) 1 [0: 0: 0: 0] time. 57 [59: 61: 63: 65] sts.

Row 8: Using yarn A P23 [24: 25: 26: 27], work 11 sts as row 8 of sleeve chart, using yarn A P23 [24: 25: 26: 27].

Row 9: Using yarn A (inc in first st) 0 [1: 1: 1: 1] time, K23 [23: 24: 25: 26], work 11 sts as row 9 of sleeve chart, using yarn A K23 [23: 24: 25: 26], (inc in last st) 0 [1: 1: 1: 1] time. 57 [61: 63: 65: 67] sts.

Row 10: Using yarn A P23 [25: 26: 27: 28], work 11 sts as row 10 of sleeve chart, using yarn A P23 [25: 26: 27: 28].

These 10 rows complete colour stripe and chevron, and beg sleeve shaping.

Break off yarn B and cont in st st, beg with a K row, using yarn A **only** as folls:

Inc 1 st at each end of 3rd and every foll 6th [4th: 4th: 4th: 4th] row to 83 [65: 71: 85: 99] sts, then on every foll 8th [6th: 6th: 6th: 6th] row until there are 87 [93: 97: 103: 109] sts.

Cont straight until sleeve meas 35 [35: 36: 36: 36] cm, ending with RS facing for next row.

Shape top

Cast off 4 [5: 6: 7: 8] sts at beg of next 2 rows. 79 [83: 85: 89: 93] sts.

Dec 1 st at each end of next 5 rows, then on foll 5 alt rows, then on 2 [3: 5: 5: 6] foll 4th rows. 55 [57: 55: 59: 61] sts.

Work 1 row.

Dec 1 st at each end of next and every foll alt row until 37 sts rem, then on foll 7 rows, ending with RS facing for next row.

Cast off rem 23 sts.

MAKING UP

Press as described on the information page.

Join right shoulder seam using back stitch, or mattress stitch if preferred.

Neckband

With RS facing and using 2¼mm (US 1) needles and yarn A, pick up and knit 22 [22: 24: 24: 26] sts down left side of front neck, K across 33 sts on front holder, pick up and knit 22 [22: 24: 24: 26] sts up right side of front neck, and 7 sts down right side of back neck, K across 45 [45: 47: 47: 49] sts on back holder, then pick up and knit 7 sts up left side of back neck. 136 [136: 142: 142: 148] sts.

Work in g st for 10 rows, ending with **WS** facing for next row.

Cast off knitwise (on **WS**).

See information page for finishing instructions, setting in sleeves using the set-in method.

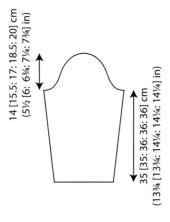

14 [15.5: 17: 18.5: 20] cm
(5½ [6: 6¾: 7¼: 7¾] in)

35 [35: 36: 36: 36] cm
(13¾ [13¾: 14¼: 14¼: 14¼] in)

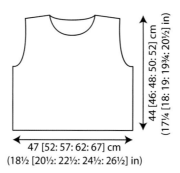

44 [46: 48: 50: 52] cm
(17¼ [18: 19: 19¾: 20½] in)

47 [52: 57: 62: 67] cm
(18½ [20½: 22½: 24½: 26½] in)

Body

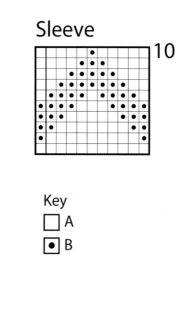

26

20

10

Sleeve

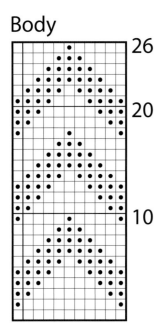

10

Key

☐ A

⊡ B

SIZING GUIDE

When you knit and wear a Rowan design we want you to look and feel fabulous. This all starts with the size and fit of the design you choose. To help you to achieve a great knitting experience we have looked at the sizing of our womens and menswear patterns. This has resulted in the introduction of our new sizing guide which includes the following exciting features:

Our sizing now conforms to standard clothing sizes. Therefore if you buy a standard size 12 in clothing, then our medium patterns will fit you perfectly.

The menswear designs are now available to knit in menswear sizes XSmall through to 2XL ie. 38" to 50" chest.

We have now added a UNISEX sizing guide. This is the SAME as the Mens standard sizing guide with an XXSmall size being added.

Dimensions in the charts below are body measurements, not garment dimensions, therefore please refer to the measuring guide to help you to determine which is the best size for you to knit.

STANDARD WOMENS SIZING GUIDE

The sizing within this chart is also based on the larger size within the range, ie. M will be based on size 14.

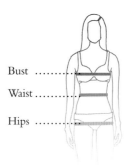

UK SIZE DUAL SIZE	S 8/10	M 12/14	L 16/18	XL 20/22	XXL 24/26	
To fit bust	32 – 34	36 – 38	40 – 42	44 – 46	48 – 50	inches
	81 – 86	91 – 97	102 – 107	112 – 117	122 – 127	cm
To fit waist	24 – 26	28 – 30	32 – 34	36 – 38	40 – 42	inches
	61 – 66	71 – 76	81 – 86	91 – 97	102 – 107	cm
To fit hips	34 – 36	38 – 40	42 – 44	46 – 48	50 – 52	inches
	86 – 91	97 – 102	107 – 112	117 – 122	127 – 132	cm

Bust ....
Waist ....
Hips ....

MEASURING GUIDE

For maximum comfort and to ensure the correct fit when choosing a size to knit, please follow the tips below when checking your size.

Measure yourself close to your body, over your underwear and don't pull the tape measure too tight!
Bust/chest – measure around the fullest part of the bust/chest and across the shoulder blades.
Waist – measure around the natural waistline, just above the hip bone.
Hips – measure around the fullest part of the bottom.

If you don't wish to measure yourself, note the size of a favourite jumper that you like the fit of. Our sizes are now comparable to the clothing sizes from the major high street retailers, so if your favourite jumper is a size Medium or size 12, then our size Medium should be approximately the same fit.

To be extra sure, measure your favourite jumper and then compare these measurements with the Rowan size diagram given at the end of the individual instructions.

Finally, once you have decided which size is best for you, please ensure that you achieve the tension required for the design you wish to knit.
Remember if your tension is too loose, your garment will be bigger than the pattern size and you may use more yarn. If your tension is too tight, your garment could be smaller than the pattern size and you will have yarn left over.

Furthermore if your tension is incorrect, the handle of your fabric will be too stiff or floppy and will not fit properly. It really does make sense to check your tension before starting every project.

SIZING & SIZE DIAGRAM NOTE

The instructions are given for the smallest size. Where they vary, work the figures in brackets for the larger sizes. One set of figures refers to all sizes. Included with most patterns in this magazine is a 'size diagram' - see image on the right, of the finished garment and its dimensions. The measurement shown at the bottom of each 'size diagram' shows the garment width 2.5cm

below the armhole shaping. To help you choose the size of garment to knit please refer to the sizing guide. Generally in the majority of designs the welt width (at the cast on edge of the garment) is the same width as the chest. However, some designs are 'A-Line' in shape or have a flared edge and in these cases the welt width will be wider than the chest width.

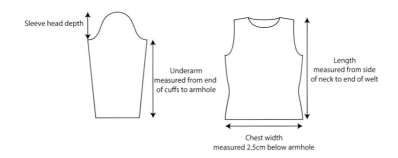

Sleeve head depth

Underarm measured from end of cuffs to armhole

Length measured from side of neck to end of welt

Chest width measured 2.5cm below armhole

TENSION

Obtaining the correct tension is perhaps the single factor which can make the difference between a successful garment and a disastrous one. It controls both the shape and size of an article, so any variation, however slight, can distort the finished garment. Different designers feature in our books and it is their tension, given at the start of each pattern, which you must match. We recommend that you knit a square in pattern and/or stocking stitch (depending on the pattern instructions) of perhaps 5 - 10 more stitches and 5 - 10 more rows than those given in the tension note. Mark out the central 10cm square with pins. If you have too many stitches to 10cm try again using thicker needles, if you have too few stitches to 10cm try again using finer needles. Once you have achieved the correct tension your garment will be knitted to the measurements indicated in the size diagram shown at the end of the pattern.

CHART NOTE

Many of the patterns in the book are worked from charts. Each square on a chart represents a stitch and each line of squares a row of knitting. Each colour used is given a different letter and these are shown in the materials section, or in the key alongside the chart of each pattern. When working from the charts, read odd rows (K) from right to left and even rows (P) from left to right, unless otherwise stated. When working lace from a chart it is important to note that all but the largest size may have to alter the first and last few stitches in order not to lose or gain stitches over the row.

WORKING A LACE PATTERN

When working a lace pattern it is important to remember that if you are unable to work both the increase and corresponding decrease and vica versa, the stitches should be worked in stocking stitch.

KNITTING WITH COLOUR

There are two main methods of working colour into a knitted fabric: **Intarsia** and **Fairisle** techniques. The first method produces a single thickness of fabric and is usually used where a colour is only required in a particular area of a row and does not form a repeating pattern across the row, as in the fairisle technique.

Fairisle type knitting: When two or three colours are worked repeatedly across a row, strand the yarn not in use loosely behind the stitches being worked. If you are working with more than two colours, treat the "floating" yarns as if they were one yarn and always spread the stitches to their correct width to keep them elastic. It is advisable not to carry the stranded or "floating" yarns over more than three stitches at a time, but to weave them under and over the colour you are working. The "floating" yarns are therefore caught at the back of the work.

Intarsia: The simplest way to do this is to cut short lengths of yarn for each motif or block of colour used in a row. Then joining in the various colours at the appropriate point on the row, link one colour to the next by twisting them around each other where they meet on the wrong side to avoid gaps. All ends can then either be darned along the colour join lines, as each motif is completed or then can be "knitted-in" to the fabric of the knitting as each colour is worked into the pattern. This is done in much the same way as "weaving- in" yarns when working the Fairisle technique and does save time darning-in ends. It is essential that the tension is noted for intarsia as this may vary from the stocking stitch if both are used in the same pattern.

After working for hours knitting a garment, it seems a great pity that many garments are spoiled because such little care is taken in the pressing and finishing process. Follow the text below for a truly professional-looking garment.

Block out each piece of knitting and following the instructions on the ball band press the garment pieces, omitting the ribs. Tip: Take special care to press the edges, as this will make sewing up both easier and neater. If the ball band indicates that the fabric is not to be pressed, then covering the blocked out fabric with a damp white cotton cloth and leaving it to stand will have the desired effect. Darn in all ends neatly along the selvage edge or a colour join, as appropriate.

STITCHING

When stitching the pieces together, remember to match areas of colour and texture very carefully where they meet. Use a seam stitch such as back stitch or mattress stitch for all main knitting seams and join all ribs and neckband with mattress stitch, unless otherwise stated.

CONSTRUCTION

Having completed the pattern instructions, join left shoulder and neckband seams as detailed above. Sew the top of the sleeve to the body of the garment using the method detailed in the pattern, referring to the appropriate guide:

Straight cast-off sleeves: Place centre of cast-off edge of sleeve to shoulder seam. Sew top of sleeve to body, using markers as guidelines where applicable.

Square set-in sleeves: Place centre of cast-off edge of sleeve to shoulder seam. Set sleeve head into armhole, the straight sides at top of sleeve to form a neat right-angle to cast-off sts at armhole on back and front.

Shallow set-in sleeves: Place centre of cast off edge of sleeve to shoulder seam. Match decreases at beg of armhole shaping to decreases at top of sleeve. Sew sleeve head into armhole, easing in shapings.

Set-in sleeves: Place centre of cast-off edge of sleeve to shoulder seam. Set in sleeve, easing sleeve head into armhole. Join side and sleeve seams. Slip stitch pocket edgings and linings into place. Sew on buttons to correspond with buttonholes. Ribbed welts and neckbands and any areas of garter stitch should not be pressed.

ABBREVIATIONS

K	knit
P	purl
st(s)	stitch(es)
inc	increas(e)(ing)
dec	decreas(e)(ing)
st st	stocking stitch (1 row K, 1 row P)
g st	garter stitch (K every row)
beg	begin(ning)
foll	following
rem	remain(ing)
rev st st	reverse stocking stitch (1 row K , 1 row P)
rep	repeat
alt	alternate
cont	continue
patt	pattern
tog	together
mm	millimetres
cm	centimetres
in(s)	inch(es)
RS	right side
WS	wrong side
sl 1	slip one stitch
psso	pass slipped stitch over
p2sso	pass 2 slipped stitches over
tbl	through back of loop
M1	make one stitch by picking up horizontal loop before next stitch and knitting into back of it
M1P	make one stitch by picking up horizontal loop before next stitch and purlinginto back of it
yfwd	yarn forward
yrn	yarn round needle
meas	measures
0	no stitches, times or rows
–	no stitches, times or rows for that size
yo	yarn over needle
yfrn	yarn forward round needle
wyib	with yarn at back
sl2togK	slip 2 stitches together knitways

CROCHET TERMS

UK crochet terms and abbreviations have been used throughout. The list below gives the US equivalent where they vary.

ABBREV.	UK (US)
dc (sc)	double crochet (single crochet)
htr (hdc)	half treble (half double crochet)
tr (dc)	treble (double crochet)
dtr (tr)	double treble (treble)

EXPERIENCE RATING

(For guidance only)

• Beginner Techniques

For the beginner knitter, basic garment shaping and straight forward stitch technique.

• • Simple Techniques

Simple straight forward knitting, introducing various, shaping techniques and garments.

• • • Experienced Techniques

For the more experienced knitter, using more advanced shaping techniques at the same time as colourwork or more advanced stitch techniques.

• • • • Advanced Techniques

Advanced techniques used, using advanced stitches and garment shapings and more challenging techniques

BUTTONS & RIBBON

Groves & Banks

Eastern Bypass
Thame
Oxfordshire
OX9 3FU
www.grovesltd.co.uk
groves@stockistenquiries.co.uk

Bedecked Haberdashery

Bedecked Haberdashery
The Coach House
Barningham Park
RICHMOND
DL11 7DW
Tel: +44 (0)1833 621 451
eMail:Judith.lewis@bedecked.co.uk
www.bedecked.co.uk

WASH CARE INFORMATION

You may have noticed over the last season that the wash care symbols on our ball bands and shade cards have changed. This is to bring the symbols we use up to date and hopefully help you to care for your knitting and crochet more easily. Below are the symbols you are likely to see and a brief explanation of each.

MACHINE WASH SYMBOLS

HAND WASH SYMBOLS

DRY CLEAN SYMBOLS

IRONING SYMBOLS

DO NOT BLEACH SYMBOL

DRYING SYMBOLS

Anemone

Seite 4

Garn

Rowan Summerlite 4ply

A Pepper Pot 431	6	x 50 g
B Green Bay 445	6	x 50 g
C Seashell 437	6	x 50 g

Nadeln

1 Häkelndl Nr. 3

Maschenprobe

22 M und 12 R = 10 x 10 cm, im Stäbchenmuster gehäkelt mit Ndl Nr. 3.

Fertige Größe

Das fertige Schultertuch ist am äußeren Rand 375 cm breit und 86 cm lang.

Spezielle Abkürzungen

LfM = Luftmasche, **Stb** = Stäbchen.

SCHULTERTUCH

11 LfM mit Ndl Nr. 3 und Fbe A häkeln.

Basis-R (Hinr): 1 Stb in die 4. LfM ab der Ndl, je 1 Stb in die nächsten 7 LfM, Arb wenden = 9 M.

In folg Streifenmuster weiterhäkeln:

R 1: Mit Fbe B 3 LfM (zählt als 1 Stb), das Stb unterhalb der 3 LfM überschl, 4 x (3 Stb in das nächste Stb, 1 St in das nächste Stb), das Stb am Ende der letzten Musterwiederholung in die oberste der 3 LfM am Anf der unteren R häkeln, Arb wenden = 17 M.

R 2: Mit Fbe C 3 LfM (zählt als 1 Stb), das Stb unterhalb der 3 LfM überschl, 1 Stb in das nächste Stb, 3 x (3 Stb in das nächste Stb, je 1 Stb in die nächsten 3 Stb), 3 Stb in das nächste Stb, 1 Stb in das nächste Stb, 1 Stb in die oberste der 3 LfM am Anf der unteren R, Arb wenden = 25 M.

R 3: Mit Fbe A 3 LfM (zählt als 1 Stb), das Stb unterhalb der 3 LfM überschl, je 1 Stb in die nächsten 2 Stb, 3 x (3 Stb in das nächste Stb, je 1 Stb in die nächsten 5 Stb), 3 Stb in das nächste Stb, je 1 Stb in die nächsten 2 Stb, 1 Stb in die oberste der 3 LfM am Anf der unteren R, Arb wenden = 33 M.

R 4: Mit Fbe B 3 LfM (zählt als 1 Stb), das Stb unterhalb der 3 LfM überschl, je 1 Stb in die nächsten 3 Stb, 3 x (3 Stb in das nächste Stb, je 1 Stb in die nächsten 7 Stb), 3 Stb in das nächste Stb, je 1 Stb in die nächsten 3 Stb, 1 Stb in die oberste der 3 LfM am Anf der unteren R, Arb wenden = 41 M.

R 5: Mit Fbe C 3 LfM (zählt als 1 Stb), das Stb unterhalb der 3 LfM überschl, je 1 Stb in die nächsten 4 Stb, 3 x (3 Stb in das nächste Stb, je 1 Stb in die nächsten 9 Stb), 3 Stb in das nächste Stb, je 1 Stb in die nächsten 4 Stb, 1 Stb in die oberste der 3 LfM am Anf der unteren R, Arb wenden = 49 M.

R 6: Mit Fbe A 3 LfM (zählt als 1 Stb), das Stb unterhalb der 3 LfM überschl, je 1 Stb in die nächsten 5 Stb, 3 x (3 Stb in das nächste Stb, je 1 Stb in die nächsten 11 Stb), 3 Stb in das nächste Stb, je 1 Stb in die nächsten 5 Stb, 1 Stb in die oberste der 3 LfM am Anf der unteren R, Arb wenden = 57 M.

Diese 6 R bilden das Muster mit gleichzeitiger Formgebung.

Das Streifenmuster korrekt einhalten, je 1 R in den Farben B, C und A häkeln, dabei **gleichzeitig** in jeder R wie angegeben 8 M zun, dabei vor und nach jeder Zun je 1 M mehr häkeln und je 2 M mehr zwischen jedem Zun-Abschnitt, weitere 95 R häkeln, enden mit folg R:

Nächste R (Rückr): Mit Fbe C 3 LfM (zählt als 1 Stb), das Stb unterhalb der 3 LfM überschl, je 1 Stb in die nächsten 100 Stb, 3 x (3 Stb in das nächste Stb, je 1 Stb in die nächsten 201 Stb), 3 Stb in das nächste Stb, je 1 Stb in die nächsten 100 Stb, 1 Stb in die oberste der 3 LfM am Anf der unteren R, Arb wenden = 817 M.

Nächste R: Mit Fbe C 3 LfM (zählt als 1 Stb), das Stb unterhalb der 3 LfM überschl, je 1 Stb in die nächsten 101 Stb, 3 x (3 Stb in das nächste Stb, je 1 Stb in die nächsten 203 Stb), 3 Stb in das nächste Stb, je 1 Stb in die nächsten 101 Stb, 1 Stb in die oberste der 3 LfM am Anf der unteren R, Arb wenden = 825 M.

Den Fd abschneiden.

FERTIGSTELLUNG

Das Tuch dämpfen, siehe Informationsseite.

Archer •••

Seite 8

Größe
Passend für Oberweite

81-86	91-97	102-107	112-117	122-127	cm

Gestrickte Oberweite

90	101,5	113,5	122	134	cm

Garn
Rowan Summerlite 4ply
A Seashell 437

2	2	2	2	3	x 50 g

B Touch of Gold 439

2	2	2	2	2	x 50 g

C Green Bay 445

1	2	2	2	2	x 50 g

D Vintage Claret 443

1	2	2	2	2	x 50 g

E Langoustino 440

1	2	2	2	2	x 50 g

Nadeln
1 Häkelndl Nr. 3

Maschenprobe
27 M und 16 R = 10 x 10 cm, im Muster gehäkelt mit Ndl Nr. 3.

Spezielle Abkürzungen
LfM = Luftmasche, **fM** = feste M, **fM2zus** = 2 x (Ndl in die angegebene M, Fd durchziehen), Fd holen und durch alle 3 Schlingen auf der Ndl ziehen, **hStb** = halbes Stäbchen, **Stb** = ein Stäbchen, **Stb2zus** = 2 x (Fd um die Ndl, Ndl in die angegebene M, Fd holen und durchziehen, Fd holen und durch 2 Schlingen auf der Ndl ziehen), Fd holen und durch alle 3 Schlingen auf der Ndl ziehen, **Stb3zus** = 3 x (Fd um die Ndl, Ndl in die angegebene M, Fd holen und durchziehen, Fd holen und durch 2 Schlingen auf der Ndl ziehen), Fd holen und durch alle 4 Schlingen auf der Ndl ziehen, **Zw** = Zwischenraum, **Kettm** = Kettmasche.

Streifenmuster
R 1: Mit Fbe A.
R 2: Mit Fbe B.
R 3: Mit Fbe C.
R 4: Mit Fbe D.
R 5: Mit Fbe E.

Diese 5 R bilden das Streifenmuster und werden fortlfd wdhl.

RÜCKENTEIL
122 (138: 154: 166: 182) LfM mit Ndl Nr. 3 und Fbe A häkeln.
Basis-R (Rückr): 1 fM in die 2. LfM ab der Ndl, *1 LfM, 1 LfM überschl, 1 fM in die nächste LfM, ab * wdhl bis zum Ende, Arbeit wenden = 121 (137: 153: 165: 181) M.
Fd A abschneiden und mit Fbe B wie folgt häkeln:
R 1 (Hinr): Mit Fbe B 3 LfM, 1 Stb in den nächsten LfM-Zw (zählt als 1 Stb2zus), *1 LfM, Stb2zus, dabei das 1. Beinchen in denselben LfM-Zw wie die vorherige M, das 2. Beinchen in den nächsten LfM-Zw häkeln, ab * wdhl bis das 2. Beinchen des Stb2zus in den letzten LfM-Zw gehäkelt wurde, 1 LfM, Stb2zus, dabei das 1. Beinchen in denselben LfM-Zw, in den das 1. Beinchen der vorherigen M gehäkelt wurde und das 2. Beinchen in die letzte fM häkeln, Arbeit wenden.
R 2: Mit Fbe C 1 LfM (zählt nicht als M), 1 fM in die 1. M, *1 fM in den nächsten LfM-Zw, 1 LfM, die nächste M überschl, ab * wdhl bis zum letzten LfM-Zw, 1 fM in den letzten LfM-Zw, 1 fM in die letzte M, Arb wenden.
R 3: Mit Fbe D 3 LfM (zählen als 1 Stb), Stb2zus, dabei das 1. Beinchen in denselben LfM-Zw häkeln wie die vorherige M, das 2. Beinchen in den nächsten LfM-Zw häkeln, *1 LfM, Stb2zus, dabei das 1. Beinchen in denselben LfM-Zw wie die vorherige M häkeln, das 2. Beinchen in den nächsten LfM-Zw häkeln, ab * wdhl bis das 2. Beinchen des letzten Stb2zus in die letzte M gehäkelt wurde, 1 Stb in dieselbe M, Arb wenden.
R 4: Mit Fbe E 1 LfM (zählt nicht als M), 1 fM in die 1. M, *1 LfM, die nächste M überschl, 1 fM in den nächsten LfM-Zw, ab * wdhl, die letzte fM in die oberste der 3 LfM vom Anf der unteren R häkeln, Arb wenden.
Diese 4 R bilden das Muster in R 2-5 des Streifenmusters.
Mit R 1 des Streifenmusters beg und im Muster häkeln wie folgt:
Nach 6 (6: 10: 10: 14) R enden mit R 2 des Musters.
Seitl Abnahmen
Nächste R (Hinr): 3 LfM, die ersten 2 M überschl, 1 Stb in den nächsten LfM-Zw (zählt als 1 Stb2zus) = 1 Abn, im Muster häkeln bis das 2. Beinchen des letzten Stb2zus in die letzte M gehäkelt wurde − 1 Abn, Arb wenden = 119 (135: 151: 163: 179) M.
Nächste R: 1 LfM, 1 fM in die 1. M, *1 fM in den nächsten LfM-Zw, 1 LfM, die nächste M überschl, ab * wdhl bis zum letzten LfM-Zw, 1 fM in den letzten LfM-Zw, 1 fM in die oberste der 3 LfM der unteren R, Arb wenden.

Die beiden letzten R noch 3 x wdhl = 113 (129: 145: 157: 173) M. Mit R 3 des Musters beg und 12 R gerade häkeln, enden mit R 2 des Muster = Rückr.

Nächste R (Hinr): 4 LfM (zählen als 1 Stb und 1 LfM) = 1 Zun, Stb2zus, dabei das 1. Stb in die M unterhalb der 4 LfM und das 2. Stb in den nächsten LfM-Zw häkeln, im Muster häkeln bis das 2. Beinchen des letzten Stb2zus in die letzte M gehäkelt wurde, 1 LfM, 1 Stb in dieselbe M = 1 Zun, Arb wenden = 115 (131: 147: 159: 175) M.

Nächste R: 1 LfM (zählt nicht als M), 1 fM in die 1. M, *1 fM in den nächsten LfM-Zw, 1 LfM, die nächste M überschl, ab * wdhl bis zum letzten LfM-Zw, 1 fM in den letzten LfM-Zw, 1 fM in die 3. der 4 LfM vom Anf der unteren R, Arb wenden.

Die beiden letzten R noch 3 x wdhl = 121 (137: 153: 165: 181) M. Mit R 3 des Musters beg und 9 R gerade häkeln, enden mit R 3 des Musters = Hinr und nach 1 R in Fbe C (C: B: B: A). (Das Rückenteil sollte ca. 30 (30: 32,5: 32,5: 35) cm lang sein.)

Armausschnitte

Das Streifenmuster korrekt einhalten, wie folgt fortfahren:

Nächste R (Rückr): Je 1 Kettm in die ersten 9 (9: 13: 13: 17) M = 9 (9: 13: 13: 17) M Abn, 1 LfM (zählt nicht als M), 1 fM in die nächste M, 1 fM in den nächsten LfM-Zw, *1 LfM, die nächste M überschl, 1 fM in den nächsten LfM-Zw, ab * wdhl bis zu den letzten 10 (10: 14: 14: 18) M, 1 fM in die nächste M, Arb wenden, die restl 9 (9: 13: 13: 17) M frei lassen = 9 (9: 13: 13: 17) M Abn = 103 (119: 127: 139: 147) M.

Größe 91-97, 102-107, 112-117 und 122-127 speziell

Nächste R (Hinr): 3 LfM, die ersten 2 M überschl, 1 Stb in den nächsten LfM-Zw (zählt als 1 Stb2zus) = 1 Abn, im Muster bis zum Ende, das 2. Beinchen des letzten Stb2zus in die letzte M häkeln = 1 Abn, Arb wenden = - (117: 125: 137: 145) M.

Nächste R: 1 LfM (zählt nicht als M), fM2zus in die 1. M und den 1. LfM-Zw = 1 Abn, *1 LfM, die nächste M überschl, 1 fM in die nächste M, ab * wdhl bis zu den letzten 3 M, 1 LfM, die nächste M überschl, fM2zus in den letzten LfM-Zw und die oberste der 3 LfM am Anf der unteren R = 1 Abn, Arb wenden = - (115: 123: 135: 143) M.

Nächste R: 3 LfM, die M unterhalb der 3 LfM überschl, 1 Stb in den 1. LfM-Zw (zäht als 1 Stb2zus) = 1 Abn, Stb2zus, dabei das 1. Beinchen in denselben LfM-Zw wie die vorherige M, das 2. Beinchen in den nächsten LfM-Zw häkeln, im Muster häkeln, bis das 2. Beinchen des Stb2zus in den letzten LfM-Zw gehäkelt wurde, Stb2zus, dabei das 1. Beinchen in denselben LfM-Zw häkeln wie die vorherige M, das 2. Beinchen in die letzte M häkeln = 1 Abn, Arb wenden = - (113: 121: 133: 141) M.

Nächste R: 1 LfM (zählt nicht als M), fM2zus in die ersten 2 M = 1 Abn, 1 fM in den nächsten LfM-Zw, *1 LfM, die nächste M überschl, 1 fM in den nächsten LfM-Zw, ab * wdhl bis zu den letzten 2 M, fM2zus in die letzten 2 M = 1 Abn, Arb wenden = - (111: 119: 131: 139) M.

Die letzten 4 R noch 1 x wdhl = - (103: 111: 123: 131) M.

Alle Größen

Nächste R: 3 LfM, die ersten 2 M überschl, 1 Stb in den nächsten LfM-Zw (zählt als Stb2zus) = 1 Abn, im Muster bis zum Ende, das 2. Beinchen des letzten Stb2zus in die letzte M häkeln = 1 Abn, Arb wenden = 101 (101: 109: 121: 129) M.

Nächste R: 1 LfM (zählt nicht als M), 1 fM in die 1. M, *1 fM in den nächsten LfM-Zw, 1 LfM, die nächste M überschl, ab * wdhl

bis zum letzten LfM-Zw, 1 fM in den letzten LfM-Zw, 1 fM in die oberste der 3 LfM am Anf der unteren R, Arb wenden.

Die beiden letzten R noch 6 (2: 2: 4: 4) x wdhl, enden mit einer Rückr = 89 (97: 105: 113: 121) M.

Mit R 3 des Musters beg und gerade weiterhäkeln bis zu einer Armausschnittlänge von 21 (22,5: 24: 25,5: 27) cm, enden mit einer Rückr.

Den Fd abschneiden. Für den Halsausschnitt die mittl 5 (6,5: 7,5: 9: 10) cm der letzten R bds mit einem Fd markieren, der Halsausschnitt müsste ca. 23 (23: 24: 24: 25) cm breit sein.)

VORDERTEIL

Linker seitl Abschnitt

5 LfM mit Häkelndl Nr. 3 und Fbe A häkeln.

Basis-R (Hinr): 1 Stb in die 5. LfM ab der Ndl (zählt als 1 Stb, 1 LfM, 1 Stb), Arb wenden = 3 M.

Das Muster wie folgt häkeln:

R 1 (Rückr): Mit Fbe B 1 LfM (zählt nicht als M), 1 fM in die 1. M, 1 LfM = 1 Zun, 1 fM in den LfM-Zw, 1 LfM, 1 fM in die 3. der 4 LfM am Anf der unteren R = 1 Zun, Arb wenden = 5 M.

R 2: Mit Fbe C 4 LfM (zählen als 1 Stb und 1 LfM) = 2 Zun, Stb2zus, dabei das 1. Stb in die M unterhalb der 4 LfM häkeln und das 2. Beinchen in den 1. LfM-Zw häkeln, 1 LfM, Stb2zus, dabei das 1. Beinchen in denselben LfM-Zw wie die vorherige M, das 2. Beinchen in den nächsten LfM-Zw häkeln, 1 LfM, Stb2zus, dabei das 1. Beinchen in den LfM-Zw wie die vorherige M häkeln und das 2. Beinchen in die letzte M häkeln, 1 LfM, 1 Stb in die letzte M = 2 Zun, Arb wenden = 9 M.

R 3: Mit Fbe D 1 LfM (zählt nicht als M), 1 fM in die 1. M, 1 LfM = 1 Zun, 3 x (1 fM in den nächsten LfM-Zw, 1 LfM, die nächste M überschl), 1 fM in den letzten LfM-Zw, 1 fM in die 3. der 4 LfM am Anf der unteren R = 1 Zun, Arb wenden = 11 M.

R 4: Mit Fbe E 4 LfM (zählen als 1 Stb und 1 LfM) = 2 Zun, Stb2zus, dabei das 1. Beinchen in die M unterhalb der 4 LfM häkeln und das 2. Beinchen in den 1. LfM-Zw, 4 x (1 LfM, Stb2zus, dabei das 1. Beinchen in denselben LfM-Zw wie die vorherige M, das 2. Beinchen in den nächsten LfM-Zw häkeln), 1 LfM, Stb2zus, dabei das 1. Beinchen in denselben LfM-Zw wie die vorherige M, das 2. Beinchen in die letzte M häkeln, 1 LfM, 1 Stb in die letzte M häkeln = 2 Zun, Arb wenden = 15 M.

R 5: Mit Fbe A 1 LfM (zählt nicht als M), 1 fM in die 1. M, 1 LfM = 1 Zun, 6 x (1 fM in den nächsten LfM-Zw, 1 LfM, die nächste M überschl), 1 fM in den letzten LfM-Zw, 1 LfM, 1 fM in die 3. der 4 LfM vom Anf der unteren R = 1 Zun, Arb wenden = 17 M.

Die beiden letzten R bilden das Muster in der Streifenfolge mit je 2 Zun am Anf und Ende jeder Hinr und je 1 Zun an beiden Seiten in jeder Rückr.

Mit R 2 des Streifenmusters im Muster weiterhäkeln wie folgt:

R 6 (Hinr): 4 LfM (zählen als 1 Stb und 1 LfM) = 2 Zun, Stb2zus, dabei das 1. Beinchen in die M unterhalb der 4 LfM häkeln und das 2. Beinchen in den 1. LfM-Zw, *1 LfM, Stb2zus, dabei das 1. Beinchen in denselben LfM-Zw wie die vorherige M, das 2. Beinchen in den nächsten LfM-Zw häkeln, ab * wdhl bis das 2. Beinchen des letzten Stb2zus in den letzten LfM-Zw gehäkelt wurde, 1 LfM, Stb2zus, dabei das 1. Beinchen in denselben LfM-Zw wie die vorherige M, das 2. Beinchen in die letzte M häkeln, 1 LfM, 1 Stb in die letzte M = 2 Zun, Arb wenden.

R 7: 1 LfM (zählt nicht als M); 1 fM in die 1. M, 1 LfM = 1 Zun,

1 fM in den 1. LfM-Zw, *1 LfM, die nächste M überschl, 1 fM in den nächsten LfM-Zw, ab * wdhl bis 1 fM in den letzten LfM-Zw gehäkelt wurde, 1 LfM, 1 fM in die 3. der 4 LfM am Anf der unteren R häkeln = 1 Zun, Arb wenden.

R 6 und 7 noch 8 (10: 11: 13: 14) x wdhl, danach R 6 noch 1 x häkeln, enden nach 1 R mit Fbe E (D: A: E: B), enden mit einer Hinr. = 75 (87: 93: 105: 111) M.

Den Fd abschneiden.

Rechter seitl Abschnitt

Genauso häkeln wie den li seitl Abschnitt, am Ende der letzten R den Fd **nicht** abschneiden.

Verbinden der beiden Abschnitte

Nächste R (Rückr): Mit Fbe A (E: B: A: C) den re seitl Abschnitt wie folgt häkeln: 1 LfM (zählt nicht als M), 1 fM in die 1. M, 36 (42: 45: 51: 54) x (1 fM in den nächsten LfM-Zw, 1 LfM, die nächste M überschl), 1 fM in den letzten LfM-Zw, 1 fM in die 3. der 4 LfM am Anf der unteren R, 1 LfM, diese M mit einem Fd markieren, danach in einer Rückr den li seitl Abschnitt häkeln wie folgt: 1 fM in die 1. M, 1 LfM, 36 (42: 45: 51: 54) x (1 fM in den nächsten LfM-Zw, 1 LfM, die nächste M überschl), 1 fM in den letzten LfM-Zw, 1 fM in die 3. der 4 LfM am Anf der unteren R, Arb wenden = 153 (177: 189: 213: 225) M.

Mit R 2 (1: 3: 2: 4) des Streifenmusters beg, wie folgt fortfahren:

Nächste R (Hinr): 4 LfM (zählen als 1 Stb und 1 LfM), Stb2zus, dabei das 1. Beinchen in die M unterhalb der 4 LfM und das 2. Beinchen in den nächsten LfM-Zw häkeln, 36 (42: 45: 51: 54) x (1 LfM, Stb2zus, dabei das 1. Beinchen in denselben LfM-Zw wie die vorherige M, das 2. Beinchen in den nächsten LfM-Zw häkeln), 1 LfM, Stb3zus, dabei das 1. Beinchen in denselben LfM-Zw wie die vorherige M, das 2. Beinchen in die Mitte der beiden Abschnitte in die mark M häkeln und das 3. Beinchen in den nächsten LfM-Zw häkeln, 36 (42: 45: 51: 54) x (1 LfM, Stb2zus, dabei das 1. Beinchen in denselben LfM-Zw wie die vorherige M, das 2. Beinchen in den nächsten LfM-Zw häkeln), 1 LfM, Stb2zus, dabei das 1. Beinchen in denselben LfM-Zw wie die vorherige M, das 2. Beinchen in die letzte M häkeln, 1 LfM, 1 Stb in die letzte M, Arb wenden.

Nächste R: 1 LfM (zählt nicht als M), 2 fM in die 1. M, 1 LfM, 1 fM in den 1. LfM-Zw, 35 (41: 44: 50: 53) x (1 LfM, die nächste M überschl, 1 fM in den nächsten LfM-Zw), 1 LfM, die nächste M überschl, fM2zus in die nächsten 2 LfM-Zw, 1 LfM, das nächste Stb3zus in der vord Mitte überschl, fM2zus in die nächsten 2 LfM-Zw, 35 (41: 44: 50: 53) x (1 LfM, die nächste M überschl, 1 fM in den nächsten LfM-Zw), 1 LfM, die letzten Stb2zus überschl, 1 fM in den letzten LfM-Zw, 1 LfM, 2 fM in die 3. der 4 LfM am Anf der unteren R, Arb wenden.

Die beiden letzten R bilden das Muster mit den Abn an den seitl Rändern und in der vord Mitte.

Die beiden letzten R wdhl, bis der seitl Rand genauso lang ist wie das Rückenteil vor Beg der Armausschnitte, enden mit einer Rückr..

Anf und Ende der letzten R für den Beg der Armausschnitte mit einem Fd markieren.

Für die vord Mitte in der letzten R den LfM-Zw zwischen den beiden mittl fM2zus markieren.

Armausschnitte

R 1 (Hinr): 3 LfM, die ersten 2 M überschl, Stb2zus, dabei das 1. Beinchen in den 1. LfM-Zw und das 2. Beinchen in den nächsten LfM-Zw häkeln (zählt als 1 Stb3zus) = 4 Abn, *1 LfM, Stb2zus,

dabei das 1. Beinchen in denselben LfM-Zw wie die vorherige M, das 2. Beinchen in den nächsten LfM-Zw häkeln*, von * -* wdhl, bis das 2. Beinchen des Stb2zus in den LfM-Zw vor dem mark LfM-Zw gehäkelt wurde, 1 LfM, Stb3zus, dabei das 1. Beinchen in denselben LfM-Zw wie die vorherige M, das 2. Beinchen in den mark LfM-Zw und das 3. Beinchen in den nächsten LfM-Zw häkeln, die Markierung in das zuletzt gehäkelte 3Stbzus versetzen, von * bis * noch 1 x wdhl bis das Stb2zus in den vorletzten LfM-Zw gehäkelt wurde, 1 LfM, Stb3zus, dabei das 1. Beinchen in denselben LfM-Zw wie die vorherige M, das 2. Beinchen in den nächsten LfM-Zw und das 3. Beinchen in die letzte M = 4 Abn, Arb wenden = 145 (169: 181: 205: 217) M.

R 2: 1 LfM (zählt als M), 2 fM in die 1. M, 1 LfM, 1 fM in den 1. LfM-Zw, *1 LfM, die nächste M überschl, 1 fM in den nächsten lfM-Zw*, von * bis * wdhl bis 1 fM in den 3. LfM-Zw vor dem mark Stb3zus gehäkelt wurde, 1 LfM, die nächste M überschl, fM2zus in die nächsten 2 LfM-Zw, 1 LfM, die Markierung in den gerade gehäkelten LfM-Zw versetzen, das nächsten 3Stbzus in der vord Mitte überschl, fM2zus in die nächsten 2 LfM-Zw, von * bis * wdhl bis 1 fM in den letzten LfM-Zw gehäkelt wurde, 1 LfM, 2 fM in die letzte M, Arb wenden.

Die beiden letzten R noch 1 (3: 3: 4: 4) x wdhl, enden mit einer Rückr = 137 (145: 157: 173: 185) M.

Nächste R (Hinr): 3 LfM (zählen als 1 Stb), Stb2zus, dabei das 1. Beinchen in die M unterhalb der 3 LfM, das 2. Beinchen in den 1. LfM-Zw häkeln = 1 Abn, *1 LfM, Stb2zus, dabei das 1. Beinchen in denselben LfM-Zw wie die vorherige M, das 2. Beinchen in den nächsten LfM-Zw häkeln*, von * bis * wdhl bis das 2. Beinchen des Stb2zus in den LfM-Zw vor dem mark LfM-Zw in der vord Mitte gehäkelt wurde, 1 LfM, Stb3zus, dabei das 1. Beinchen in denselben LfM-Zw wie die vorherige M, das 2. Beinchen in den mark LfM-Zw und das 3. Beinchen in den nächsten LfM-Zw häkeln, die Markierung in das gerade gehäkelte Stb3zus versetzen, von * bis * noch 1 x wdhl bis das 2. Beinchen des Stb3zus in den letzten LfM-Zw gehäkelt wurde, 1 LfM, Stb2zus, dabei das 1. Beinchen in denselben LfM-Zw wie die vorherige M, das 2. Beinchen in den letzten LfM-Zw häkeln, 1 Stb in die letzte M = 1 Abn, Arb wenden = 135 (143: 155: 171: 183) M.

Nächste R: 1 fM (zählt nicht als M), (1 fM, 1 LfM, 1 fM) in die 1. M, *1 LfM, die nächste M überschl, 1 fM in den nächsten LfM-Zw*, von * bis * wdhl bis 1 fM in den 3. LfM-Zw vor dem mark Stb3zus gehäkelt wurde, 1 LfM, die nächste M überschl, fM2zus in die nächsten 2 LfM-Zw, 1 LfM, die Markierung in den zuletzt gehäkelten LfM-Zw versetzen, das nächste Stb3zus überschl, fM2zus in die nächsten 2LfM-Zw, von * bis * wdhl bis 1 fM in den letzten LfM-Zw gehäkelt wurde, 1 LfM, das letzte Stb2zus überschl, (1 fM, 1 LfM, 1 fM) in die oberste der 3 LfM am Anf der Rde häkeln, Arb wenden.

Nächste R: 3 LfM, 1 Stb in den 1. LfM-Zw (zählt als 1 Stb2zus) = 1 Abn, *1 LfM, Stb2zus, dabei das 1. Beinchen in denselben LfM-Zw wie die vorherige M, das 2. Beinchen in den nächsten LfM-Zw häkeln*, von * bis * wdhl bis das 2. Beinchen des Stb2zus in den LfM-Zw vor dem mark LfM-Zw gehäkelt wurde, 1 LfM, Stb3zus, dabei das 1. Beinchen in denselben LfM-Zw wie die vorherige M, das 2. M in den mark LfM-Zw und das 3. Beinchen in den nächsten LfM-Zw häkeln, die Markierung in das zuletzt gehäkelte 3Stbzus versetzen, von * bis * wdhl bis das 2. Beinchen des Stb2zus in den letzten LfM-Zw gehäkelt wurde, 1 LfM, Stb2zus, dabei das

1. Beinchen in denselben LfM-Zw wie die vorherige M, das 2. Beinchen in die letzte M häkeln = 1 Abn, Arb wenden = 133 (141: 153: 169: 181) M.

Nächste R: 1 LfM (zählt nicht als M), 2 fM in die 1. M, 1 LfM, 1 fM in den 1. LfM-Zw, *1 LfM, die nächste M überschl, 1 fM in den nächsten LfM-Zw*, von * bis * wdhl bis 1 fM in die 3. LfM-Zw vor dem mark Stb3zus gehäkelt wurde, 1 LfM, die nächsten Stb2zus überschl, fM2zus in die nächsten 2 LfM-Zw, 1 LfM, die Mark in den zuletzt gehäkelten LfM-Zw versetzen, die nächsten Stb3zus überschl, fM2zus in die nächsten 2 LfM-Zw, von * bis * wdhl bis 1 fM in den letzten LfM-Zw gehäkelt wurde, 1 LfM, 2 fM in die letzten M, Arb wenden, die restl 3 LfM am Anf der unteren R frei lassen.

Die letzten 4 R noch 3 (2: 2: 3: 3) x wdhl, enden mit einer Rückr = 121 (133: 145: 157: 169) M.

Die Armausschnittrundung ist beendet.

Weiter im Muster und der Streifenfolge mit den Abn in der vord Mitte und den Seiten wie folgt häkeln:

Nächste R (Hinr): 4 LfM (zählt als 1 Stb und 1 LfM), Stb2zus, dabei das 1. Beinchen in die M unterhalb der 4 LfM, das 2. Beinchen in den 1. LfM-Zw häkeln, *1 LfM, Stb2zus, dabei das 1. Beinchen in denselben LfM-Zw wie die vorherige M, das 2. Beinchen in den nächsten LfM-Zw häkeln*, von * bis * wdhl, bis das 2. Beinchen des Stb2zus in den LfM-Zw vor dem mark LfM-Zw gehäkelt wurde, 1 LfM, Stb3zus, dabei das 1. Beinchen in denselben LfM-Zw, das 2. Beinchen in den mark LfM-Z und das 3. Beinchen in den nächsten LfM-Zw häkeln, die Markierung in das zuletzt gehäkelte 3Stbzus versetzen, von * bis * wdhl bis das 2. Beinchen des Stb2zus in den letzten LfM-Zw gehäkelt wurde, Stb2zus, dabei das 1. Beinchen in denselben LfM-Zw wie die vorherige M, das 2. Beinchen in die letzte M häkeln, 1 LfM, 1 Stb in die letzte M, Arb wenden.

Nächste R: 1 LfM (zählt nicht als M), 2 fM in die 1. M, 1 LfM, 1 fM in den 1. LfM-Zw, *1 LfM, die nächste M überschl, 1 fM in den nächsten LfM-Zw*, von * bis * wdhl bis 1 fM in das Stb3zus vor dem mark Stb3zus gehäkelt wurden, 1 LfM, die nächste M überschl, fM2zus in die nächsten 2 LfM-Zw, 1 LfM, die Markierung in den zuletzt gehäkelten LfM-Zw versetzen, das nächste Stb3zus in der vord Mitte überschl, fM2zus in die nächsten 2 LfM-Zw, von * bis * wdhl bis 1 fM in den letzten LfM-Zw gehäkelt wurde, 1 LfM, 2 fM in die 3. der 4 LfM am Anf der unteren R, Arb wenden.

Die beiden R teilen das Muster und die seitl Abn sowie die Abn in der Mitte ein, die beiden R wdhl bis zu einer Armausschnittlänge von 19 (20,5: 22: 23,5: 25) cm, enden mit einer Rückr. (Das Vorderteil sollte in der vord Mitte ca. 32,5 (33: 35,5: 36: 37) cm lang sein.)

Teilen der Arbeit für den Halsausschnitt

Nächste R (Hinr): 4 LfM (zählen als 1 Stb und 1 LfM), Stb2zus, dabei das 1. Beinchen in die M unterhalb der 4 LfM und das 2. Beinchen in den 1.LfM-Zw häkeln, 4 (6: 8: 10: 12) x (1 LfM, Stb2zus, dabei das 1. Beinchen in denselben LfM-Zw wie die vorherige M, das 2. Beinchen in den nächsten LfM-Zw häkeln), 1 LfM, 1 U, die Ndl in denselben LfM-Zw wie die vorherige M, Fd holen, Fd durch 2 Schlingen auf der Ndl ziehen, 1 U, Ndl in den nächsten LfM-Zw, Fd holen und durch 2 Schlingen auf der Ndl ziehen, 2 U, Ndl in den nächsten LfM-Zw, Fd holen und durchziehen, 2 x (Fd holen und durch 2 Schlingen auf der Ndl ziehen), Fd holen und durch alle 4 Schlingen auf der Ndl ziehen, Arb wenden = 13 (17: 21: 25: 29) M.

Beide Seiten getrennt beenden.

Nächste R (Rückr): 1 LfM (zählt nicht als M), 1 fM in die 1. M, 1 fM in den 1. LfM-Zw, 5 (7: 9: 11: 13) x (1 LfM, die nächste M überschl, 1 fM in den nächsten LfM-Zw), 1 fM in die 3. der 4 LfM am Anf der unteren R, Arb wenden.

Nächste R: 4 LfM (zählen als 1 Stb und 1 LfM), Stb2zus, dabei das 1. Beinchen in die M unterhalb der 4 LfM und das 2. Beinchen in den 1. LfM-Zw häkeln, 4 (6: 8: 10: 12) x (1 LfM, Stb2zus, dabei das 1. Beinchen in denselben LfM-Zw wie die vorherige M, das 2. Beinchen in den nächsten LfM-Zw häkeln), 1 LfM, Stb2zus, dabei das 1. Beinchen in denselben LfM-Zw wie die vorherige M, das 2. Beinchen in die letzte M häkeln, Arb wenden.

Nächste R: 1 LfM (zählt nicht als M), 1 fM in die 1. M, 1 fM in den 1. LfM-Zw, 2 (4: 6: 8: 10) x (1 LfM, die nächste M überschl, 1 fM in den nächsten LfM-Zw), 1 LfM, die nächste M überschl, fM2zus in die nächsten 2 LfM-Zw, Arb wenden, die restl 3 M frei lassen = 8 (12: 16: 20: 24) M.

Größe 81-86 speziell

Nächste R (Hinr): 1 LfM (zählt nicht als M), die 1. M überschl, Ndl in den 1. LfM-Zw, Fd holen und durchziehen, 1 U, Ndl in den nächsten LfM-Zw, Fd holen und durchziehen, Fd holen und durch alle 4 Schlingen auf der Ndl ziehen, 1 LfM, 1 U, Ndl in denselben LfM-Zw wie die letzte M, Fd holen und durchziehen, 1 U, Ndl in den nächsten LfM-Zw, Fd holen und durchziehen, Fd holen und 2 Schlingen auf der Ndl ziehen, Fd holen und durch alle 4 Schlingen auf der Ndl ziehen, 1 LfM, Stb2zus, dabei das 1. Beinchen in denselben LfM-Zw wie die vorherige M, das 2. Beinchen in die letzte M = 5 M.

Größe 91-97, 102-107, 112-117 und 122-127 speziell

Nächste R (Hinr): 1 LfM (zählt nicht als M), die 1. M überschl, Ndl in den 1. LfM-Zw, Fd holen und durchziehen, 1 U, Ndl in den nächsten LfM-Zw, Fd holen und durchziehen, Fd holen und durch alle 4 Schlingen auf der Ndl ziehen, 1 LfM, 1 U, Ndl in denselben LfM-Zw wie die letzte M, Fd holen und durchziehen, 1 U, Ndl in den nächsten LfM-Zw, Fd holen und durchziehen, Fd holen und durch 2 Schlingen auf der Ndl ziehen, Fd holen und durch alle 4 Schlingen auf der Ndl ziehen, – (2: 4: 6: 8) x (1 LfM, Stb2zus, dabei das 1. Beinchen in denselben LfM-Zw wie die vorherige M, das 2. Beinchen in den nächsten LfM-Zw häkeln), 1 LfM, Stb2zus, dabei das 1. Beinchen in denselben LfM-Zw wie die vorherige M, das 2. Beinchen in die letzte M häkeln, = – (9: 13: 17: 21) M.

Nächste R: 1 LfM (zählt nicht als M), 1 fM in die 1. M, 1 fM in den 1. LfM-Zw, – (1: 3: 5: 7) x (1 LfM, die nächste M überschl, 1 fM in den nächsten LfM-Zw), 1 LfM, 1 M überschl, fM2zus in die nächsten 2 LfM-Zw, Arb wenden, die restl M frei lassen = – (6: 10: 14: 18) M.

Größe 91-97 speziell

Nächste R (Hinr): 1 LfM (zählt nicht als M), die 1. M überschl, Ndl in den 1. LfM-Zw, Fd holen und durchziehen, 1 U, Ndl in den nächsten LfM-Zw, Fd durchziehen, Fd holen und durch alle 4 Schlingen auf der Ndl ziehen, 1 LfM, 1 U, Ndl in denselben LfM-Zw wie die letzte M, Fd holen und durchziehen, 1 U, Ndl in die letzte M, Fd holen und durchziehen, Fd holen und durch 2 Schlingen auf der Ndl ziehen, Fd holen und durch alle 4 Schlingen auf der Ndl ziehen = 3 M.

Größe 102-107 speziell

Nächste R (Hinr): 1 LfM (zählt nicht als M), die 1. M überschl, fM2zus über die ersten 2 LfM-Zw, 1 LfM, Ndl in denselben LfM-

Zw wie die letzte M, Fd holen und durchziehen, 1 U, Ndl in den nächsten LfM-Zw, Fd holen und durch ziehen, Fd holen und durch alle 4 Schlingen auf der Ndl ziehen, 1 LfM, 1 U, Ndl in denselben LfM-Zw wie die vorherige M, Fd holen und durchziehen, 1 U, Ndl in den nächsten LfM-Zw, Fd holen und durchziehen, Fd holen und durch alle 5 Schlingen auf der Ndl ziehen, 1 LfM, 1 U, Nd in denselben LfM-Zw wie die vorherige M, Fd holen und durchziehen, 1 U, Ndl In die letzte M, Fd holen und durchziehen, Fd holen und durch 2 Schlingen ziehen, Fd holen und durch alle 4 Schlingen auf der Ndl ziehen = 7 M.

Größe 112-117 speziell

Nächste R (Hinr): 1 LfM (zählt nicht als M), die 1. M überschl, fM2zus über die ersten 2 LfM-Zw, 1 LfM, Ndl in denselben LfM-Zw wie die letzte M, Fd holen und durchziehen, 1 U, Ndl in den nächsten LfM-Zw, Fd holen und durchziehen, Fd holen und durch alle 4 Schlingen auf der Ndl ziehen, 1 LfM, 1 U, Ndl in denselben LfM-Zw wie die letzte M, Fd holen und durchziehen, 1 U, Ndl in den nächsten LfM-Zw, Fd holen und durchziehen, Fd holen und durch alle 5 Schlingen auf der Ndl ziehen, 1 LfM, 1 U, Ndl in denselben LfM-Zw wie die vorherige M, Fd holen und durchziehen, 1 U, Ndl in den nächsten LfM-Zw, Fd holen und durchziehen, Fd holen und durch 2 Schlingen auf der Ndl ziehen, Fd holen und durch alle 4 Schlingen auf der Ndl ziehen, 1 LfM, Stb2zus, dabei das 1. Beinchen in denselben LfM-Zw wie die vorherige M, das 2. Beinchen in den nächsten LfM-Zw, 1 LfM, 1 U, Ndl in denselben LfM-Zw wie die letzte M, Fd holen und durchziehen, Fd holen und durch 2 Schlingen auf der Ndl ziehen, 2 U, Ndl in die letzte M, Fd holen und durchziehen, 2 x (Fd holen und durch 2 Schlingen auf der Ndl ziehen), Fd holen und durch alle 3 Schlingen auf der Ndl ziehen = 11 M.

Größe 122-127 speziell

Nächste R (Hinr): 1 LfM (zählt nicht als M), die 1. M überschl, fM2zus in die ersten 2 LfM-Zw, 1 LfM, fM2zus in denselben LfM-Zw wie die vorherige M und den nächsten LfM-Zw, 1 LfM, Ndl in denselben LfM-Zw wie die vorherige M, Fd holen und durchziehen, 1 U, Ndl in den nächsten LfM-Zw, Fd holen und durchziehen, Fd holen und durch alle 4 Schlingen auf der Ndl ziehen, 1 LfM, 1 U, Ndl in denselben LfM-Zw wie die letzte M, Fd holen und durchziehen, 1 U, Ndl in den nächsten LfM-Zw, Fd holen und durchziehen, Fd holen und durch alle 5 Schlingen auf der Ndl ziehen, 1 LfM, 1 U, Ndl in denselben LfM-Zw wie die vorherige M, Fd holen und durchziehen, 1 U, Ndl in den nächsten LfM-Zw, Fd holen und durchziehen, Fd holen und durch 2 Schlingen ziehen, Fd holen und durch alle 4 Schlingen auf der Ndl ziehen, 2 x (1 LfM, Stb2zus, dabei das 1. Beinchen in denselben LfM-Zw wie die vorherige M, das 2. Beinchen in den nächsten LfM-Zw), 1 LfM, Stb2zus, dabei das 1. Beinchen in denselben LfM-Zw wie die vorherige M, das 2. Beinchen in die letzte M, Arb wenden = 15 M.

Nächste R: 1 LfM (zählt nicht als M), 1 fM in die 1. M, 1 fM in den 1. LfM-Zw, 4 x (1 LfM, 1 M überschl, 1 fM in den nächsten LfM-Zw), 1 LfM, 1 M überschl, fM2zus in die nächsten 2 LfM-Zw, Arb wenden, die restl M frei lassen = 12 M.

Nächste R: 1 LfM (zählt nicht als M), die 1. M überschl, fM2zus über die ersten 2 LfM-Zw, 1 LM, fM2zus über denselben LfM-Zw wie die vorherige M und dem nächsten LfM-Zw, 1 LfM, Ndl in denselben LfM-Zw wie die vorherige M, Fd holen und durchziehen, 1 U, Ndl in den nächsten LfM-Zw, Fd holen und

durchziehen, Fd holen und durch alle 4 Schlingen auf der Ndl ziehen, 1 LfM, 1 U, Ndl in denselben LfM-Zw wie die vorherige M, Fd holen und durchziehen, 1 U, Ndl in den nächsten LfM-Zw, Fd holen und durchziehen, Fd holen und durch 2 Schlingen auf der Ndl ziehen, Fd holen und durch alle 4 Schlingen auf der Ndl ziehen, 1 LfM, Stb2zus, dabei das 1. Beinchen in denselben LfM-Zw wie die vorherige M, das 2. Beinchen in die letzte M = 9 M.

Alle Größen

Den Fd abschneiden.

Zurück zur letzten vollständigen R, die nächsten 45 (47: 49: 51: 53) LfM-Zw überschl, den Fd in der entsprechenden Fbe am nächsten LfM-Zw befestigen, 4 LfM (zählen nicht als M), Stb2zus, dabei das 1. Beinchen in den nächsten LfM-Zw und das 2. Beinchen in den folg LfM-Zw, 4 (6: 8: 10: 12) x (1 LfM, Stb2zus, dabei das 1. Beinchen in denselben LfM-Zw wie die vorherige M, das 2. Beinchen in den nächsten LfM-Zw), 1 LfM, Stb2zus, dabei das 1. Beinchen in denselben LfM-Zw wie die vorherige M, das 2. Beinchen in die letzte M, 1 LfM, 1 Stb in die letzte M, Arb wenden = 13 (17: 21: 25: 29) M.

Nächste R (Rückr): 1 LfM (zählt nicht als M), 1 fM in die 1. M, 1 fM in den 1. LfM-Zw, 5 (7: 9: 11: 13) x (1 LfM, 1 M überschl, 1 fM in den nächsten LfM-Zw), 1 fM in die letzte M, Arb wenden, die restl 4 Lfm vom Anf der unteren R frei lassen.

Nächste R: 3 LfM, die ersten 2 M überschl, 1 Stb in den nächsten LfM-Zw (zählen als 1 Stb2zus), 4 (6: 8: 10: 12) x (1 LfM, Stb2zus, dabei das 1. Beinchen in denselben LfM-Zw wie die vorherige M, das 2. Beinchen in den nächsten LfM-Zw häkeln), 1 LfM, Stb2zus, dabei das 1. Beinchen in denselben LfM-Zw wie die vorherige M, das 2. Beinchen in die letzte M, 1 LfM, 1 Stb in die letzte M, Arb wenden.

Nächste R: Mit Kettm bis in das 1. Stb2zus, 1 LfM (zählt nicht als M), fM2zus in den die nächsten 2 LfM-Zw, 3 (5: 7: 9: 11) x (1 LfM, 1 M überschl, 1 fM in den nächsten LfM-Zw), 1 fM in die letzte M, Arb wenden, die restl 3 LfM am Anf der unteren R frei lassen = 8 (12: 16: 20: 24) M.

Größe 81-86 speziell

Nächste R (Hinr): 3 LfM, die ersten 2 M überschl, 1 Stb in den nächsten LfM-Zw (zählt als 1 Stb2zus), 1 LfM, 1 U, Ndl in denselben LfM-Zw wie die vorherige M, Fd holen und durchziehen, Fd holen und durch 2 Schlingen auf der Ndl ziehen, 1 U, Ndl in den nächsten LfM, Fd holen und durchziehen, Fd holen und durch alle 4 Schlingen auf der Ndl ziehen, 1 LfM, 1 U, Ndl in denselben LfM-Zw wie die vorherige M, Fd holen und durchziehen, Ndl in den nächsten LfM-Zw, Fd holen und durchziehen, Fd holen und durch alle 4 Schlingen auf der Ndl ziehen = 5 M.

Größe 91-97, 102-107, 112-117 und 122-127 speziell

Nächste R (Hinr): 3 LfM, die ersten 2 M überschl, 1 Stb in den 1. LfM-Zw, (zählt als 1 Stb2zus), - (2: 4: 6: 8) x (1 LfM, Stb2zus, dabei das 1. Beinchen in denselben LfM-Zw wie die vorherige M, das 2. Beinchen in den nächsten LfM-Zw), 1 LfM, 1 U, Ndl in denselben LfM-Zw wie die letzte M, Fd holen und durchziehen, Fd holen und durch 2 Schlingen auf der Ndl ziehen, 1 U, Ndl in den nächsten LfM-Zw, Fd holen und durchziehen, Fd holen und durch alle 4 Schlingen auf der Ndl ziehen, 1 LfM, 1 U, Ndl in denselben LfM-Zw wie die vorherige M, Fd holen und durchziehen, Ndl in den nächsten LfM-Zw, Fd holen und durchziehen, Fd holen und durch alle 4 Schlingen auf der Ndl ziehen, Arb wenden, die restl M frei lassen = - (9: 13: 17: 21) M.

Nächste R: 1 LfM (zählt nicht als M), die 1. M überschl, fM2zus in die ersten 2 LfM-Zw, - (2: 4: 6: 8) x (1 LfM, 1 M überschl, 1 fM in den nächsten LfM-Zw), 1 fM in die letzte M, Arb wenden = - (6: 10: 14: 18) M.

Größe 91-97 speziell
Nächste R (Hinr): 3 LfM (zählen nicht als M), die ersten 2 M überschl, 1 hStb in den 1. LfM-Zw, 1 LfM, 1 U, Ndl in denselben LfM-Zw wie die letzte M, Fd holen und durchziehen, Ndl in den nächsten LfM-Zw, Fd holen und durchziehen, Fd holen und durch 4 Schlingen auf der Ndl ziehen, die restl 3 M frei lassen, Arb wenden = 3 M.

Größe 102-107 speziell
Nächste R (Hinr): 3 LfM (zählen nicht als M), die ersten 2 M überschl, 1 hStb in den 1. LfM-Zw, 1 LfM, 1 U, Ndl in denselben LfM-Zw wie die vorherige M, Fd holen und durchziehen, 1 U, Ndl in den nächsten LfM-Zw, Fd holen und durchziehen, Fd holen und durch alle 5 Schlingen auf der Ndl ziehen, 1 LfM, 1 U, Ndl in denselben LfM-Zw wie die vorherige M, Fd holen und durchziehen, Ndl in den nächsten LfM-Zw, Fd holen und durchziehen, Fd holen und durch alle 4 Schlingen auf der Ndl ziehen, 1 LfM, fM2zus in denselben LfM-Zw wie die vorherige M und den nächsten LfM-Zw, die restl M frei lassen = 7 M.

Größe 112-117 speziell
Nächste R (Hinr): 4 LfM (zählt nicht als M), die ersten 2 M frei lassen, 1 Stb in den 1. LfM-Zw, 1 LfM, Stb2zus, dabei das 1. Beinchen in denselben LfM-Zw wie die vorherige M, das 2. Beinchen in den nächsten LfM-Zw, 1 LfM, 1 U, Ndl denselben LfM-Zw wie die vorherige M, Fd holen und durchziehen, Fd holen und durch 2 Schlingen ziehen, 1 U, Ndl in den nächsten LfM-Zw, Fd holen und durch alle 4 Schlingen auf der Ndl ziehen, 1 LfM, 1 U, Ndl in denselben LfM-Zw wie die vorherige M, Fd holen und durchziehen, 1 U, Ndl in den nächsten LfM-Zw, Fd holen und durchziehen, Fd holen und durch alle 5 Schlingen auf der Ndl ziehen, 1 LfM, 1U, Ndl in denselben LfM-Zw wie die vorherige M, Fd holen und durchziehen, Ndl in den nächsten LfM-Zw, Fd holen und durchziehen, Fd holen und durch alle 4 Schlingen auf der Ndl ziehen, 1 LfM, fM2zus in denselben LfM-Zw wie die vorherige M und den nächsten LfM-Zw, die restl M frei lassen = 11 M.

Größe 122-127 speziell
Nächste R (Hinr): 3 LfM, die ersten 2 M überschl, 1 Stb in den nächsten LfM-Zw (zählt als 1 Stb3zus), 2 x (1 LfM, Stb3zus, dabei das 1. Beinchen in denselben LfM-Zw wie die vorherige M, das 2. Stb in den nächsten LfM-Zw), 1 LfM, 1 U, Fd in denselben LfM-Zw wie die vorherige M, Fd holen und durchziehen, Fd holen und durch 2 Schlingen ziehen, 1 U, Ndl in den nächsten LfM-Zw, Fd holen und durch alle 4 Schlingen auf der Ndl ziehen, 1 LfM, 1 U, Ndl in denselben LfM-Zw wie die vorherige M, Fd holen und durchziehen, 1 U, Ndl in den nächsten LfM-Zw, Fd holen und durchziehen, Fd holen und durch alle 5 Schlingen auf der Ndl ziehen, 1 LfM, 1 U, Ndl in denselben LfM-Zw wie die vorherige M, Fd holen und durchziehen, Ndl in den nächsten LfM-Zw, Fd holen und durchziehen, Fd holen und durch alle 4 Schlingen auf der Ndl ziehen, 2 x (1 LfM, fM2zus über die nächsten 2 LfM-Zw), Arb wenden, die restl M frei lassen = 15 M.

Nächste R: 1 LfM (zählt nicht als M), die 1. M überschl, fM2zus über die ersten 2 LfM-Zw, 5 x (1 LfM, 1 M überschl, 1 fM in den nächsten LfM-Zw), 1 fM in die letzte M, Arb wenden = 12 M.

Nächste R: 3 LfM, die ersten 2 M überschl, 1 Stb in den nächsten

LfM-Zw (zählt als 1 Stb3zus), 1 LfM, Ndl in denselben LfM-Zw wie die vorherige M, Fd durchziehen, Fd holen und durch 2 Schlingen auf der Ndl ziehen, 1 U, Ndl in den nächsten LfM-Zw, Fd durchziehen, Fd holen und durch alle 4 Schlingen auf der Ndl ziehen, 1 LfM, 1 U, Ndl in denselben LfM-Zw wie die vorherige M, Fd durchziehen, Ndl in den nächsten LfM-Zw, Fd durchziehen, Fd holen und durch alle 4 Schlingen auf der Ndl ziehen, 2 x (1 LfM, fM2zus über die nächsten 2 LfM-Zw), die restl M frei lassen = 9 M.

Alle Größen
Den Fd abschneiden.

FERTIGSTELLUNG
Alle Teile dämpfen, siehe Informationsseite.
Beide Schulternähte schließen.

Halsblende
Von re mit Ndl Nr. 3 den Fd in Fbe A an der li Schulternaht befestigen, 1 LfM (zählt nicht als M), 1 Rde in fM um die ganze Halsausschnittkante häkeln, 1 Kettm in die 1. fM, Arb nicht wenden.
Nächste Rde (Hinr): 1 LfM (zählt nicht als M), jetzt von li nach rechts anstelle von re nach li je 1 fM in jede fM der unteren Rde häkeln, 1 Kettm in die 1. fM.
Den Fd abschneiden.
Die Seitennähte schließen.

Armausschnittblenden (beide gleich)
Von re mit Ndl Nr. 3 den Fd in Fbe A an der oberen Seitennaht befestigen, 1 LfM (zählt nicht als M), 1 Rde in fM um die ganze Armausschnittkante häkeln, 1 Kettm in die 1. fM, Arb nicht wenden.
Weiterhäkeln wie bei der Halsblende angegeben.

Saumblende
Von re mit Ndl Nr. 3 den Fd in Fbe A an der unteren li Seitennaht befestigen, 1 LfM (zählt nicht als M), 1 Rde in fM um den ganzen unteren Rand häkeln, 1 Kettm in die 1. fM, Arb nicht wenden.
Weiterhäkeln wie bei der Halsblende angegeben.

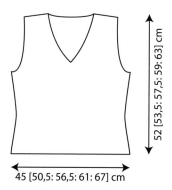

52 [53,5: 57,5: 59: 63] cm

45 [50,5: 56,5: 61: 67] cm

Avocet

Seite 16

Größe

Passend für Oberweite

| 81-86 | 91-97 | 102-107 | 112-117 | 122-127 | cm |

Gestrickte Oberweite

| 94 | 106 | 117 | 128 | 139 | cm |

Garn

Rowan Summerlite DK

A Khaki 461

| 10 | 11 | 13 | 14 | 15 | x 50 g |

B Linen 460

| 1 | 1 | 1 | 1 | 1 | x 50 g |

Nadeln

1 Paar Nr. 3 ¼
1 Paar Nr. 3 ¾
1 Häkelndl Nr. 3

Maschenprobe

22 M und 30 R = 10 x 10 cm, glatt re gestr mit Ndl Nr. 3 ¾.

RÜCKENTEIL

110 (124: 136: 148: 160) M mit Ndl Nr. 3 ¼ und Fbe A anschl.

R 1 (Hinr): 0 (0: 1: 0: 1) M re, 2 (1: 2: 1: 2) M li, ★2 M re, 2 M li, ab ★ wdhl bis zu den letzten 0 (3: 1: 3: 1) M, 0 (2: 1: 2: 1) M re, 0 (1: 0: 1: 0) M li.

R 2: 0 (0: 1: 0: 1) M li, 2 (1: 2: 1: 2) M re, ★2 M li, 2 M re, ab ★ wdhl bis zu den letzten 0 (3: 1: 3: 1) M, 0 (2: 1: 2: 1) M li, 0 (1: 0: 1: 0) M re.

Die beiden R bilden das Rippenmuster, nach weiteren 27 R enden mit einer Hinr.

R 30 (Rückr): 2 M zus-str, 2 x [52 (59: 65: 71: 77) M im Muster, 2 M zus-str] = 107 (121: 133: 145: 157) M.

Wechseln zur Ndl Nr. 3 ¾.

Mit einer Rechtsr beg und fortlfd glatt re str bis zu einer Länge von 20 (20,5: 21: 21,5: 22) cm, enden mit einer Rückr.

Nächste R (Hinr): 2 M re, übzAbn, re bis zu den letzten 4 M, 2 M rezus-str, 2 M re.

Alle seitl Abn str wie in der letzten R angegeben: In der 10. R und 1 x in der folg 10. R bds je 1 M abn, danach 3 x in jeder folg 8. R bds je 1 M abn = 95 (109: 121: 133: 145) M.

Nach 15 R enden mit einer Rückr.

Nächste R (Hinr): 3 M re, 1 M zun, re bis zu den letzten 3 M; 1 M zun, 3 M re.

Alle seitl Zun str wie in der letzten R angegeben: In der 10. R und 1 x in der folg 10. R bds je 1 M zun, danach 1 x in der 12. R bds je 1 M zun = 103 (117: 129: 141: 153) M.

Nach 13 R enden mit einer Rückr.

Armausschnitte

Am Anf der nächsten 2 R je 4 (5: 6: 7: 8) M abk = 95 (107: 117: 127: 137) M.

Nächste R (Hinr): 2 M re, übzAbn, re bis zu den letzten 4 M, 2 M rezus-str, 2 M re.

Nächste R: 2 M li, 2 M li zus-str, li bis zu den letzten 4 M, 2 M li verschr zus-str, 2 M li.

Alle seitl Abn str wie in den letzten 2 R angegeben: In den nächsten 3 (7: 9: 9: 9) R bds je 1 M abn, danach 5 (5: 5: 6: 7) x in jeder folg 2. R bds je 1 M abn = 75 (79: 85: 93: 101) M.

Nach einer Armausschnittlänge von 20 (21,5: 23: 24,5: 26) cm enden mit einer Rückr.

Schulterschrägen

Am Anf der nächsten 6 R je 5 (6: 6: 7: 8) M abk, danach am Anf der folg 2 R je 6 (5: 7: 8: 8) M abk = 33 (33: 35: 35: 37) M.

Rückw Halsblende

Wechseln zur Ndl Nr. 3 ¼.

Nächste R (Hinr): 1 M re, ★1 M li, 1 M re, ab ★ wdhl bis zum Ende.

Nächste R: 1 M li, ★1 M re, 1 M li, ab ★ wdhl bis zum Ende.

Alle M im Rippenmuster abk.

VORDERTEIL

108 (122: 134: 146: 158) M mit Ndl Nr. 3 ¼ und Fbe A anschl.

R 1 (Hinr): 0 (0: 1: 0: 1) M re, 2 (1: 2: 1: 2) M li, 11 (13: 14: 16: 17) x (2 M re, 2 M li), 4 x (2 M re zus-str, 2 U, übzAbn), 11 (13: 14: 16: 17) x (2 M li, 2 M re), 2 (1: 2: 1: 2) M li, 0 (0: 1: 0: 1) M re.

R 2: 0 (0: 1: 0: 1) M li, 2 (1: 2: 1: 2) M re, 11 (13: 14: 16: 17) x (2 M li, 2 M re), 4 x (1 M li, in die beiden U der unteren R 1 x von vorne und 1 x von hinten je 1 M li str, 1 M li), 11 (13: 14: 16: 17) x (2 M re, 2 M li), 2 (1: 2: 1: 2) M re, 0 (0: 1: 0: 1) M li.

Die beiden R bilden das Muster: Die mittl M werden im Lochmuster gestr, die je 16 M an beiden Seiten im Rippenmuster.

Weitere 28 R str, enden mit einer Rückr, dabei in der letzten R bds je 1 M abn, enden mit einer Rückr = 106 (120: 132: 144: 156) M.

Wechseln zur Ndl Nr. 3 ¾, im Muster str wie folgt:

R 1 (Hinr): 45 (52: 58: 64: 70) M re, 4 x (2 M re zus-str, 2 U, übzAbn), 45 (52: 58: 64: 70) M re.

R 2: 45 (52: 58: 64: 70) M li, 4 x (1 M li, in die beiden U der unteren R 1 x von vorne und 1 x von hinten je 1 M li str, 1 M li), 45 (52: 58: 64: 70) M li.

Das Muster korrekt einhalten, nach einer Länge von 20 (20,5: 21: 21,5: 22) cm enden mit einer Rückr.

Alle seitl Abn str wie beim Rückenteil angegeben: In der nächsten R und 2 x in der folg 10. R bds je 1 M abn, danach 3 x in jeder folg 8. R bds je 1 M abn = 94 (108: 120: 132: 144) M.

Nach 15 R enden mit einer Rückr.

Alle seitl Zun str wie beim Rückenteil angegeben: In der nächsten R und 2 x in jeder folg 10. R bds je 1 M zun = 100 (114: 126: 138: 150) M.

Nach 11 R enden mit einer Rückr.

Vord Halsausschnitt

Nächste R (Hinr): 3 M re, 1 M zun, 37 (44: 50: 56: 62) M re, 2 M re zus-str, 8 M im Muster, 1 M anschl, Arbeit wenden, die restl M auf einer Hilfsndl stilllegen, beide Seiten getrennt beenden = 51 (58: 64: 70: 76) M.

Nächste R: 1 M re, 8 M im Muster, li bis zum Ende.

Nächste R: Re bis zu den letzten 9 M, 8 M im Muster, 1 M re.

Nächste R: 1 M re, 8 M im Muster, li bis zum Ende.

Nächste R (Hinr): Re bis zu den letzten 11 M, 2 M re zus-str, 8 M im Muster, 1 M re.

Diese 4 bilden die Abn 9 M innerhalb vom vord Rand entfernt, die Randmasche wird fortlfd re gestr.

Die letzten 4 R noch 2 x wdhl, danach die 1. der 4 R noch 1 x str, enden mit einer Rückr = 48 (55: 61: 67: 73) M.

Armausschnitt

Am Anf der nächsten R 4 (5: 6: 7: 8) M abk = 44 (50: 55: 60: 65) M. 1 R str.

Alle Abn für die Armausschnittrundung str wie beim Rückenteil angegeben: In den nächsten 5 (9: 11: 11: 11) R je 1 M abn, danach 5 (5: 5: 6: 7) x in jeder folg 2. R je 1 M abn, **gleichzeitig** am inneren Rand in der nächsten R und 3 (4: 5: 5: 6) x in jeder folg 4. R wie angegeben 9 M vom vord Rand entfernt je 1 M abn = 30 (31: 33: 37: 40) M.

Nach 1 (1: 3: 3: 5) R enden mit einer Rückr.

Nur noch am vord Rand in der nächsten R und 5 (2: 1: 0: 0) x in jeder folg 4. R je 1 M abn, danach 2 (4: 5: 6: 6) x in jeder folg 6. R je 1 M abn = 22 (24: 26: 30: 33) M.

Nach einer Armausschnittlänge von 20 (21,5: 23: 24,5: 26) cm enden mit einer Rückr.

Schulterschräge

Am Anf der nächsten R und 2 x am Anf jeder folg 2. R je 5 (6: 6: 7: 8) M abk.

Nach 1 R die restl 7 (6: 8: 9: 9) M abk.

Die stillgelegten M aufn, mit neuem Fd in einer Hinr zuerst 1 M anschl, danach 8 M im Muster, übzAbn, 37 (44: 50: 56: 62) M re, 1 M zun, 3 M re = 51 (58: 64: 70: 76) M.

Die 2. Seite gegengleich beenden, dabei am Halsausschnitt statt 2 M re zus-str jetzt eine übzAbn str.

ÄRMEL

54 (54: 58: 58: 58) M mit Ndl Nr. 3 ¼ und Fbe A anschl.

R 1 (Hinr): 2 M re, ★2 M li, 2 M re, ab ★ wdhl bis zum Ende.

R 2: 2 M li, ★2 M re, 2 M li, ab ★ wdhl bis zum Ende.

Weitere 16 R im Rippenmuster str, dabei am Ende der letzten R 1 M abn (zun: abn: abn: zun), enden mit einer Rückr = 53 (55: 57: 57: 59) M.

Wechseln zur Ndl Nr. 3 ¾.

Mit einer Rechtsr beg und fortlfd glatt re str.

Armschrägen

In der 9. (9.: 9.: 7.: 7.) R und in jeder folg 10. (8.: 8.: 6.: 6.) R bds je 1 M zun bis 75 (67: 85: 73: 83) M erreicht sind, danach in jeder folg – (10.: –: 8.: 8.) R bds je 1 M abn bis – (79: –: 89: 93) M erreicht sind.

Nach einer Länge von 46 (46: 47: 47: 47) cm enden mit einer Rückr.

Armkugel

Am Anf der nächsten 2 R je 4 (5: 6: 7: 8) M abk = 67 (69: 73: 75: 77) M.

Alle seitl Abn str wie bei den Abn für die Armausschnittrundungen angegeben: In den nächsten 3 R bds je 1 M abn, danach 2 x in jeder folg 2. R und 3 (4: 5: 6: 7) x in jeder folg 4. R bds je 1 M abn = 51 (51: 53: 53: 53) M.

Nach 1 R enden mit einer Rückr.

In der nächsten R und in jeder folg 2. R bds je 1 M abn bis 31 M übrig sind, und in den folg 7 R bds je 1 M abn, enden mit einer Rückr.

Die restl 17 M abk.

FERTIGSTELLUNG

Alle Teile dämpfen, siehe Informationsseite.

Mit der Häkelndl Nr. 3 und Fbe B 4 Luftmaschenketten häkeln, jede so lang, dass sie beim Vorderteil von der Anschlagkante bis zum oberen Rand der Schulter durch die Löcher des Lochmusters passt. Die Luftmaschenketten durch die Löcher ziehen und auf der Rückseite sichern.

Die oberen Ränder der Vorderteilblenden an die seitl Ränder der rückw Halsblende nähen, die Schulternähte schließen. Die Ärmel in die Armausschnitte nähen, Seiten- und Unterarmnähte schließen.

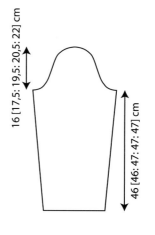

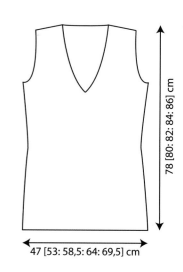

16 [17,5: 19,5: 20,5: 22] cm

46 [46: 47: 47: 47] cm

78 [80: 82: 84: 86] cm

47 [53: 58,5: 64: 69,5] cm

Blenny ••••

Seite 25

Größe
Passend für Oberweite

| 81-86 | 91-97 | 102-107 | 112-117 | 122-127 | cm |

Gestrickte Oberweite

| 91 | 102 | 112 | 122 | 132 | cm |

Garn
Rowan Summerlite 4ply

A Still Grey 422

| 6 | 7 | 7 | 8 | 9 | x 50 g |

B Touch of Gold 439

| 1 | 1 | 1 | 1 | 1 | x 50 g |

C Anchor Grey 446

| 1 | 1 | 1 | 1 | 1 | x 50 g |

Nadeln
1 Paar Nr. 2 ¼
1 Paar Nr. 3

Maschenprobe
28 M und 36 R = 10 x 10 cm, glatt re gestr, 26 M und 40 R = 10 x 10 cm, im Hebemaschenmuster gestr, 25 M und 40 R = 10 x 10 cm, im Perlmuster gestr, alle mit Ndl Nr. 3.

Spezielle Abkürzungen
Bei allen im Muster abgehobenen M liegt der Fd immer auf der Rückseite der Arbeit = in der Hinr liegt der Fd hinter der M, in der Rückr liegt der Fd vor der M.

RÜCKENTEIL
126 (142: 158: 170: 186) M mit Ndl Nr. 2 ¼ und Fbe A anschl.
R 1 (Hinr): 2 M re, ★2 M li, 2 M re, ab ★ wdhl bis zum Ende.
R 2: 2 M li, ★2 M re, 2 M li, ab ★ wdhl bis zum Ende.
Die beiden R bilden das Rippenmuster und werden wdhl bis zu einer Länge von 6 cm, dabei am Ende der letzten R 1 M zun (zun: abn: zun: abn), enden mit einer Rückr = 127 (143: 157: 171: 185) M. Wechseln zur Ndl Nr. 3.
Mit einer Rechtsr beg und fortlfd glatt re str bis zu einer Länge von 33,5 (34: 34,5: 35: 35,5) cm, enden mit einer Rückr.
Raglanschrägen
Am Anf der nächsten R 4 (5: 6: 7: 8) M abk = 123 (138: 151: 164:

177) M.
Nächste R (Rückr): 4 (5: 6: 7: 8) M abk, li str bis 6 (7: 4: 6: 6) M auf der re Ndl sind, 2 M li zus-str, 7 (9: 9: 11: 11) x [13 (11: 13: 11: 12) M li, 2 M li zus-str], 6 (7: 4: 6: 7) M li = 111 (123: 135: 145: 157) M.
Im Hebemaschenmuster in folg Streifen fortfahren:
R 1 (Hinr): Mit Fbe B 2 M re, übzAbn, 3 (1: 3: 0: 2) M re, ★1 M abh (s Hinweis), 3 M re, ab ★ wdhl bis zu den letzten 8 (6: 8: 5: 7) M, 1 M abh, 3 (1: 3: 0: 2) M re, 2 M re zus-str, 2 M re = 109 (121: 133: 143: 155) M.
R 2: Mit Fbe B 6 (4: 6: 3: 5) M li, ★1 M abh (s Hinweis), 3 M li, ab ★ wdhl bis zu den letzten 7 (5: 7: 4: 6) M, 1 M abh, 6 (4: 6: 3: 5) M li.
R 3: Mit Fbe A re.
R 4: Mit Fbe A li.
R 5: Mit Fbe C 2 M re, übzAbn, 0 (2: 0: 1: 3) M re, ★1 M abh, 3 M re, ab ★ wdhl bis zu den letzten 5 (7: 5: 6: 8) M, 1 M abh, 0 (2: 0: 1: 3) M re, 2 M re zus-str, 2 M re = 107 (119: 131: 141: 153) M.
R 6: Mit Fbe C 3 (5: 3: 4: 6) M li, ★1 M abh, 3 M li, ab ★ wdhl bis zu den letzten 4 (6: 4: 5: 7) M, 1 M abh, 3 (5: 3: 4: 6) M li.
R 7: Mit Fbe C 3 (5: 3: 4: 6) M re, ★1 M abh, 3 M re, ab ★ wdhl bis zu den letzten 4 (6: 4: 5: 7) M, 1 M abh, 3 (5: 3: 4: 6) M re.
R 8: Wie R 6.
R 9: Mit Fbe A 2 M re, übzAbn, re bis zu den letzten 4 M, 2 M re zus-str, 2 M re = 105 (117: 129: 139: 151) M.
R 10: Mit Fbe A li.
Diese 10 R bilden das Hebemaschenmuster mit gleichzeitigen Abn für die Raglanschrägen.
Das Muster korrekt einhalten, weitere 13 R str, dabei in der 3. (3.: 3.: 3.: nächsten) R und 2 (2: 2: 0: 0) x in jeder folg 4. R wie angegeben bds je 1 M abn, danach 0 (0: 1: 5: 6) x in jeder folg 2. R bds je 1 M abn, enden mit R 3 des Hebemaschenmusters, enden mit einer Hinr = 99 (111: 121: 127: 137) M.
Fbe B und C abschneiden und nur noch mit Fbe A wie folgt str:
Nächste R (Rückr): 11 (12: 14: 14: 10) M li, 2 M li zus-str, 3 (3: 3: 3: 5) x [23 (26: 28: 30: 21) M li, 2 M li zus-str], 11 (13: 15: 15: 10) M li = 95 (107: 117: 123: 131) M.
Im Perlmuster str wie folgt:
R 1 (Hinr): 2 M re, übzAbn, 1 M li, ★1 M re, 1 M li, ab ★ wdhl bis zu den letzten 4 M, 2 M re zus-str, 2 M re = 93 (105: 115: 121: 129) M.
R 2: 4 M li, 1 M re, ★1 M li, 1 M re, ab ★ wdhl bis zu den letzten

4 M, 4 M li.

Die beiden R bilden das Perlmuster und werden fortlfd wdhl, dabei für die seitl Abn in der 3. (3.: nächsten: nächsten: nächsten) R und 3 (0: 0: 0: 0) x in jeder folg 4. R bds je 1 M abn, danach 20 (29: 33: 36: 39) x in jeder folg 2. R bds je 1 M abn.

Nach 1 R enden mit einer Rückr.

Die restl 45 (45: 47: 47: 49) M auf einer Hilfsndl stilllegen.

VORDERTEIL

Das Vorderteil str wie das Rückenteil bis 65 (65: 71: 71: 77) M innerhalb der Raglanschrägen übrig sind.

Nach 1 R enden mit einer Rückr.

Vord Halsausschnitt

Nächste R (Hinr): 2 M re, übzAbn, 14 (14: 17: 17: 20) M im Muster, Arbeit wenden, die restl M auf einer Hilfsndl stilllegen, beide Seiten getrennt beenden.

Am Halsausschnitt in den nächsten 6 R je 1 M abn, danach 2 x in jeder folg 2. R und 0 (0: 1: 1: 2) x in jeder folg 4. R je 1 M abn, **gleichzeitig** an der Raglanschräge in der 2. R und 4 (4: 6: 6: 8) x in jeder folg 2. R je 1 M abn = 4 M.

Nächste R (Rückr): 4 M li.

Nächste R: 2 M re, übzAbn.

Nächste R: 3 M li.

Nächste R: 1 M re, übzAbn.

Nächste R: 2 M li.

Nächste R: 2 M re zus-str, den Fd abschneiden.

Die stillgelegten M aufn, die mittl 29 M auf einer Hilfsndl stilllegen, mit neuem Fd im Muster bis zu den letzten 4 M, 2 M re zus-str, 2 M re.

Die 2. Seite gegengleich beenden.

ÄRMEL

66 (70: 74: 74: 78) M mit Ndl Nr. 2 ¼ und Fbe A anschl.

6 cm im Rippenmuster str so wie beim Rückenteil angegeben, dabei am Ende der letzten R 1 M zun (zun: abn: abn: abn), enden mit einer Rückr = 67 (71: 73: 73: 77) M.

Wechseln zur Ndl Nr. 3.

Mit einer Rechtsr beg und 6 (6: 4: 4: 4) R glatt re str, enden mit einer Rückr.

Nächste R (Hinr): 3 M re, 1 M zun, re bis zu den letzten 3 M; 1 M zun, 3 M re.

Alle seitl Zun str wie in der letzten R angegeben: In der 6. (6.: 4.: 4.: 4.) R und in jeder folg 6. (6.: 4.: 4.: 4.) R bds je 1 M zun bis 87 (99: 83: 101: 111) M erreicht sind, danach in jeder folg 8. (-: 6.: 6.: 6.) R bds je 1 M zun bis 93 (-: 105: 111: 117) M erreicht sind.

Nach einer Länge von 33 (33: 34: 34: 34) cm enden mit einer Rückr.

Raglanschrägen

Am Anf der nächsten R je 4 (5: 6: 7: 8) M abk = 89 (94: 99: 104: 109) M.

Nächste R (Rückr): 4 (5: 6: 7: 8) M abk, li str bis 6 (6: 5: 7: 7) M auf der re Ndl sind, 2 M li zus-str, 5 x [12 (13: 14: 14: 15) M li, 2 M li zus-str], 7 (6: 6: 8: 7) M li = 79 (83: 87: 91: 95) M.

Im Hebemaschenmuster str wie folgt:

R 1 (Hinr): Mit Fbe B 2 M re, übzAbn, 3 (1: 3: 1: 3) M re, *1 M abh, 3 M re, ab * wdhl bis zu den letzten 8 (6: 8: 6: 8) M, 1 M abh, 3 (1: 3: 1: 3) M re, 2 M re zus-str, 2 M re = 77 (81: 85: 89: 93) M.

R 2: Mit Fbe B 6 (4: 6: 4: 6) M li, *1 M abh, 3 M li, ab * wdhl bis zu den letzten 7 (5: 7: 5: 7) M, 1 M abh, 6 (4: 6: 4: 6) M li.

R 3: Mit Fbe A re.

R 4: Mit Fbe A li.

R 5: Mit Fbe C 2 M re, übzAbn, 0 (2: 0: 2: 0) M re, *1 M abh, 3 M re, ab * wdhl bis zu den letzten 5 (7: 5: 7: 5) M, 1 M abh, 0 (2: 0: 2: 0) M re, 2 M re zus-str, 2 M re = 75 (79: 83: 87: 91) M.

R 6: Mit Fbe C 3 (5: 3: 5: 3) M li, *1 M abh, 3 M li, ab * wdhl bis zu den letzten 4 (6: 4: 6: 4) M, 1 M abh, 3 (5: 3: 5: 3) M li.

R 7: Mit Fbe C 3 (5: 3: 5: 3) M re, *1 M abh, 3 M re, ab * wdhl bis zu den letzten 4 (6: 4: 6: 4) M, 1 M abh, 3 (5: 3: 5: 3) M re.

R 8: Wie R 6.

R 9: Mit Fbe A 2 M re, übzAbn, re bis zu den letzten 4 M, 2 M re zus-str, 2 M re = 73 (77: 81: 85: 89) M.

R 10: Mit Fbe A li.

Diese 10 R bilden das Hebemaschenmuster mit gleichzeitigen seitl Abnahmen.

Weitere 13 R str, dabei in der 3. R und 2 x in jeder folg 4. R bds je 1 M abn, enden mit R 3 des Hebemaschenmusters = Hinr = 67 (71: 75: 79: 83) M.

Fbe B und C abschneiden und nur noch mit Fbe A fortfahren wie folgt:

Nächste R (Rückr): 16 (17: 18: 19: 20) M li, 2 M li zus-str, 31 (33: 35: 37: 39) M li, 2 M li zus-str, 16 (17: 18: 19: 20) M li = 65 (69: 73: 77: 81) M.

Im Perlmuster str wie folgt:

R 1 (Hinr): 2 M re, übzAbn, 1 M li, *1 M re, 1 M li, ab * wdhl bis zu den letzten 4 M, 2 M re zus-str, 2 M re = 63 (67: 71: 75: 79) M.

R 2: 4 M li, 1 M re, *1 M li, 1 M re, ab * wdhl bis zu den letzten 4 M, 4 M li.

Die beiden R fortlfd wdhl, dabei in der 3. R und 3 (4: 5: 6: 7) x in jeder folg 4. R bds je 1 M abn, danach 18 (19: 20: 21: 22) x in der folg 2. R bds je 1 M abn = 19 M.

Nach 1 R enden mit einer Rückr.

Linker Ärmel speziell

Nächste R (Hinr): 2 M re, übzAbn, im Muster bis zu den letzten 4 M, 2 M re zus-str, 2 M re = 17 M.

Nächste R: 5 M abk, im Muster bis zu den letzten 3 M, 3 M li = 12 M.

Nächste R: 2 M re, übzAbn, im Muster bis zum Ende = 11 M.

Nächste R: 6 M abk, im Muster bis zu den letzten 3 M, 3 M li.

Rechter Ärmel speziell

Nächste R (Hinr): 6 M abk, im Muster bis zu den letzten 4 M, 2 M re zus-str, 2 M re = 12 M.

Nächste R: 3 M li, im Muster bis zum Ende.

Die beiden letzten R noch 1 x wdhl.

Beide Ärmel

Die restl 5 M abk.

FERTIGSTELLUNG

Alle Teile dämpfen, siehe Informationsseite.

Die beiden vord und die re rückw Raglannähte schließen.

Halsblende

Von re mit Ndl Nr. 2 ¼ und Fbe A aus dem oberen Rand des li Ärmels 17 M aufn und re str, aus der li vord Halsausschnittkante 12 (12: 15: 15: 18) M aufn und re str, die 29 M auf der Hilfsndl in der vord Mitte wie folgt str: 4 M re, 1 M zun, 2 x (10 M re, 1 M zun), 5 M re, aus der re vord Halsausschnittkante 12 (12: 15: 15: 18) M aufn und re str, aus dem oberen Rand des re Ärmels 17 M aufn und re str, zuletzt die 45 (45: 47: 47: 49) M auf der Hilfsndl im Rückenteil wie folgt str: 4 (4: 3: 3: 4) M re, 1 M zun, 4 x [9 (9: 10: 10: 10) M re,

1 M zun], 5 (5: 4: 4: 5) M re = 140 (140: 148: 148: 156) M.
Mit einer Linksr beg und 9 R glatt re str, danach in der folg Hinr alle M mit Ndl Nr. 3 re abk.
Die li rückw Raglannaht und die seitl Blendennaht schließen. Die Seiten- und Unterarmnähte schließen.

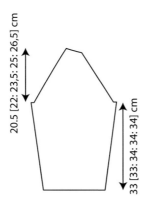

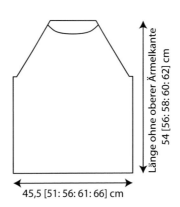

Cormorant ••

Seite 22

Garn
Rowan Summerlite 4ply

A Duck Egg 419	3	x 50 g
B Langoustino 440	2	x 50 g
C Vintage Claret 443	2	x 50 g
D Bossom 444	1	x 50 g
E Rooibos 441	1	x 50 g
F Pinched Pink 426	2	x 50 g
G Blushes 420	1	x 50 g

Nadeln
1 Paar Nr. 4
1 Häkelndl Nr. 2,5

Maschenprobe
28 M und 25 R = 10 x 10 cm, mehrfarbig glatt re gestr mit Ndl Nr. 4.

Fertige Größe
Der Schal ist 56 cm breit und ca. 234 cm lang (einschließlich Blenden und Fransen).

SCHAL
151 M mit Ndl Nr. 4 und Fbe A anschl, dabei mindestens 15 cm des Anschlagfadens hängen lassen.
Nächste R (Rückr): Li.
Wie folgt mehrfarbig glatt re weiterstr, dabei beim Farbwechsel die Fäden auf der Rückseite kreuzen:
R 1 (Hinr): Mit Fbe A 1 M re, *mit Fbe B 1 M re, mit Fbe A 1 M re, ab * wdhl bis zum Ende.
R 2: Mit Fbe B 1 M li, *mit Fbe A 1 M li, mit Fbe B 1 M li, ab * wdhl bis zum Ende.
R 3 und 4: Wie R 1 und 2.
R 5: Mit Fbe A 1 M re, *mit Fbe C 1 M re, mit Fbe A 1 M re, ab * wdhl bis zum Ende.
R 6: Mit Fbe C 1 M li, *mit Fbe A 1 M li, mit Fbe C 1 M li, ab * wdhl bis zum Ende.
R 7: Mit Fbe B 1 M re, *mit Fbe C 1 M re, mit Fbe B 1 M re, ab * wdhl bis zum Ende.
R 8: Mit Fbe C 1 M li, *mit Fbe B 1 M li, mit Fbe C 1 M li, ab * wdhl bis zum Ende.
R 9: Wie R 7.
R 10: Mit Fbe C 1 M li, *mit Fbe D 1 M li, mit Fbe C 1 M li, ab

* wdhl bis zum Ende.

R 11: Mit Fbe D 1 M re, *mit Fbe C 1 M re, mit Fbe D 1 M re, ab * wdhl bis zum Ende.

R 12: Wie R 10.

R 13: Mit Fbe D 1 M re, *mit Fbe E 1 M re, mit Fbe D 1 M re, ab * wdhl bis zum Ende.

R 14: Mit Fbe E 1 M li, *mit Fbe D 1 M li, mit Fbe E 1 M li, ab * wdhl bis zum Ende.

R 15: Mit Fbe F 1 M re, *mit Fbe E 1 M re, mit Fbe F 1 M re, ab * wdhl bis zum Ende.

R 16: Mit Fbe E 1 M li, *mit Fbe F 1 M li, mit Fbe E 1 M li, ab * wdhl bis zum Ende.

R 17: Mit Fbe F 1 M re, *mit Fbe C 1 M re, mit Fbe F 1 M re, ab * wdhl bis zum Ende.

R 18: Mit Fbe C 1 M li, *mit Fbe A 1 M li, mit Fbe C 1 M li, ab * wdhl bis zum Ende.

R 19: Wie R 5.

R 20: Mit Fbe F 1 M li, *mit Fbe A 1 M li, mit Fbe F 1 M li, ab * wdhl bis zum Ende.

R 21: Mit Fbe A 1 M re, *mit Fbe F 1 M re, mit Fbe A 1 M re, ab * wdhl bis zum Ende.

R 22: Wie R 20.

R 23: Mit Fbe A 1 M re, *mit Fbe E 1 M re, mit Fbe A 1 M re, ab * wdhl bis zum Ende.

R 24: Mit Fbe E 1 M li, *mit Fbe A 1 M li, mit Fbe E 1 M li, ab * wdhl bis zum Ende.

R 25: Mit Fbe B 1 M re, *mit Fbe E 1 M re, mit Fbe B 1 M re, ab * wdhl bis zum Ende.

R 26: Mit Fbe E 1 M li, *mit Fbe B 1 M li, mit Fbe E 1 M li, ab * wdhl bis zum Ende.

R 27: Wie R 25.

R 28: Mit Fbe C 1 M li, *mit Fbe B 1 M li, mit Fbe C 1 M li, ab * wdhl bis zum Ende.

R 29: Mit Fbe B 1 M re, *mit Fbe C 1 M re, mit Fbe B 1 M re, ab * wdhl bis zum Ende.

R 30: Mit Fbe C 1 M li, *mit Fbe E 1 M li, mit Fbe C 1 M li, ab * wdhl bis zum Ende.

R 31: Mit Fbe E 1 M re, *mit Fbe C 1 M re, mit Fbe E 1 M re, ab * wdhl bis zum Ende.

R 32: Mit Fbe C 1 M li, *mit Fbe A 1 M li, mit Fbe C 1 M li, ab * wdhl bis zum Ende.

R 33: Mit Fbe A 1 M re, *mit Fbe C 1 M re, mit Fbe A 1 M re, ab * wdhl bis zum Ende.

R 34: Mit Fbe F 1 M li, *mit Fbe G 1 M li, mit Fbe F 1 M li, ab * wdhl bis zum Ende.

R 35: Mit Fbe G 1 M re, *mit Fbe F 1 M re, mit Fbe G 1 M re, ab * wdhl bis zum Ende.

R 36 –39: Wie R 34 und 35, 2 x str.

R 40: Mit Fbe C 1 M li, *mit Fbe G 1 M li, mit Fbe C 1 M li, ab * wdhl bis zum Ende.

R 41: Mit Fbe G 1 M re, *mit Fbe C 1 M re, mit Fbe G 1 M re, ab * wdhl bis zum Ende.

R 42: Mit Fbe C 1 M li, *mit Fbe F 1 M li, mit Fbe C 1 M li, ab * wdhl bis zum Ende.

R 43: Mit Fbe F 1 M re, *mit Fbe C 1 M re, mit Fbe F 1 M re, ab * wdhl bis zum Ende.

R 44: Mit Fbe C 1 M li, *mit Fbe B 1 M li, mit Fbe C 1 M li, ab * wdhl bis zum Ende.

R 45: Mit Fbe B 1 M re, *mit Fbe C 1 M re, mit Fbe B 1 M re, ab * wdhl bis zum Ende.

R 46: Wie R 44.

R 47: Mit Fbe B 1 M re, *mit Fbe A 1 M re, mit Fbe B 1 M re, ab * wdhl bis zum Ende.

R 48: Mit Fbe A 1 M li, *mit Fbe B 1 M li, mit Fbe A 1 M li, ab * wdhl bis zum Ende.

R 49 und 50: Wie R 47 und 48.

R 51: Wie R 47.

R 52: Wie R 26.

R 53: Wie R 25.

R 54: Wie R 26.

R 55 und 56: Wie R 15 und 16.

R 57: Mit Fbe F 1 M re, *mit Fbe D 1 M re, mit Fbe F 1 M re, ab * wdhl bis zum Ende.

R 58: Mit Fbe D 1 M li, *mit Fbe F 1 M li, mit Fbe D 1 M li, ab * wdhl bis zum Ende.

R 59 und 60: Wie R 57 und 58.

Diese 60 R bilden das Muster und werden noch 8 x wdhl, danach R 1-4 noch 1 x str, enden mit einer Rückr.
Mit Fbe A alle M abk.

FERTIGSTELLUNG

Den Schal dämpfen, siehe Informationsseite.

BLENDE

Mit der Häkelndl Nr. 2,5 und Fbe A von re den Fd an der 1. Anschlagmasche befestigen und wie folgt häkeln: 1 LfM (zählt nicht als M), 2 fM in dieselbe M, in der der Fd befestigt wurde, 147 fM in die Anschlagmaschen häkeln bis zur letzten M, 3 fM in die letzte M, weiter in fM entlang der Längskante bis zur Abkettkante des Schal häkeln (die Maschenzahl muss teilbar sein durch 3), 3 fM in die 1. M der Abkettkante, 147 fM in die Abkettkante bis zur letzten M häkeln, 3 fM in die letzte M häkeln, weiter fM in die nächste Längskante bis zur Anschlagkante häkeln (die Maschenzahl muss teilbar sein durch 3), 1 fM in dieselbe M wie die ersten 2 fM, 1 Kettm in die 1. fM.

Nächste Rde: 3 LfM, 1 Kettm in die fM unterhalb der 3 LfM (für ein Pikot), *je 1 Kettm in die nächsten 3 fM, 3 LfM, 1 Kettm in dieselbe M wie die letzte Kettm, ab * wdhl bis zu den letzten 2 M, je 1 Kettm in die nächsten 2 M, 1 Kettm in die M unterhalb des 1. Pikots.

Den Fd abschneiden.

Fransen

Für jede Franse je 3 Fäden in Fbe A schneiden, jeder 15 cm lang. Je 3 Fäden zusammennehmen und mit Hilfe der Häkelndl durch das 1. Pikot an der Ecke knüpfen und festziehen. Wie angegeben je eine Franse in jedes Pikot der Anschlag- und Abkettkante knüpfen. Die Fransen alle bis auf 6 cm abschneiden.

Kittiwake ••

Seite 10

Größe
Passend für Oberweite

81–86	91–97	102–107	112–117	122–127	cm

Gestrickte Oberweite

87,5	99,5	109	119,5	129	cm

Garn
Rowan Summerlite 4ply

A Navy Ink 429

2	2	2	2	3	x 50 g

B Pure White 417

2	2	2	2	3	x 50 g

C Aqua 433

2	2	2	2	3	x 50 g

D Periwinkle 424

2	2	2	2	3	x 50 g

E Touch of Gold 439

2	2	2	2	2	x 50 g

Nadeln
1 Paar Nr. 2 ¼
1 Paar Nr. 3

Maschenprobe
34 M und 40 R = leicht gedehnt 10 x 10 cm, im Muster gestr mit Ndl Nr. 3.

Streifenmuster
Rde 1–10: Mit Fbe B
Rde 11–20: Mit Fbe C
Rde 21–30: Mit Fbe D
Rde 31–40: Mit Fbe E
Diese 40 Runden bilden das Streifenmuster und werden fortlfd wdhl.

RÜCKENTEIL
118 (134: 146: 162: 174) M mit Ndl Nr. 2 ¼ und Fbe A anschl.
R 1 (Hinr): 2 M re, ★2 M li, 2 M re, ab ★ wdhl bis zum Ende.
R 2: 2 M li, ★2 M re, 2 M li, ab ★ wdhl bis zum Ende.
Die beiden R bilden das Rippenmuster und werden wdhl bis zu einer Länge von 10 cm, enden mit einer Hinr.

Größe 81–86, 91–97 und 112–117 speziell
Nächste R (Rückr): 4 (2: –: 1: –) M im Ripp-Muster, 1 M zun, ★5 M im Ripp-Muster, 1 M zun, ab ★ wdhl bis zu den letzten 4 (2: –: 1: –) M, 4 (2: –: 1: –) M im Ripp-Muster = 141 (161: –: 195: –) M.

Größe 102–107 und 122–127 cm speziell
Nächste R (Rückr): 1 M im Ripp-Muster, 1 M zun, – (–: 2: –: 0) x (5 M im Ripp-Muster, 1 M zun), ★4 M im Ripp-Muster, 1 M zun, 3 x (5 M im Ripp-Muster, 1 M zun), ab ★ wdhl bis zu den letzten 2 M, 2 M im Ripp-Muster = – (–: 177: –: 211) M.

Alle Größen
Fbe A abschneiden, wechseln zur Ndl Nr. 3.
Mit R 1 des Streifenmusters wie folgt beg:
R 1 (Hinr): Mit Fbe B 1 (0: 0: 0: 0) M li, 2 (1: 1: 2: 2) M re, ★2 M li, 2 M re, ab ★ wdhl bis zu den letzten 2 (0: 0: 1: 1) M, 2 (0: 0: 1: 1) M li.
R 2: Mit Fbe B 1 (0: 0: 0: 0) M re, 2 (1: 1: 2: 2) M li, ★2 M re, 2 M li, ab ★ wdhl bis zu den letzten 2 (0: 0: 1: 1) M, 2 (0: 0: 1: 1) M re.
Die beiden R bilden das Muster, nach 16 R enden mit einer Rückr.
In der nächsten R und 3 x in jeder folg 18. R bds je 1 M zun, alle Zun im Musterverlauf str = 149 (169: 185: 203: 219) M.
Nach einer Länge von ca. 32,5 (33: 33,5: 34: 34,5) cm enden mit R 10 (12: 14: 16: 18) des Streifenmusters, enden mit einer Rückr.

Armausschnitte
Am Anf der nächsten beiden R je 4 (6: 7: 8: 9) M abk = 141 (157: 171: 187: 201) M.
Für die Armausschnittrundungen in den nächsten 5 (9: 11: 15: 15) R bds je 1 M abn, danach 7 (7: 7: 6: 7) x in jeder folg 2. R und 1 x in der folg 4. R bds je 1 M abn = 115 (123: 133: 143: 155) M.
Nach einer Armausschnittlänge von 19,5 (21: 22,5: 24: 25,5) cm enden mit einer Rückr.

Rückw Halsausschnitt
Nächste R (Hinr): 30 (34: 37: 42: 47) M im Muster, Arbeit wenden, die restl M auf einer Hilfsndl stilllegen, beide Seiten getrennt beenden.
Am Halsausschnitt in der nächsten R 1 M abn = 29 (33: 36: 41: 46) M.

Schulterschräge
Am Anf der nächsten R und am Anf der folg 2. R je 6 (7: 8: 9: 10) M abk, **gleichzeitig** am Halsausschnitt in den nächsten 3 R je 1 M abn = 14 (16: 17: 20: 23) M.
Nach 1 R am Anf der folg R 6 (7: 8: 9: 11) M abk und am Ende

der R 1 M abn.

Nach 1 R die restl 7 (8: 8: 10: 11) M abk.

Die stillgelegten M aufn, die mittl 55 (55: 59: 59: 61) M auf einer Hilfsndl stilllegen, mit neuem Fd in einer Hinr im Muster str bis zum Ende.

Die 2. Seite gegengleich beenden.

VORDERTEIL

Das Vorderteil str wie das Rückenteil bis 42 (42: 46: 46: 50) R unterhalb der Schulterschrägen, enden mit einer Rückr.

Vord Halsausschnitt

Nächste R (Hinr): 44 (48: 52: 57: 63) M im Muster, Arbeit wenden, die restl M auf einer Hilfsndl stilllegen, beide Seiten getrennt beenden.

Am Halsausschnitt in den nächsten 10 R je 1 M abn, danach 6 x in jeder folg 2. R und 3 (3: 4: 4: 5) x in jeder folg 4. R je 1 M abn = 25 (29: 32: 37: 42) M.

Nach 7 R enden mit einer Rückr.

Schulterschräge

Am Anf der nächsten R und 2 (2: 2: 2: 1) x in jeder folg 2. R je 6 (7: 8: 9.10) M abk, danach − (-: -: -: 1) x in der folg 2. R − (-: -: -: 11) M abk.

Nach 1 R die restl 7 (8: 8: 10: 11) M abk.

Die stillgelegten M aufn, die mittl 27 (27: 29: 29: 29) M auf einer Hilfsndl stilllegen, mit neuem Fd in einer Hinr im Muster str bis zum Ende.

Die 2. Seite gegengleich beenden.

ÄRMEL

78 (82: 90: 94: 102) M mit Ndl Nr. 2 ¼ und Fbe A anschl.

5 cm im Rippenmuster str so wie beim Rückenteil angegeben, enden mit einer Hinr.

Größe 81-86, 91-97, 102-107 und 112-117 cm speziell

Nächste R (Rückr): 3(2: 3: 2: -) M im Rippenmuster, 1 M zun, ★1 (2: 1: 1: -) x (4 M im Rippenmuster, 1 M zun), 1 (1: 2: 1: -) x (5 M im Rippenmuster, 1 M zun), ab ★ wdhl bis zu den letzten 3 (2: 3: 2: -) M, 3 (2: 3: 2: -) M im Rippenmuster = 95 (101: 109: 115: -) M.

Größe 122-127 speziell

Nächste R (Rückr): 1 M im Rippenmuster, 1 M zun, ★5 M im Rippenmuster, 1 M zun, ab ★ wdhl bis zu den letzten 5 M, 1 M im Rippenmuster = 123 M.

Alle Größen

Fbe A abschneiden, wechseln zur Ndl Nr. 3.

Mit R **21** des Streifenmusters beg und im Muster str wie folgt:

R 1 (Hinr): Mit Fbe D 2 (1: 1: 0: 0) M li, 2 M re, ★2 M li, 2 M re, ab ★ wdhl bis zu den letzten 3 (2: 2: 1: 1) M, 2 (2: 2: 1: 1) M li, 1 (0: 0: 0: 0) M re.

R 2: 2 (1: 1: 0: 0) M re, 2 M li, ★2 M re, 2 M li, ab ★ wdhl bis zu den letzten 3 (2: 2: 1: 1) M, 2 (2: 2: 1: 1) M re, 1 (0: 0: 0: 0) M li.

Das Muster korrekt einhalten, dabei für die

Armschrägen

in der nächsten R und 6 (7: 4: 5: 2) in jeder folg 2. R bds je 1 M zun, danach 3 (3: 5: 5: 7) x in jeder folg 4. R bds je 1 M zun, alle Zun im Musterverlauf str = 115 (123: 129: 137: 143) M.

Nach 3 R enden mit R 10 (12: 14: 16: 18) des Streifenmusters, enden mit einer Rückr, (der Ärmel müsste ca. 12,5 (13: 13,5: 14:

14,5) cm lang sein.

Armkugel

Am Anf der nächsten 2 R je 4 (6: 7: 8: 9) M abk = 107 (111: 115: 121: 125) M.

In den nächsten 13 R bds je 1 M abn, danach 5 x in jeder folg 2. R und 3 (4: 5: 5: 6) x in jeder folg 4. R bds je 1 M abn = 65 (67: 69: 75: 77) M.

1 R str.

In der nächsten R und in jeder folg 2. R bds je 1 M abn bis 49 M übrig sind, danach in den folg 11 R bds je 1 M abn, enden mit einer Rückr.

Die restl 27 M abk.

FERTIGSTELLUNG

Die Teile nicht dämpfen.

Die re Schulternaht schließen.

Halsblende

Von re mit Ndl Nr. 2 ¼ und Fbe A aus der li vord Halsausschnittkante 35 (35: 39: 39: 42) M aufn und re str, die 27 (27: 29: 29: 29) M auf der Hilfsndl in der vord Mitte wie folgt str: 2 (2: 1: 1: 1) M re, 2 M re zus-str, 4 x [3 (3: 4: 4: 4) M re, 2 M re zus-str], 3 (3: 2: 2: 2) M re; aus der re vord Halsausschnittkante 35 (35: 39: 39: 42) M aufn und re str, aus der re rückw Halsausschnittkante 6 M aufn und re str, die 55 (55: 59: 59: 61) M auf der Hilfsndl im Rückenteil wie folgt str: 2 (2: 3: 3: 4) M re, 2 M re zus-str, 8 (8: 10: 10: 10) x [4 (4: 3: 3: 3) M re, 2 M re zus-str], 3 (3: 4: 4: 5) M re, zuletzt aus der li rückw Halsausschnittkante 6 M aufn und re str = 150 (150: 162: 162: 170) M.

Mit R 2 des Rippenmusters beg so wie beim Rückenteil angegeben, nach 11 R alle M im Muster abk.

Die li Schulternaht und die seitl Blendennaht schließen.

Die Seiten- und Unterarmnähte schließen, die Ärmel in die Armausschnitte nähen.

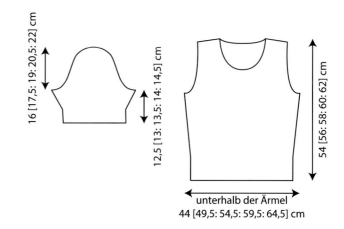

16 [17,5: 19: 20,5: 22] cm

12,5 [13: 13,5: 14: 14,5] cm

54 [56: 58: 60: 62] cm

unterhalb der Ärmel
44 [49,5: 54,5: 59,5: 64,5] cm

Lionfish ••••

Seite 32

Größe

Passend für Oberweite

| 81-86 | 91-97 | 102-107 | 112-117 | 122-127 | cm |

Gestrickte Oberweite

| 100 | 111 | 121 | 131 | 141 | cm |

Garn

Rowan Summerlite 4ply

A Still Grey 422

| 7 | 8 | 9 | 9 | 10 | x 50 g |

B Touch of Gold 439

| 3 | 3 | 3 | 3 | 4 | x 50 g |

Nadeln

1 Rundstrickndl Nr. 2 ¾, mindestens 120 cm lang
1 Rundstrickndl Nr. 3, mindestens 120 cm lang.
1 Nadelspiel Nr. 2 ¾
1 Nadelspiel Nr. 3

Maschenprobe

28 M und 36 R = 10 x 10 cm, glatt re gestr mit Ndl Nr. 3.

Streifenmuster

Rde 1–10: Mit Fbe A
Rde 11: Mit Fbe B
Rde 12: Mit Fbe A
Rde 13: Mit Fbe B
Rde 14–19: Wie R 12 und 13, 3 x str.
Rde 20–29: Mit Fbe A
Rde 30: Mit Fbe B
Rde 31: Mit Fbe A
Rde 32: Mit Fbe B
Rde 33–38: Wie R 31 und 32, 3 x str.
Diese 38 Runden bilden das Streifenmuster und werden fortlfd wdhl.

RÜCKEN- und VORDERTEIL

(werden bis zu den Armausschnitten in einem Stück gestr)
280 (312: 340: 368: 396) M mit der Rundstrickndl Nr. 2 ¾ und Fbe A anschl.
In Runden str wie folgt, dabei beachten, dass in der 1. Rde die M

nicht verdreht sind.
Rde 1 (Hinr): Re.
Anf und Ende der Rde markieren, gleichzeitig wird die rückw Mitte markiert.
Weitere 5 Runden glatt re str.
Wechseln zur Rundstrickndl Nr. 3.
Mit Rde 1 des Streifenmusters beg, fortlfd im Streifenmuster glatt re str bis zu einer Länge von 45 cm, enden mit Rde 5 des Streifenmusters.

Armausschnitte

Nächste Rde: 65 (73: 80: 87: 94) M re, diese M für die li Rückenteilhälfte auf einer Hilfsndl stilllegen, 10 M re, diese 10 M für den li Armausschnitt auf einer weiteren Hilfsndl stilllegen, 130 (146: 160: 174: 188) M re, diese M für das Vorderteil auf einer Hilfsndl stilllegen, 10 M re, diese 10 M für den re Armausschnitt auf einer Hilfsndl stilllegen, 65 (73: 80: 87: 94) M re, diese M für die re Rückenteilhälfte auf einer Hilfsndl stilllegen, den Fd abschneiden.

ÄRMEL

56 (58: 60: 60: 62) M mit dem Nadelspiel Nr. 2 ¾ und Fbe A anschl.
In Runden str wie folgt, dabei beachten, dass in der 1. Rde die M nicht verdreht sind.
Rde 1: Re.
Anf und Ende der Rde markieren, gleichzeitig wird die Unterarmnaht markiert.
Weitere 4 Runden re str.
Rde 6 (Hinr): 2 (3: 4: 4: 5) M re, 1 M zun, ★3 M re, 1 M zun, ab ★ wdhl bis zu den letzten 3 (4: 5: 5: 6) M, 3 (4: 5: 5: 6) M re = 74 (76: 78: 78: 80) M.
Wechseln zum Nadelspiel Nr. 3.
Mit Rde 1 des Streifenmusters beg, 10 (8: 8: 6: 6) Runden str.
Nächste Rde (Hinr): 1 M re, 1 M zun, re bis zur letzten M, 1 M zun, 1 M re = 76 (78: 80: 80: 82) M.
Alle Zun für die Armschrägen str wie in der letzten Rde angegeben:
In der 10. (8.: 8.: 6.: 6.) Rde und 4 (1: 11: 6: 14) x in jeder folg 10. (8.: 8.: 6.: 6.) Rde bds je 1 M zun, danach 7 (12: 4: 12: 6) x in jeder folg 12. (10.: 10.: 8.: 8.) Rde bds je 1 M zun = 100 (106: 112: 118: 124) M.
Nach einer Länge von 45 cm (mit eingerolltem Rand) enden mit Rde 5 des Streifenmusters.
Nächste Rde: 5 M re, diese M für den Armausschnitt auf einer

Hilfsndl stilllegen, re bis zu den letzten 5 M, die restl 5 M auf dieselbe Hilfsndl heben wie die ersten 5 M = 10 M für den Armausschnitt. Den Fd abschneiden, die restl 90 (96: 102: 108: 114) M auf einer Hilfsndl stilllegen.

PASSE

Von re mit der Rundstrickndl Nr. 3 und Fbe A zuerst die 65 (73: 80: 87: 94) M der li Rückenteilhälfte re str, die 90 (96: 102: 108: 114) M des li Ärmels re str, die 130 (146: 160: 174: 188) M des Vorderteils re str, die 90 (96: 102: 108: 114) M des re Ärmels re str, zuletzt die 65 (73: 80: 87: 94) M der re Rückenteilhälfte re str = 440 (484: 524: 564: 604) M.

Anf und Ende der Rde markieren, gleichzeitig wird die rückw Mitte markiert.

Mit Rde 8 des Streifenmusters beg, 1 Rde str.

Nächste Rde: 26 (21: 19: 22: 26) M re, 2 M re zus-str, ★53 (38: 42: 45: 48) M re, 2 M re zus-str, ab ★ wdhl bis zu den letzten 27 (21: 19: 23: 26) M, 27 (21: 19: 23: 26) M re = 432 (472: 512: 552: 592) M.

Nach weiteren 9 (9: 11: 11: 11) Runden enden mit Rde 18 (18: 20: 20: 20) des Streifenmusters.

(**Hinweis:** Wechseln zum Nadelspiel, wenn nicht mehr genug M für die Rundstrickndl vorhanden sind.)

Größe 81-86, 102-107 und 112-117) cm

Nächste Rde: 5 (-: 1: 8: -) M re, 2 M re zus-str, ★10 (-: 11: 11: -) M re, 2 M re zus-str, ab ★ wdhl bis zu den letzten 5 (-: 2: 9: -) M, 5 (-: 2: 9: -) M re = 396 (-: 472: 510: -) M.

Größe 91-97 und 122-127 speziell

Nächste Rde: - (3: -: -: 5) M re, 2 M re zus-str, ★11 M re, 2 M re zus-str, - (10: -: -: 12) M re, 2 M re zus-str, ab ★ wdhl bis zu den letzten − (17: -: -: 18) M, 11 M re, 2 M re zus-str, - (4: -: -: 5) M re = - (434: -: -: 548) M.

Alle Größen

Weitere 9 (9: 11: 11: 11) Runden str, enden mit Rde 28 (28: 32: 32: 32) des Streifenmusters.

Größe 81-86 und 112-117 cm

Nächste Rde: 11 (-: -: 6: -) M re, 2 M re zus-str, ★10 (-: -: 9: -) M re, 2 M re zus-str, ab ★ wdhl bis zu den letzten 11 (-: -: 7: -) M, 11 (-: -: 7: -) M re = 364 (-: -: 464: -) M.

Größen 91-97, 102-107 und 122-127 speziell

Nächste Rde: - (9: 9: -: 5) M re, 2 M re zus-str, ★- (11: 9: -: 9) M re, 2 M re zus-str, - (10: 8: -: 8) M re, 2 M re zus-str, ab ★ wdhl bis zu den letzten − (23: 20: -: 16) M, - (11: 9: -: 9) M re, 2 M re zus-str, - (10: 9: -: 5) M re = - (400: 428: -: 496) M.

Alle Größen

Nach 9 (9: 11: 11: 11) Runden enden mit Rde 38 (38: 6: 6: 6) des Streifenmusters.

Größen 81-86, 91-97, 102-107 und 112-117 cm speziell

Nächste Rde: 3 (5: 5: 6: -) M re, 2 M re zus-str, ★9 (10: 6: 6: -) M re, 2 M re zus-str, 10 (11: 7: 7: -) M re, 2 M re zus-str, ab ★ wdhl bis zu den letzten 14 (18: 13: 14: -) M, 9 (19: 6: 6: -) M re, 2 M re zus-str, 3 (6: 5: 6: -) M re = 332 (368: 378: 410: -) M.

Größe 122-127 speziell

Nächste Rde: 8 M re, 2 M re zus-str, ★7 M re, 2 M re zus-str, ab ★ wdhl bis zu den letzten 9 M, 9 M re = 442 M.

Alle Größen

Nach 9 (9: 11: 11: 11) Runden enden mit Rde 10 (10: 16: 18: 18) des Streifenmusters.

Größe 81-86, 91-97 und 102-107 cm speziell

Nächste Rde: 7 (8: 3: -: -) M re, 2 M re zus-str, ★7 (8: 8: -: -) M re, 2 M re zus-str, ab ★ wdhl bis zu den letzten 8 (8: 3-: -) M, 8 (8: 3: -: -:) M re = 296 (332: 340: -: -) M.

Größe 112-117 und 122-127 speziell

Nächste Rde: - (-: -: 9: 5) M re, 2 M re zus-str, ★8 M re, 2 M re zus-str, - (-: -: 7: 9) M re, 2 M re zus-str, ab ★ wdhl bis zu den letzten − (-: -: 19: 15) M, 8 M re, 2 M re zus-str, - (-: -: 9: 5) M re = - (-: -: 368: 400) M.

Alle Größen

Nach 9 (9: 9: 11: 11) Runden enden mit Rde 20 (20: 26: 30: 30) des Streifenmusters.

Größe 81-86, 91-97 und 122-127 cm speziell

Nächste Rde: 7 (1: -: -: 3) M re, 2 M re zus-str, ★6 M re, 2 M re zus-str, ab ★ wdhl bis zu den letzten 7 (1: -: -: 3) M, 7 (1: -: -: 3) M re = 260 (290: -: -: 350) M.

Größe 102-107 und 112-117 speziell

Nächste Rde: - (-: 8: 7: -) M re, 2 M re zus-str, ★5 M re, 2 M re zus-str, 6 M re, 2 M re zus-str, ab ★ wdhl bis zu den letzten − (-: 15: 14: -) M, 5 M re, 2 M re zus-str, - (-: 8: 7: -) M re = - (-: 296: 320: -) M.

Alle Größen

Nach 9 (9: 9: 11: 11) Runden enden mit Rde 30 (30: 36: 4: 4) des Streifenmusters.

Nächste Rde: 5 (4: 7: 6: 2) M re, 2 M re zus-str, ★6 (6: 6: 4: 5) M re, 2 M re zus-str, ab ★ wdhl bis zu den letzten 5 (4: 7: 6: 3) M, 5 (4: 7: 6: 3) M re = 228 (254: 260: 268: 300) M.

Nach 7 (9: 9: 9: 11) Runden enden mit Rde 38 (2: 8: 14: 16) des Streifenmusters.

Größe 81-86, 91-97, 102-107 und 122-127 speziell

Nächste Rde: 4 (2: 5: 2: -: 2) M re, 2 M re zus-str, ★5 (6: 6: -: 4) M re, 2 M re zus-str, ab ★ wdhl bis zu den letzten 5 (2: 5: -: 2) M, 5 (2: 5: -: 2) M re = 196 (222: 228: -: 250) M.

Größe 112-117 speziell

Nächste Rde: 2 M re, 2 M re zus-str, ★5 M re, 2 M re zus-str, 6 M re, 2 M re zus-str, ab ★ wdhl bis zu den letzten 9 M, 5 M re, 2 M re zus-str, 2 M re = 232 M.

Alle Größen

Nach 7 (9: 9: 9: 11) Runden enden mit Rde 8 (12: 18: 24: 28) des Streifenmusters.

Nächste Rde: 2 (5: 2: 4: 1) M re, 2 M re zus-str, ★5 (4: 4: 4: 3) M re, 2 M re zus-str, ab ★ wdhl bis zu den letzten 3 (5: 2: 4: 2) M, 3 (5: 2: 4: 2) M re = 168 (186: 190: 194: 200) M.

Nach 7 (9: 9: 9: 11) Runden enden mit Rde 16 (22: 28: 34: 2) des Streifenmusters.

Größe 81-86 und 102-107 speziell

Nächste Rde: 2 (-: 1: -: -) M re, 2 M re zus-str, ★5 (-: 3: -: -) M re, 2 M re zus-str, ab ★ wdhl bis zu den letzten 3 (-: 2: -: -) M, 3 (-: 2: -: -) M re = 144 (-: 152: -: -) M.

Größe 91-97 speziell

Nächste Rde: 2 M re, 2 M re zus-str, ★2 M re, 2 M re zus-str, 6 x (3 M re, 2 M re zus-str), ab ★ wdhl bis zu den letzten 12 M, 2 M re, 2 M re zus-str, 3 M re, 2 M re zus-str, 3 M re = 148 M.

Größe 112-117 und 122-127 speziell

Nächste Rde: - (-: -: 4: 2) M re, 2 M re zus-str, ★2 M re, 2 M re zus-str, 3 M re, 2 M re zus-str, ab ★ wdhl bis zu den letzten – (-: -: 8: 7) M, 2 M re, 2 M re zus-str, - (-: -: 4: 3) M re = - (-: -: 152: 156) M.

Alle Größen
Fbe B abschneiden und nur noch mit Fbe A fortfahren.

Halsblende
Wechseln zum Nadelspiel Nr. 2 ¾.
Nach 6 R in kraus re mit Ndl Nr. 3 alle M abk.

FERTIGSTELLUNG
Das Teil dämpfen.
Die je 10 M an den Armausschnitten entweder zusammennähen oder im Maschenstich miteinander verbinden.

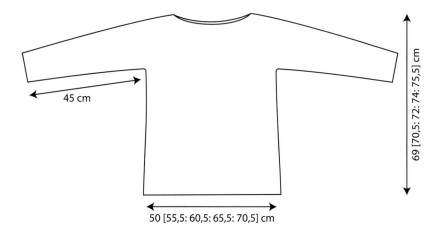

Pipefish ●●●

Seite 28

Größe
Passend für Oberweite

| 81-86 | 91-97 | 102-107 | 112-117 | 122-127 | cm |

Gestrickte Oberweite

| 90 | 101,5 | 111,5 | 121,5 | 131,5 | cm |

Garn
Rowan Summerlite 4ply

A Still Grey 422

| 4 | 5 | 5 | 6 | 6 | x 50 g |

B Sand Dune 438

| 1 | 1 | 1 | 1 | 1 | x 50 g |

C Anchor Grey 446

| 1 | 1 | 1 | 1 | 1 | x 50 g |

D Duck Egg 419

| 1 | 1 | 1 | 1 | 1 | x 50 g |

Nadeln
1 Paar Nr. 3
1 Rundstrickndl Nr. 3, mindestens 100 (100: 100: 120: 120) cm lang.

Maschenprobe
28 M und 36 R = 10 x 10 cm, glatt re gestr, 27 M und 50 R = 10 x 10 cm, im Blendenmuster gestr, beide mit Ndl Nr. 3.

RÜCKENTEIL
121 (137: 151: 163: 177) M mit Ndl Nr. 3 und Fbe A anschl.
Die Blende in folg Streifenmuster str:
R 1 (Hinr): Mit Fbe A 1 M re, ★1 M li abh, dabei liegt der Fd vor der M, 1 M re, ab ★ wdhl bis zum Ende.
R 2: Mit Fbe A li.
R 3 und 4: Mit Fbe B wie R 1 und 2.
R 5 und 6: Mit Fbe C wie R 1 und 2.
R 7 und 8: Mit Fbe D wie R 1 und 2.
Diese 8 R bilden das Blendenmuster, weitere 21 R str, enden mit R 5 des Musters, enden mit einer Hinr.
R 30 (Rückr): Mit Fbe C 12 (12: 15: 9: 10) M li, 1 M zun, 4 (4: 4: 6: 6) x [24 (28: 30: 24: 26) M li, 1 M zun], 13 (13: 16: 10: 11) M li = 126 (142: 156: 170: 184) M.
Fbe C abschneiden.
Mit einer Rechtsr beg und nur noch mit Fbe A glatt re weiterstr.

Nach einer Länge von 27 (27,5: 28: 28,5: 29) cm enden mit einer Rückr.

Armausschnitte

Am Anf der nächsten 2 R je 6 (7: 8: 9: 10) M abk = 114 (128: 140: 152: 164) M.

In den nächsten 7 (11: 13: 15: 15) R bds je 1 M abn, danach 4 (4: 4: 4: 5) x in jeder folg 2. R bds je 1 M abn = 92 (98: 106: 114: 124) M.
Nach einer Armausschnittlänge von 19 (20,5: 22: 23,5: 25) cm enden mit einer Rückr.

Schulterschrägen

Am Anf der nächsten 2 R je 4 (4: 5: 6: 6) M abk, danach am Anf der folg 2 R je 4 (4: 5: 6: 7) M abk = 76 (82: 86: 90: 98) M.

Rückw Halsausschnitt

Nächste R (Hinr): 4 (5: 5: 6: 7) M abk, re str bis 11 (13: 14: 15: 17) M auf der re Ndl sind, Arbeit wenden, die restl M auf einer Hilfsndl stilllegen, beide Seiten getrennt beenden.

Am Halsausschnitt in den nächsten 3 R je 1 M abn, **gleichzeitig** am Anf der 2. R 4 (5: 5: 6: 7) M abk.
Die restl 4 (5: 6: 6: 7) M abk.
Die stillgelegten M aufn, die mittl 46 (46: 48: 48: 50) M auf einer Hilfsndl stilllegen, mit neuem Fd in einer Hinr re str bis zum Ende.
Die 2. Seite gegengleich beenden.

LINKES VORDERTEIL

53 (61: 67: 75: 81) M mit Ndl Nr. 3 und Fbe A anschl.
29 R im Blendenmuster str so wie beim Rückenteil angegeben, enden mit R 5 des Blendenmusters, enden mit einer Hinr.

Nächste R (Rückr): Mit Fbe C 13 (15: 10: 19: 13) M li, 1 M zun, 1 (1: 2: 1: 2) x [27 (31: 23: 37: 27) M li, 1 M zun], 13 (15: 11: 19: 14) M li = 55 (63: 70: 77: 84) M.
Fbe C abschneiden.
Mit einer Rechtsr beg und nur mit Fbe A glatt re weiterstr.
Nach einer Länge von 27 (27,5: 28: 28,5: 29) cm enden mit einer Rückr.

Armausschnitt und vord Schräge

Am Anf der nächsten R 6 (7: 8: 9.10) M abk und am Ende der R 1 M abn = 48 (55: 61: 67: 73) M.
1 R str.
Am Armausschnitt in den nächsten 7 (11: 13: 15: 15) R je 1 M abn, danach 4 (4: 4: 4: 5) x in jeder folg 2. R je 1 M abn, **gleichzeitig** am vord Rand in der nächsten (nächsten: nächsten: 3.: 3.) R und 4 (1: 0: 0: 0) x in jeder folg 2. R je 1 M abn, danach 1 (4: 5: 5: 5) x in jeder folg 4. R je 1 M abn = 31 (34: 38: 42: 47) M.
Nur noch am vord Rand in der 2. (4.: 4.: 4.: 2.) R und 10 (10: 11: 10: 10) x in jeder folg 4. R je 1 M abn, danach − (−: −: 1: 2) x in jeder folg − (−: −: 6.: 6.) R je 1 M abn = 20 (23: 26: 30: 34) M.
Nach einer Armausschnittlänge von 19 (20,5: 22: 23,5: 25) cm enden mit einer Rückr.

Schulterschräge

Am Anf der nächsten R und 3 (1: 3: 3: 0) x am Anf jeder folg 2. R je 4 (4: 5: 6: 6) M abk, danach − (2: −: −: 3) x am Anf jeder folg 2 R je − (5: −: −: 7) M abk.
Nach 1 R die restl 4 (5: 6: 6: 7) M abk.

RECHTES VORDERTEIL

Genauso str wie das li Vorderteil, alle Abn gegengleich str.

ÄRMEL

71 (77: 83: 89: 97) M mit Ndl Nr. 3 und Fbe A anschl.
29 R im Blendenmuster str so wie beim Rückenteil angegeben, enden mit R 5 des Streifenmusters, enden mit einer Hinr.

Nächste R (Rückr): Mit Fbe C 11 (12: 13: 14: 16) M li, 1 M zun, 2 x [24 (26: 28: 30: 32) M li, 1 M zun], 12 (13: 14: 15: 17) M li = 74 (80: 86: 92: 100) M.
Fbe C abschneiden.
Mit einer Rechtsr beg und nur noch mit Fbe A glatt re weiterstr, dabei für die

Armschrägen

in der 3. (3.: 5.: 5.: 5.) R und in jeder folg 4. R bds je 1 M zun bis 90 (96: 96: 102: 104) M erreicht sind, danach in jeder folg − (−: 6.: 6.: 6.) R bds je 1 M zun bis − (−: 100: 106: 112) M erreicht sind.
Nach 3 (3: 5: 5: 5) R enden mit einer Rückr. (Der Ärmel müsste ca. 15 (15: 16: 16: 16) cm lang sein.)

Armkugel

Am Anf der nächsten 2 R je 6 (7: 8: 9: 10) M abk = 78 (82: 84: 88: 92) M.
In den nächsten 3 R bds je 1 M abn, danach 5 x in jeder folg 2. R und 3 (4: 5: 6: 7) x in jeder folg 4. R bds je 1 M abn = 56 (58: 58: 60: 62) M.
1 R str.
In der nächsten R und in jeder folg 2. R bds je 1 M abn bis 36 M übrig sind, und in den folg 7 R bds je 1 M abn, enden mit einer Rückr.
Die restl 22 M abk.

FERTIGSTELLUNG

Alle Teile dämpfen, siehe Informationsseite.
Beide Schulternähte schließen.

Hals- und Vorderteilblenden

Von re mit der Rundstrickndl Nr. 3 und Fbe A die M wie folgt aufn und re str, beg und enden an den Anschlagkanten der Vorderteile:
Aus der re Vorderteilkante bis zum Beg der vord Schräge 73 (74: 76: 77: 78) M, aus der re vord Schräge 60 (64: 68: 72: 76) M, aus der re rückw Halsausschnittkante 3 M, die 46 (46: 48: 48: 50) M auf der Hilfsndl im Rückenteil re str, dabei in der Mitte 1 M abn, aus der li rückw Halsausschnittkante 3 M, aus der li vord Schräge 60 (64: 68: 72: 76) M und aus der restl li Vorderteilkante 73 (74: 76: 77: 78) M = 317 (327: 341: 351: 363) M.
Mit R 2 des Blendenmusters beg so wie beim Rückenteil angegeben, 29 R str, enden mit R 6 des Musters, enden mit einer Rückr.
In der folg R alle M mit Fbe C abk.
Die Ärmel in die Armausschnitte nähen, die Seiten- und Unterarmnähte schließen.

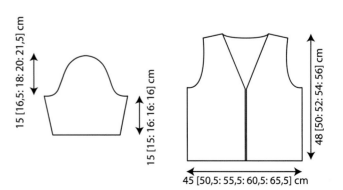

Puffin ••••

Seite 18

Größe

Passend für Oberweite

81-86	91-97	102-107	112-117	122-127	cm

Gestrickte Oberweite

103	113	123	133	143	cm

Garn

Rowan Summerlite DK

A Coral Blush 467

1	1	2	2	2	x 50 g

B Favourite Denims 469

1	1	1	2	2	x 50 g

C Summer 453

1	1	1	2	2	x 50 g

D Silvery Blue 468

1	1	1	2	2	x 50 g

E Pink Powder 472

1	1	1	2	2	x 50 g

F Khaki 461

1	1	1	1	2	x 50 g

G White 465

1	1	1	1	1	x 50 g

H Black 464

2	3	3	3	4	x 50 g

Nadeln

1 Paar Nr. 3 ¼
1 Paar Nr. 3 ¾

Maschenprobe

20 M und 38 R = 10 x 10 cm, im Muster gestr mit Ndl Nr. 3 ¾.

RÜCKENTEIL

103 (113: 123: 133: 143) M mit Ndl Nr. 3 ¼ und Fbe H anschl.
R 1 (Hinr): 1 M re, *1 M li, 1 M re, ab * wdhl bis zum Ende.
R 2: 1 M li, *1 M re, 1 M li, ab * wdhl bis zum Ende.
Die beiden R bilden das Rippenmuster, nach weiteren 14 R enden mit einer Rückr.
Fbe H abschneiden.
Wechseln zur Ndl Nr. 3 ¾ und das Muster in folg Streifenmuster str:

R 1 (Hinr): Mit Fbe A re.
R 2: Mit Fbe A li.
R 3 und 4: Mit Fbe B re.
R 5: Mit Fbe A 2 M re, *1 U, 2 M re zus-str, ab * wdhl bis zur letzten M, 1 M re.
R 6: Mit Fbe A re.
R 7: Mit Fbe B li.
R 8: Mit Fbe B re.
R 9-16: wie R 1-8, aber mit Fbe C anstatt Fbe A und Fbe D anstatt Fbe B str.
R 17-24: Wie R 1-8, aber mit Fbe E anstatt mit Fbe A und Fbe F anstatt Fbe B str.
R 25-32: Wie R 1-8, aber mit Fbe G anstatt mit Fbe A und Fbe H anstatt Fbe B str.
Diese 32 R bilden das Muster und werden fortlfd wdhl.
Nach einer Länge von 44 (46: 48: 50: 52) cm enden mit einer Rückr.
Schulterschrägen
Am Anf der nächsten 4 R je 3 (3: 4: 4: 5) M abk, danach am Anf der folg 2 R je 3 (4: 4: 5: 5) M abk = 85 (93: 99: 107: 113) M.
Rückw Halsausschnitt
Nächste R (Hinr): 3 (4: 4: 5: 5) M abk, im Muster str bis 23 (26: 28: 31: 33) M auf der re Ndl sind, Arbeit wenden, die restl M auf einer Hilfsndl stilllegen, beide Seiten getrennt beenden.
Am Halsausschnitt in den nächsten 4 R je 1 M abn, danach 2 x in jeder folg 2. R je 1 M abn, **gleichzeitig** am Anf der 2. R und 2 (3: 2: 3: 2) x am Anf jeder folg 2. R je 3 (4: 4: 5: 5) M abk, danach 1 (-: 1: -: 1) x in der folg 2. R 4 (-: 5: -: 6) M abk.
Nach 1 R die restl 4 (4: 5: 5: 6) M abk.
Die stillgelegten M aufn, die mittl 33 (33: 35: 35: 37) M auf einer Hilfsndl stilllegen, mit neuem Fd in einer Hinr im Muster str bis zum Ende.
Die 2. Seite gegengleich beenden.

VORDERTEIL

Das Vorderteil str wie das Rückenteil bis 12 (12: 16: 16: 20) R unterhalb des Beg der Schulterschrägen, enden mit einer Rückr.
Vord Halsausschnitt
Nächste R (Hinr): 38 (43: 48: 53: 58) M im Muster, Arbeit wenden, die restl M auf einer Hilfsndl stilllegen, beide Seiten getrennt beenden.
Am Halsausschnitt in den nächsten 6 R je 1 M abn, danach 2 (2: 3:

3: 3) x in jeder folg 2. R und 0 (0: 0: 0: 1) x in der folg 4. R je 1 M abn = 30 (35: 39: 44: 48) M.

Nach 1 (1: 3: 3: 3) R enden mit einer Rückr.

Schulterschräge

Am Anf der nächsten R 3 (3: 4: 4: 5) M abk und am Ende der R 1 M abn = 26 (31: 34: 39: 42) M.

1 R str.

Am Anf der nächsten R und 5 (0: 5: 0: 5) x am Anf jeder folg 2. R je 3 (3: 4: 4: 5) M abk, danach 1 (6: 1: 6: 1) x am Anf jeder folg 2. R je 4 (4: 5: 5: 6) M abk.

Nach 1 R die restl 4 (4: 5: 5: 6) M abk.

Die stillgelegten M aufn, die mittl 27 M auf einer Hilfsndl stilllegen, mit neuem Fd in entsprechender Fbe im Muster str bis zum Ende. Die 2. Seite gegengleich beenden.

ÄRMEL

73 (79: 85: 91: 97) M mit Ndl Nr. 3 ¼ und Fbe H anschl.

16 R im Rippenmuster str so wie beim Rückenteil angegeben, enden mit einer Rückr.

Fbe H abschneiden und wechseln zur Ndl Nr. 3 ¾.

Das Muster im Streifenmuster str so wie beim Rückenteil angegeben bis zu einer Länge von 15 (15: 16: 16: 16) cm, enden mit einer Rückr.

Alle M mit der Fbe der unteren R abk.

FERTIGSTELLUNG

Alle Teile dämpfen, siehe Informationsseite.

Die re Schulternaht schließen.

Halsblende

Von re mit Ndl Nr. 3 ¼ und Fbe H die M wie folgt aufn und re str: Aus der li vord Halsausschnittkante 21 (21: 24: 24: 27) M, die 27 M auf der Hilfsndl in der vord Mitte re str, aus der re vord Halsausschnittkante 21 (21: 24: 24: 27) M, aus der re rückw Halsausschnittkante 8 M, die 33 (33: 35: 35: 37) M auf der Hilfsndl im Rückenteil re str, dabei in der Mitte 1 M zun und aus der li rückw Halsausschnittkante 8 M = 119 (119: 127: 127: 135) M.

Mit R 2 des Rippenmusters beg so wie beim Rückenteil angegeben, nach 9 R alle M im Rippenmuster abk.

Die li Schulternaht und die seitl Blendennaht schließen. An allen seitl Rändern von den Schulternähten abwärts je 18,5 (20: 21,5: 23: 24,5) cm abmessen und markieren. Die Ärmel mit der Mitte der Abkettkante auf die Schulternähte heften und an den seitl Rändern zwischen den Markierungen festnähen. Die Seiten- und Unterarmnähte schließen.

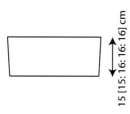

15 [15: 16: 16: 16] cm

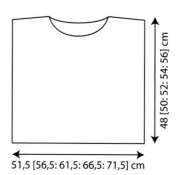

48 [50: 52: 54: 56] cm

51,5 [56,5: 61,5: 66,5: 71,5] cm

Redshank ●●●

Seite 30

Größe

Passend für Oberweite

81-86	91-97	102-107	112-117	122-127	cm

Gestrickte Oberweite

141	152	162	172	182	cm

Garn

Rowan Summerlite 4ply

A Seashell 437

5	6	6	7	7	x 50 g

B Still Grey 422

5	6	6	7	7	x 50 g

C Anchor Grey 446

3	3	3	4	4	x 50 g

Nadeln

1 Paar Nr. 2 ¾

1 Paar Nr. 3 ¼

1 Rundstrickndl Nr. 3 ¼, mindestens 120 cm lang

Maschenprobe

34 M und 68 R = 10 x 10 cm, im Perlmuster mit abgehobenen M gestr mit Ndl Nr. 3 ¼.

32 M und 44 R = 10 x 10 cm, im Rippenmuster gestr mit Ndl Nr. 2 ¾.

Streifenmuster A

R 1 und 2: Mit Fbe A

R 3 und 4: Mit Fbe B

R 5-12: Wie R 1-4, 2 x str.

R 13 und 14: Mit Fbe A

R 15 und 16: Mit Fbe C.

R 17-24: Wie R 13-16, 2 x str

Diese 24 R bilden das Streifenmuster A und werden fortlfd wdhl.

Streifenmuster B

R 1 und 2: Mit Fbe A.

R 3 und 4: Mit Fbe B.

R 5-24: Wie R 1-4, 5 x str.

R 25 und 26: Mit Fbe A.

R 27 und 28: Mit Fbe C.

R 29-48: Wie R 25-28, 5 x str.

Diese 48 R bilden das Streifenmuster B und werden fortlfd wdhl.

RÜCKENTEIL

237 (257: 273: 293: 309) M mit Ndl Nr. 2 ¾ und Fbe B anschl.

R 1 (Hinr): *2 M li, 2 M re, ab * wdhl bis zur letzten M, 1 M li.

R 2: *2 M re, 2 M li, ab * wdhl bis zur letzten M, 1 M re.

Die beiden R bilden das Rippenmuster und werden wdhl bis zu einer Länge von 10 cm, dabei in der letzten R bds je 1 (1: 1: 0: 0) M zun, enden mit einer Rückr = 239 (259: 275: 293: 309) M.

Wechseln zur Ndl Nr. 3 ¼.

Das Streifenmuster A im Perlmuster mit abgehobenen M wie folgt str:

R 1 (Hinr): Mit Fbe A 1 M re, *1 M li abh, dabei liegt der Fd hinter der M, 1 M re, ab * wdhl bis zum Ende.

R 2: Mit Fbe A 1 M re, 1 M li abh, dabei liegt der Fd vor der M, 1 M re, ab * wdhl bis zum Ende.

R 3: Mit Fbe B 2 M re, *1 M li abh, dabei liegt der Fd hinter der M, 1 M re, ab * wdhl bis zur letzten M, 1 M re.

R 4: Mit Fbe B 2 M re, *1 M li abh, dabei liegt der Fd vor der M, 1 M re, ab * wdhl bis zur letzten M, 1 M re.

Die 4 R bilden das Perlmuster mit abgehobenen M in den ersten 4 R des Streifenmusters A.

Mit R 5 des Streifenmusters weiterstr, weitere 80 R im Muster str, enden mit R 4 des Perlmusters und R 12 des Streifenmusters A, enden mit einer Rückr.

Zunahmen für die Ärmel

Wechseln zur Rundstrickndl Nr. 3 ¼, wenn zu viele M auf der gerade Ndl sind, weiter im Streifenmuster A str, dabei in der nächsten R und 5 (6: 7: 8: 8) x in jeder folg 6. R bds je 1 M zun, danach 10 (12: 13: 12: 12) x in jeder folg 4. R und 10 (9: 11: 11: 9) x in jeder folg 2. R bds je 1 M zun, zuletzt in den folg 9 (7: 5: 5: 9) R bds je 1 M zun, enden mit einer Rückr = 309 (329: 349: 367: 387) M.

Am Anf der nächsten 8 R je 4 M anschl = 341 (361: 381: 399: 419) M.

Anf und Ende der letzten R für das Ende der Zun mit einem Fd markieren.

Weitere 24 (14: 2: 0: 0) R str, enden mit R 24 des Streifenmusters A, enden mit einer Rückr.

Mit R 1 des Streifenmusters B beg, im Muster weitere 42 (56: 70: 74: 76) R str, enden mit R 42 (8: 22: 26: 28) des Streifenmusters B, enden mit einer Rückr.

Anf und Ende der letzten R für den Beg der Abn für die Ärmel markieren.

Abnahmen für die Oberarmnaht

Am Anf der nächsten 12 (16: 20: 20: 20) R je 4 M abk = 293 (207: 301: 319: 339) M. ★★

In den nächsten 57 (53: 47: 45: 45) R bds je 1 M abn, danach 21 (17: 15: 18: 20) x in jeder folg 2. R und danach in den folg 11 (19: 25: 31: 37) R bds je 1 M abn, enden mit R 20 (34: 48: 14: 26) des Streifenmusters B = 115 (119: 127: 131: 135) M.

Rückw Halsausschnitt und Schulterschrägen

Nächste R (Hinr): 2 M zus-str, 29 (31: 33: 35: 35) M im Muster, Arbeit wenden, die restl M auf einer Hilfsndl stilllegen, beide Seiten getrennt beenden = 30 (32: 34: 36: 36) M.

Für die Halsrundung in den nächsten 4 (4: 3: 1: 1) R je 1 M abn, danach 1 (0: 0: 0: 0) x in der folg 2. R 1 M abn, **gleichzeitig** für die Oberarmnaht in den nächsten 6 (4: 3: 1: 1) R je 1 M abn = 19 (24: 28: 34: 34) M.

Größe 81-86 und 91-97 speziell

Nächste R (Rückr): Im Muster bis zu den letzten 2 M, 2 M zus-str = 18 (23: -: -: -) M.

Alle Größen

Am Anf der nächsten R und 2 (3: 4: 5: 5) x in jeder folg 2. R je 4 M abk, **gleichzeitig** am Halsausschnitt in den nächsten 1 (1: 1: 3: 3) R je 1 M abn, danach 1 (2: 3: 3: 3) x in jeder folg 2. R je 1 M abn. Nach 1 R die restl 4 M abk.

Die stillgelegten M aufn, mit neuem Fd in entsprechender Fbe die mittl 53 (53: 57: 57: 61) M abk, im Muster bis zu den letzten 2 M, 2 M zus-str = 30 (32: 34: 36: 36) M.

Die 2. Seite gegengleich beenden.

VORDERTEIL

Das Vorderteil str wie das Rückenteil, angegeben bis ★★.

In den nächsten 57 (53: 47: 45: 45) R bds je 1 M abn, danach 12 (12: 10: 16: 18) x in jeder folg 2. R bds je 1 M abn = 155 (167: 187: 197: 213) M.

Nach 1 R enden mit R 40 (6: 14: 28: 34) des Streifenmusters B, enden mit einer Rückr.

Vord Halsausschnitt und Schulterschrägen

Nächste R (Hinr): 2 M zus-str, 57 (63: 72: 77: 84) M im Muster, Arbeit wenden, die restl M auf einer Hilfsndl stilllegen, beide Seiten getrennt beenden = 58 (64: 73: 78: 85) M.

Am Oberarm in der 2. R und 7 (3: 3: 0: 0) x in jeder folg 2. R je 1 M abn, danach in den folg 18 (25: 26: 32: 38) R je 1 M abn, **gleichzeitig** am Halsausschnitt in den nächsten 6 R und 5 x in jeder folg 2. R je 1 M abn, danach 3 x in jeder folg 4. R und 1 (0: 1: 1: 2) x in jeder folg 6. R je 1 M abn, enden mit einer Hinr (Rückr: Hinr: Hinr: Hinr) = 17 (21: 28: 30: 30) M.

Größe 81-86 speziell

Nächste R (Rückr): Im Muster bis zu den letzten 2 M; 2 M zus-str = 16 M.

Am Anf der nächsten R und 2 x am Anf jeder folg 2. R je 4 M abk = 4 M.

Größe 91-97 speziell

Am Anf der nächsten R und 3 x am Anf jeder folg 2. R je 4 M abk, **gleichzeitig** am Halsausschnitt in der nächsten R 1 M abn = 4 M.

Größe 102-107 speziell

Am Oberarm in den nächsten 3 R je 1 M abn = 25 M.

Am Anf der nächsten R und 4 x am Anf jeder folg 2. R je 4 M abk, **gleichzeitig** am Halsausschnitt in der 3. R 1 M abn = 4 M.

Größe 112-117 und 122-127 speziell

Nächste R (Rückr): Im Muster bis zu den letzten 2 M, 2 M zus-str = 29 M.

Am Anf der nächsten R und 5 x am Anf jeder folg 2. R je 4 M abk, **gleichzeitig** am Halsausschnitt in der 5. R 1 M abn = 4 M.

Alle Größen

1 R str.

Die restl 4 M abk.

Die stillgelegten M aufn, mit neuem Fd in der entsprechenden Fbe die mittl 37 (37: 39: 39: 41) M abk, im Muster str bis zu den letzten 2 M, 2 M zus-str = 58 (64: 73: 78: 85) M.

Die 2. Seite gegengleich beenden.

FERTIGSTELLUNG

Alle Teile dämpfen, siehe Informationsseite.

Die re Schulter- und Oberarmnaht schließen.

Halsblende

Von re mit Ndl Nr. 2 ¾ und Fbe B die M wie folgt aufn und re str:
Aus der li vord Halsausschnittkante 21 (21: 23: 23: 26) M, aus der vord Mitte 35 (35: 36: 36: 38) M, aus der re vord Halsausschnittkante 21 (21: 23: 23: 26) M, aus der re rückw Halsausschnittkante 7 M, aus der rückw Halsausschnittkante 50 (50: 53: 53: 57) M und aus der li rückw Halsausschnittkante 7 M = 141 (141: 149: 149: 161) M.

Mit R 2 des Rippenmusters beg so wie beim Rückenteil angegeben, nach 2,5 cm alle M im Muster abk.

Die li Schulter- und Oberarmnaht sowie die seitl Blendennaht schließen.

Ärmelbündchen (beide gleich)

Von re mit Ndl Nr. 2 ¾ und Fbe B aus dem unteren Rand der Ärmel zwischen den Markierungen 61 (65: 69: 69: 73) M aufn und re str.

Mit R 2 des Rippenmusters beg so wie beim Rückenteil angegeben, nach 10 cm alle M im Muster abk.

Die Seiten- und Unterarmnähte schließen.

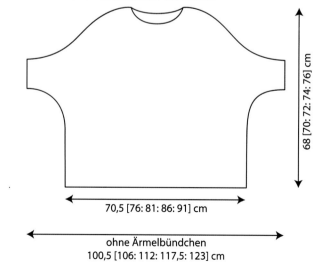

68 [70: 72: 74: 76] cm

70,5 [76: 81: 86: 91] cm

ohne Ärmelbündchen
100,5 [106: 112: 117,5: 123] cm

Ruff •

Seite 20

Garn
Rowan Summerlite DK

A White 465	2	x 50 g
B Garden 471	1	x 50 g
C Lagoon 457	2	x 50 g
D Summer 453	1	x 50 g
E Rouge 462	2	x 50 g
F Cantaloupe 456	1	x 50 g
G Fuchsia 455	2	x 50 g
H Indigo 450	1	x 50 g

Nadeln
1 Rundstrickndl Nr. 3 ¾, mindestens 120 cm lang.

Maschenprobe
22 M und 40 R = 10 x 10 cm, kraus re gestr mit Ndl Nr. 3 ¾.

Fertige Größe
Der fertige Schal ist 29,5 cm breit und 180 cm lang (ohne Fransen)

SCHAL
396 M mit Ndl Nr. 3 ¾ und Fbe A anschl, dabei ca. 15 cm des Anschlagfadens hängen lassen.
In Hin- und Rückr str wie folgt:
R 1 (Hinr): Mit Fbe A re.
Fbe A abschneiden, dabei 15 cm des Faden hängen lassen (für die Fransen).
Mit neuem Fd in Fbe A beg, dabei 15 cm des Fadens hängen lassen (für eine Franse):
R 2: Mit Fbe A re.
Fbe A abschneiden, dabei 15 cm des Faden hängen lassen (für die Fransen).
Mit neuem Fd in Fbe B beg, dabei 15 cm des Fadens hängen lassen (für eine Franse):
R 3: Mit Fbe B re.
Fbe B abschneiden, dabei 15 cm des Faden hängen lassen.
Mit neuem Fd in Fbe B beg, dabei 15 cm des Fadens hängen lassen.
R 4: Mit Fbe B re.
In folg Streifenmuster kraus re weiterstr, dabei jeweils am Anf und Ende jeder R je 15 cm des Fadens lassen.
R 5–8: Wie Fbe C re.

R 9 und 10: Mit Fbe D re.
R 11–14: Mit Fbe E re.
R 15 und 16: Mit Fbe F re.
R 17 und 18: Mit Fbe A re.
R 19–22: Mit Fbe G re.
R 23 und 24: Mit Fbe A re.
R 25 und 28: Mit Fbe H re.
R 29–32: Mit Fbe F re.
R 33–36: Mit Fbe H re.
R 37 und 38: Mit Fbe A re.
R 39–42: Mit Fbe G re.
R 43 und 44: Mit Fbe A re.
R 45 und 46: Mit Fbe F re.
R 47 und 50: Mit Fbe E re.
R 51 und 52: Mit Fbe D re.
R 53 –56: Mit Fbe C re.
R 57–58: Mit Fbe B re.
R 59–116: Wie R 1-58.
R 117: Mit Fbe A re.
Alle M abk, dabei am Anf und Ende der R je 15 cm hängen lassen.

FERTIGSTELLUNG
Den Schal **nicht dämpfen.**
Für die Fransen die Fäden in Gruppen mit je 4 Fäden verknoten.
Alle Fäden auf eine Länge von 10 cm schneiden.

Silver Moony ●●●

Seite 6

Größe

Passend für Oberweite

| 81-86 | 91-97 | 102-107 | 112-117 | 122-127 | cm |

Gestrickte Oberweite

| 88 | 99 | 110 | 121 | 132 | cm |

Garn

Rowan Summerlite DK

A Linen 460

| 8 | 9 | 10 | 11 | 12 | x 50 g |

B Indigo 450

| 1 | 1 | 1 | 1 | 1 | x 50 g |

C Black 464

| 1 | 1 | 1 | 1 | 1 | x 50 g |

D Cantaloupe 456

| 1 | 1 | 1 | 1 | 1 | x 50 g |

E Rouge 462

| 1 | 1 | 1 | 1 | 1 | x 50 g |

F Khaki 461

| 1 | 1 | 1 | 1 | 1 | x 50 g |

Nadeln

1 Paar Nr. 3 ¼

1 Paar Nr. 3 ¾

Knöpfe – 8 x 9427224190 von Groves, siehe Informationsseite.

Maschenprobe

22 M und 37 R = 10 x 10 cm, im Muster gestr mit Ndl Nr. 3 ¾

Streifenmuster

R 1 und 2: Mit Fbe A

R 3 und 4: Mit Fbe B

R 5-8: Mit Fbe A

R 9 und 10: Mit Fbe C.

R 11-14: Mit Fbe A.

R 15 und 16: Mit Fbe D.

R 17-20: Mit Fbe A.

R 21 und 22: Mit Fbe E.

R 23-26: Mit Fbe A.

R 27 und 28: Mit Fbe F.

R 29 und 30: Mit Fbe A.

Diese 30 R bilden das Streifenmuster und werden fortlfd wdhl.

RÜCKENTEIL

101 (113: 125: 137: 149) M mit Ndl Nr. 3 ¼ und Fbe A anschl.

Nach 6 R in kraus enden mit einer Rückr.

Wechseln zur Ndl Nr. 3 ¾.

Die Streifen im Muster str wie folgt:

R 1 (Hinr): Mit Fbe A re.

R 2: Mit Fbe A li.

R 3: Mit Fbe B 2 M li, ★1 M abh, dabei liegt der Fd vor der M, 1 M li, ab ★ wdhl bis zur letzten M, 1 M li.

R 4: Mit Fbe B 1 M re, ★1 M abh, dabei liegt der Fd hinter der M, 1 M re, ab ★ wdhl bis zum Ende.

R 5: Mit Fbe A re.

R 6: Mit Fbe A li.

Diese 6 R bilden das Muster in den ersten 6 R des Streifenmusters, mit R 7 im Muster weiterstr, nach weiteren 8 (8: 10: 10: 12) R enden mit einer Rückr.

In der nächsten R und 3 x in jeder folg 10. R bds je 1 M abn, danach 2 x in jeder folg 8. R bds je 1 M abn = 89 (101: 113: 125: 137) M.

Nach 17 R enden mit einer Rückr.

In der nächsten R und 2 x in jeder folg 12. R bds je 1 M zun, danach 1 x in der folg 14. R bds je 1 M abn, alle Zun im Musterverlauf str = 97 (109: 121: 133: 145) M.

Nach 15 R enden mit R 12 (12: 14: 14: 16) des Streifenmusters, enden mit einer Rückr (Das Rückenteil müsste ca. 37 (37: 37,5: 37,5: 38,5) cm lang sein).

Armausschnitte

Am Anf der nächsten beiden R je 3 (4: 5: 6: 7) M abk = 91 (101: 111: 121: 131) M.

In den nächsten 3 (7: 9: 9: 11) R bds je 1 M abn, danach 5 (4: 4: 5: 5) x in jeder folg 2. R und 1 x in der folg 4. R bds je 1 M abn = 73 (77: 83: 91: 97) M.

Nach einer Armausschnittlänge von 19,5 (21: 22,5: 24: 25,5) cm enden mit einer Rückr.

Rückw Halsausschnitt

Nächste R (Hinr): 24 (26: 28: 32: 34) M im Muster, Arbeit wenden, die restl M auf einer Hilfsndl stilllegen, beide Seiten getrennt beenden.

Am Anf der nächsten R 1 M abn = 23 (25: 27: 31: 33) M.

Schulterschräge

Am Anf der nächsten R und 2 x am Anf jeder folg 2. R je 5 (5: 6: 7: 7) M abk, **gleichzeitig** am Halsausschnitt in den nächsten 3 R je 1 M abn, danach 1 x in der folg 2. R 1 M abn.

Nach 1 R die restl 4 (6: 5: 6: 8) M abk.

Die stillgelegten M aufn, mit neuem Fd in einer Hinr in der entsprechenden Fbe die mittl 25 (25: 27: 27: 29) M abk, im Muster bis zum Ende.

Die 2. Seite gegengleich beenden.

LINKES VORDERTEIL

48 (54: 60: 66: 72) M mit Ndl Nr. 3 ¼ und Fbe A anschl.

Nach 6 R in kraus wechseln zur Ndl Nr. 3 ¾.

Die Streifen im Muster str wie folgt:

R 1 (Hinr): Mit Fbe A re.

R 2: Mit Fbe A li.

R 3: Mit Fbe B 2 M li, ⋆1 M abh, dabei liegt der Fd vor der M, 1 M li, ab ⋆ wdhl bis zum Ende.

R 4: Mit Fbe B 2 M re, ⋆1 M abh, dabei liegt der Fd hinter der M, 1 M re, ab ⋆ wdhl bis zum Ende.

R 5: Mit Fbe A re.

R 6: Mit Fbe A li.

Diese 6 R bilden das Muster in den ersten 6 R des Streifenmusters, mit R 7 weiterstr, die 6 R des Musters werden wie folgt fortlfd wdhl: Nach weiteren 8 (8: 10: 10: 12) R enden mit einer Rückr.

Am Anf der nächsten R und 3 x am Anf jeder folg 10. R je 1 M abn, danach 2 x am Anf jeder folg 8. R je 1 M abn = 42 (48: 54: 60: 66) M.

Nach 17 R enden mit einer Rückr.

Am Anf der nächsten R und 2 x am Anf jeder folg 12. R je 1 M zun, danach 1 x am Anf der folg 14. R 1 M abn, alle Zun im Musterverlauf str = 46 (52: 58: 64: 70) M.

Nach 15 R enden mit R 12 (12: 14: 14: 16) des Streifenmusters, enden mit einer Rückr (Das li Vorderteil müsste ca. 37 (37: 37,5: 37,5: 38,5) cm lang sein).

Armausschnitt

Am Anf der nächsten R 3 (4: 5: 6: 7) M abk = 43 (48: 53: 58: 63) M.

1 R str.

Am Armausschnitt in den nächsten 3 (7: 9: 9: 11) R je 1 M abn, danach 5 (4: 4: 5: 5) x in jeder folg 2. R und 1 x in der folg 4. R je 1 M abn = 34 (36: 39: 43: 46) M.

Gerade str bis 24 (24: 28: 28: 32) R unterhalb des Beg der Schulterschräge, enden mit einer Rückr.

Vord Halsausschnitt

Nächste R (Hinr): 29 (31: 34: 38: 41) M im Muster, die restl 5 M abk. Den Fd abschneiden.

Mit neuem Fd in einer Rückr beg und str wie folgt:

Am Halsausschnitt in den nächsten 6 R je 1 M abn, danach 2 x in jeder folg 2. R und 2 (2: 3: 3: 4) x in jeder folg 4. R je 1 M abn = 19 (21: 23: 27: 29) M.

Nach 5 R enden mit einer Rückr.

Schulterschräge

Am Anf der nächsten R und 2 x am Anf jeder folg 2. R je 5 (5: 6: 7: 7) M abk.

Nach 1 R die restl 4 (6: 5: 6: 8) M abk.

RECHTES VORDERTEIL

48 (54: 60: 66: 72) M mit Ndl Nr. 3 ¼ und Fbe A anschl.

Nach 6 R in kraus wechseln zur Ndl Nr. 3 ¾.

Die Streifen im Muster str wie folgt:

R 1 (Hinr): Mit Fbe A re.

R 2: Mit Fbe A li.

R 3: Mit Fbe B ⋆1 M li, 1 M abh, dabei liegt der Fd vor der M, ab ⋆ wdhl bis zu den letzten 2 M, 2 M li.

R 4: Mit Fbe B ⋆1 M re, 1 M abh, dabei liegt der Fd hinter der M, ab ⋆ wdhl bis zu den letzten 2 M, 2 M re.

R 5: Mit Fbe A re.

R 6: Mit Fbe A li.

Das Muster korrekt einhalten und das re Vorderteil gegengleich zum li Vorderteil beenden, dabei die 1. R für den Halsausschnitt str wie folgt:

Nächste R (Hinr): 5 M abk, im Muster bis zum Ende = 29 (31: 34: 38: 41) M.

ÄRMEL

51 (53: 55: 55: 57) M mit Ndl Nr. 3 ¼ und Fbe A anschl.

Nach 6 R in kraus re wechseln zur Ndl Nr. 3 ¼.

Mit R 1 des Streifenmusters beg und im Muster str so wie beim Rückenteil angegeben, dabei für die

Armschrägen

in der 13. (13.: 11.: 9.: 9.) R und in jeder folg 12. (12.: 10.: 8.: 8.) R bds je 1 M zun bis 59 (75: 63: 67: 77) M erreicht sind, danach in jeder folg 14. (14.: 12.: 10.: 10.) R bds je 1 M zun bis 73 (77: 81: 87: 91) M erreicht sind, alle Zun im Musterverlauf str.

Nach einer Länge von ca. 45 (45: 46: 46: 46,5) cm enden mit R 12 (12: 14: 14: 16) des Streifenmusters, enden mit einer Rückr.

Armkugel

Am Anf der nächsten 2 R je 3 (4: 5: 6: 7) M abk = 67 (69: 71: 75: 77) M.

In den nächsten 3 R bds je 1 M abn, danach 3 x in jeder folg 2. R und 8 (9: 11: 12: 14) x in jeder folg 4. R bds je 1 M abn = 39 (39: 37: 39: 37) M.

1 R str.

In der nächsten R und in jeder folg 2. R bds je 1 M abn bis 27 M übrig sind, danach in den folg 5 R bds je 1 M abn, enden mit einer Rückr.

Die restl 17 M abk.

FERTIGSTELLUNG

Alle Teile dämpfen, siehe Informationsseite.

Beide Schulternähte schließen.

Knopfblende

Von re mit Ndl Nr. 3 ¼ und Fbe A aus der li vord Vorderteilkante vom Halsausschnitt bis zur Anschlagkante 114 (114: 121: 121: 128) M aufn und re str.

Nach 8 R in kraus re in der folg Rückr alle M re abk.

Knopflochblende

Von re mit Ndl Nr. 3 ¼ und Fbe A aus der re vord Vorderteilkante von der Anschlagkante bis zum Halsausschnitt 114 (114: 121: 121: 128) M aufn und re str.

Nach 3 R in kraus re enden mit einer Rückr.

R 4 (Hinr): 5 M re, ★1 U, 2 M re zus-str (für ein Knopfloch), 13 (13: 14: 14: 15) M re, ab ★ 6 x wdhl, 1 U, 2 M re zus-str (für das 8. Knopfloch), 2 M re.

Nach 4 R in kraus re in der folg Rückr alle M re abk.

Halsblende

Von re mit Ndl Nr. 3 ¼ und Fbe A die M wie folgt aufn und re str: Aus dem oberen Rand der Knopfblende 5 M, aus der re vord Halsausschnittkante 28 (28: 31: 31: 34) M, aus der re rückw Halsausschnittkante 6 M, die 25 (25: 27: 27: 29) M auf der Hilfsndl im Rückenteil re str, aus der li rückw Halsausschnittkante 6 M, aus der li vord Halsausschnittkante 28 (28: 31: 31: 34) M und aus dem oberen Rand der Knopfblende 5 M = 103 (103: 111: 111: 119) M. Mit einer Linksr beg und 7 R glatt re str, enden mit einer Rückr. In der folg R mit Ndl Nr. 3 ¾ alle M re abk.

Die Seiten- und Unterarmnähte schließen, die Ärmel in die Armausschnitte nähen, die Knöpfe annähen.

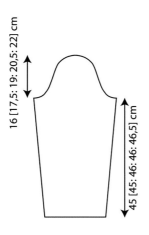

16 [17,5: 19: 20,5: 22] cm

45 [45: 46: 46: 46,5] cm

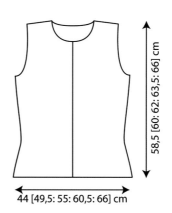

58,5 [60: 62: 63,5: 66] cm

44 [49,5: 55: 60,5: 66] cm

Stilt ••

Seite 14

Garn

Rowan Summerlite 4ply

A Seashell 437	6	x 50 g
B Periwinkle 424	4	x 50 g
C Navy Ink 429	3	x 50 g

Nadeln

1 Paar Nr. 2 ¾
1 Paar Nr. 3 ¼

Maschenprobe

34 M und 68 R = 10 x 10 cm, im Muster gestr mit Ndl Nr. 3 ¼.

Fertige Größe

Der Schal ist 45 cm breit und ca. 210 cm lang.

Streifenmuster A

R 1 und 2: Mit Fbe A
R 3 und 4: Mit Fbe B
R 5-12: Wie R 1-4, 2 x str.
R 13 und 14: Mit Fbe A
R 15 und 16: Mit Fbe C.
R 17-24: Wie R 13-16 2 x str.
Diese 24 R bilden das Streifenmuster A und werden fortlfd wdhl.

Streifenmuster B

R 1 und 2: Mit Fbe A
R 3 und 4: Mit Fbe B
R 5 –24: Wie R 1-4, 5 x str.
R 25 und 26: Mit Fbe A
R 27 und 28: Mit Fbe C.
R 29-48: Wie R 25-28, 5 x str.
Diese 48 R bilden das Streifenmuster B und werden fortlfd wdhl.

SCHAL

126 M mit Ndl Nr. 2 ¾ und Fbe A anschl.
Nach 5 R in kraus re enden mit einer Hinr.
R 6 (Rückr): 5 M re, 1 M zun, *4 M re, 1 M zun, 5 M re, 1 M zun, ab * wdhl bis zu den letzten 4 M, 4 M re = 153 M.
Wechseln zur Ndl Nr. 3 ¼.
Mit R 1 des Streifenmusters A wie folgt beg:

R 1 (Hinr): Mit Fbe A 1 M re, *1 M li abh (Fd liegt hinter der M), 1 M re, ab * wdhl bis zum Ende.
R 2: Mit Fbe A 1 M re, *1 M li abh (Fd liegt vor der M), 1 M re, ab * wdhl bis zum Ende.
R 3: Mit Fbe B 2 M re, *1 M li abh, 1 M re, ab * wdhl bis zur letzten M, 1 M re.
R 4: Mit Fbe B 2 M re, *1 M li abh, 1 M re, ab * wdhl bis zur letzten M, 1 M re.
Diese 4 R bilden das Muster A in R 1-4 des Streifenmusters.
Mit R 5 des Streifenmusters weiterstr, die 4 R des Musters fortlfd wdhl, nach weiteren 284 R enden mit R 24 des Streifenmusters A, enden mit einer Rückr.
Jetzt mit R 1 des Streifenmusters B beg, die 48 R werden 17 x wdhl, danach R 1-24 noch 1 x wdhl, enden mit einer Rückr = 840 R in Fbe B insgesamt.
Mit R 13 des Streifenmusters A beg und weitere 288 R str, enden mit R 12 des Streifenmusters, enden mit einer Rückr.
Fbe B und C abscheiden und nur noch mit Fbe A wie folgt str:
Wechseln zur Ndl Nr. 2 ¾.
Nächste R (Hinr): 4 M re, 2 M re zus-str, *3 M re, 2 M re zus-str, 4 M re, 2 M re zus-str, ab * wdhl bis zu den letzten 4 M, 4 M re = 126 M.
Nach weiteren 6 R in kraus re enden mit einer Hinr.
In der folg Rückr alle M re abk.

FERTIGSTELLUNG

Den Schal dämpfen, siehe Informationsseite.

Stingray ••

Seite 26

Größe

Passend für Oberweite

81-86	91-97	102-107	112-117	122-127	cm

Gestrickte Oberweite

94,5	105,5	116,5	127,5	138	cm

Garn

Rowan Summerlite DK

A Linen 460

9	10	11	12	13	x 50 g

B Rouge 462

1	1	1	1	1	x 50 g

C Mocha 451

1	1	1	1	1	x 50 g

D Plaster 452

1	1	1	1	1	x 50 g

Nadeln

1 Paar Nr. 3 ¼
1 Paar Nr. 3 ¾

Maschenprobe

22 M und 30 R = 10 x 10 cm, glatt re gestr mit Ndl Nr. 3 ¾

Streifenmuster für die Bündchen

R 1 und 2: Mit Fbe B
R 3 und 4: Mit Fbe C
R 5 und 6: Mit Fbe D
R 7 und 8: Mit Fbe A
R 9 und 10: Mit Fbe D
R 11 und 12: Mit Fbe C
R 13 und 14: Mit Fbe B
R 15 und 16: Mit Fbe C
R 17 und 18: Mit Fbe D
R 19 und 20: Mit Fbe A
R 21 und 22: Mit Fbe D
R 23 und 24: Mit Fbe C
R 25 und 26: Mit Fbe B
R 27 und 28: Mit Fbe C
R 29 und 30: Mit Fbe D
Diese 30 R bilden das Streifenmuster für die Bündchen.

Streifenmuster für die Halsblende

R 1 und 2: Mit Fbe D
R 3 und 4: Mit Fbe C
R 5 und 6: Mit Fbe B
R 7 und 8: Mit Fbe C
R 9 und 10: Mit Fbe D
R 11 und 12: Mit Fbe A
R 13 -36: Wie R 1-12, 2 x str
R 37 - 40: Wie R 1-4
R 41: Mit Fbe B
Diese 41 Runden bilden das Streifenmuster für die Halsblende.

RÜCKENTEIL

104 (116: 128: 140: 152) M mit Ndl Nr. 3 ¼ und Fbe A anschl.
R 1 (Hinr): 2 M re, ★1 M li, 2 M re, ab ★ wdhl bis zum Ende.
R 2: 2 M li, ★1 M re, 2 M li, ab ★ wdhl bis zum Ende.
Die beiden R bilden das Rippenmuster, weitere 2 R str, enden mit einer Rückr.
Wechseln zur Ndl Nr. 3 ¾, mit einer Rechtsr beg und fortlfd glatt re str.
Nach einer Länge von 35 (35,5: 36: 36,5: 37) cm enden mit einer Rückr.
Armausschnitte
Am Anf der nächsten 2 R je 4 (5: 6: 7: 8) M abk =96 (106: 116: 126: 136) M.
Nächste R (Hinr): 2 M re, 2 M re zus-str, re bis zu den letzten 4 M, **übzAbn**, 2 M re.
Nächste R: 2 M li, 2 M li verschr zus-str, li bis zu den letzten 4 M, 2 M li zus-str, 2 M li.
Alle Abn für die Armausschnittrundungen str wie in den letzten beiden R angegeben: In den nächsten 5 (7: 7: 9: 9) R bds je 1 M abn, danach 5 (5: 6: 6: 7) x in jeder folg 2. R bds je 1 M abn = 72 (78: 86: 92: 100) M.
Nach einer Armausschnittlänge von 21 (22,5: 24: 25,5: 27) cm enden mit einer Rückr.
Schulterschrägen und rückw Halsausschnitt
Nächste R (Hinr): 4 (5: 6: 7: 7) M abk, re str bis 18 (20: 22: 24: 27) M auf der re Ndl sind, Arbeit wenden, die restl M auf einer Hilfsndl stilllegen, beide Seiten getrennt beenden.
Alle Abn am Halsausschnitt genauso str wie die Abn am

Armausschnitt: Am Halsausschnitt in den nächsten 4 R je 1 M abn, **gleichzeitig** am Anf der 2. R 4 (5: 6: 7: 7) M abk und am Anf der folg 2. R 5 (5: 6: 7: 8) M abk.

Nach 1 R die restl 5 (6: 6: 6: 8) M abk.

Die stillgelegten M aufn, die mittl 28 (28: 30: 30: 32) M auf einer Hilfsndl stilllegen, mit neuem Fd in einer Hinr re bis zum Ende.

Die 2. Seite gegengleich beenden.

VORDERTEIL

Das Vorderteil genauso str wie das Rückenteil bis 16 (16: 18: 18: 20) R unterhalb des Beg der Schulterschrägen, enden mit einer Rückr.

Vord Halsausschnitt

Nächste R (Hinr): 25 (28: 32: 35: 39) M re, Arbeit wenden, die restl M auf einer Hilfsndl stilllegen, beide Seiten getrennt beenden.

Alle Abn am Halsausschnitt genauso str wie die Abn am Armausschnitt: Am Halsausschnitt in den nächsten 4 R je 1 M abn, danach 3 (3: 4: 4: 5) x in jeder folg 2. R je 1 M abn = 18 (21: 24: 27: 30) M.

Nach 5 R enden mit einer Rückr.

Schulterschräge

Am Anf der nächsten R und am Anf der folg 2. R je 4 (5: 6: 7: 7) M abk, und am Anf der folg 2. R 5 (5: 6: 7: 8) M abk.

Nach 1 R die restl 5 (6: 6: 6: 8) M abk.

Die stillgelegten M aufn, die mittl 22 M auf einer Hilfsndl stilllegen, mit neuem Fd in einer Hinr re str bis zum Ende.

Die 2. Seite gegengleich beenden.

ÄRMEL

42 (42: 46: 46: 50) M mit Ndl Nr. 3 ¼ und Fbe B anschl.

R 1 (Hinr): 1 (1: 0: 0: 2) M re, *1 M li, 2 M re, ab * wdhl bis zu den letzten 2 (2: 1: 1: 0) M, 1 (1: 1: 1: 0) M li, 1 (1: 0: 0: 0) M re.

R 2: 1 (1: 0: 0: 2) M li, *1 M re, 2 M li, ab * wdhl bis zu den letzten 2 (2: 1: 1: 0) M, 1 (1: 1: 1: 0) M re, 1 (1: 0: 0: 0) M li.

Die beiden R bilden das Rippenmuster, mit R 3 des Streifenmusters für das Bündchen beg, weiter im Rippenmuster str, dabei in der 3. R und 5 x in jeder folg 4. R bds je 1 M zun, danach 2 x in jeder folg 2. R, alle Zun im Musterverlauf str = 58 (58: 62: 62: 66) M.

Nach 1 R enden mit R 30 des Streifenmusters = Rückr.

Wechseln zur Ndl Nr. 3 ¾.

Mit Fbe A in einer Hinr beg und fortlfd glatt re weiterstr, nach 12 (8: 8: 6: 6) R enden mit einer Rückr.

Nächste R (Hinr): 3 M re, 1 M zun, re bis zu den letzten 3 M, 1 M zun, 3 M re.

Die seitl Zun wie angegeben in der 12. (8.: 8.: 6.: 6.) R und in jeder folg 12. (8.: 8.: 8.: 8.) R wie angegeben wdhl bis 74 (72: 72: 88: 92) M erreicht sind, danach in jeder folg – (10.:10.:–: –) R bds je 1 M zun bis – (80: 84: –: –) M erreicht sind.

Nach einer Länge von 46 (46: 47: 47: 47) cm enden mit einer Rückr.

Armkugel

Am Anf der nächsten 2 R je 4 (5: 6: 7: 8) M abk = 66 (70: 72: 74: 76) M.

Alle seitl Abn str wie bei den Armausschnitten angegeben: In den nächsten 5 R bds je 1 M abn, danach 4 x in jeder folg 2. R und 5 (5: 6: 7: 8) x in jeder folg 4. R bds je 1 M abn = 38 (42: 42: 42: 42) M.

Nach 1 R enden mit einer Rückr.

In der nächsten R und in jeder folg 2. R bds je 1 M abn bis 24 M

übrig sind, danach in den folg 3 R bds je 1 M abn, enden mit einer Rückr.

Die restl 18 M abk.

FERTIGSTELLUNG

Alle Teile dämpfen, siehe Informationsseite.

Die re Schulternaht schließen.

Halsblende

Von re mit Ndl Nr. 3 ¼ und Fbe D aus der li vord Halsausschnittkante 21 (21: 23: 23: 25) M aufn und re str, die 22 M auf der Hilfsndl in der vord Mitte re str, aus der re vord Halsausschnittkante 21 (21: 23: 23: 25) M aufn und re str, aus der re rückw Halsausschnittkante 6 M aufn und re str, die 28 (28: 30: 30: 32) M auf der Hilfsndl in der rückw Mitte re str und aus der li rückw Halsausschnittkante 6 M aufn und re str = 104 (104: 110: 110: 116) M.

Mit **R 2** des Streifenmusters und R 2 des Rippenmusters beg, weitere 40 R str, enden mit R 41 des Streifenmusters. In der folg Rückr mit Fbe B alle M abk.

Die li Schulternaht und die seitl Blendennaht schließen. Die Seiten- und Unterarmnähte schließen, die Ärmel in die Armausschnitte nähen.

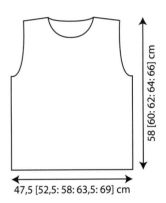

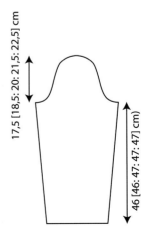

Tern •••

Seite 12

Größe

Passend für Oberweite

| 81-86 | 91-97 | 102-107 | 112-117 | 122-127 | cm |

Gestrickte Oberweite

| 94 | 104 | 114 | 124 | 134 | cm |

Garn

Rowan Summerlite 4ply

A Seashell 437

| 5 | 6 | 6 | 7 | 8 x | 50 g |

B Anchor Grey 446

| 1 | 1 | 1 | 1 | 1 | x 50 g |

Nadeln

1 Paar Nr. 2 ¼
1 Paar Nr. 3

Maschenprobe

28 M und 36 R = 10 10 cm, glatt re gestr mit Ndl Nr. 3.

RÜCKENTEIL

131 (145: 159: 173: 187) M mit Ndl Nr. 2 ¼ und Fbe A anschl.

Nach 10 R in kraus re wechseln zur Ndl Nr. 3.

Mit einer Rechtsr beg und glatt re weiterstr, nach 4 R enden mit einer Rückr.

Das Streifenmuster wie folgt str, die M des Zählmusters werdend in Intarsientechnik fortlfd glatt re gestr wie folgt:

R 1 (Hinr): Mit Fbe B 82 (89: 97: 104: 112) M re, die nächsten 11 M nach R 1 des Zählmusters, mit Fbe B 38 (45: 51: 58: 64) M re.

R 2: Mit Fbe B 38 (45: 51: 58: 64) M li, die nächsten 11 M nach R 2 des Zählmusters, mit Fbe B 82 (89: 97: 104: 112) M li.

Die beiden R platzieren das Muster, mit R 3 des Musters in folg Streifen weiterstr:

R 3 und 4: Mit Fbe B.
R 5-8: Mit Fbe A.
R 9-12: Mit Fbe B.
R 13-16: Mit Fbe A
R 17-20: Mit Fbe B.
R 21-26: Mit Fbe A:

Diese 26 R beenden das Streifenmuster und das Zickzackmuster.

Fbe B abschneiden und mit Fbe A glatt re weiterstr wie folgt:

★★ Nach einer Länge von 24 (24,5: 25: 25,5: 26) cm enden mit einer Rückr.

Armausschnitte

Am Anf der nächsten 2 R je 4 (5: 6: 7: 8) M abk = 123 (135: 147: 159: 171) M.

In den nächsten 9 (11: 13: 15: 17) R bds je 1 M abn, danach 3 x in jeder folg 2. R und 1 x in der folg 4. R bds je 1 M abn = 97 (105: 113: 121: 129) M.

Nach einer Armausschnittlänge von 18 (19,5: 21: 22,5: 24) cm enden mit einer Rückr.

Schulterschrägen und rückw Halsausschnitt

Nächste R (Hinr): 4 (5: 5: 6: 7) M abk, re str bis 22 (25: 28: 31: 33) M auf der re Ndl sind, Arbeit wenden, die restl M auf einer Hilfsndl stilllegen, beide Seiten getrennt beenden.

Am Halsausschnitt in den nächsten 4 R je 1 M abn, danach 1 x in der folg 2. R 1 M abn, **gleichzeitig** am Anf der 2. R und am Anf jeder folg 2. R 1 x 4 (5: 5: 6: 7) M abk, 1 x 4 (5: 6: 6: 7) M abk, 1 x 4 (5: 6: 7: 7) M abk und 1 x 5 (5: 6: 7: 7) M abk.

Die stillgelegten M aufn, die mittl 45 (45: 47: 47: 49) M auf einer Hilfsndl stilllegen, mit neuem Fd in einer Hinr re str bis zum Ende. Die 2. Seite gegengleich beenden.

VORDERTEIL

131 (145: 159: 173: 187) M mit Ndl Nr. 2 ¼ und Fbe A anschl.

Nach 10 R in kraus re wechseln zur Ndl Nr. 3.

Mit einer Rechtsr beg und glatt re weiterstr, nach 4 R enden mit einer Rückr.

Das Muster str wie beim Rückenteil angegeben:

R 1 (Hinr): Mit Fbe B 38 (45: 51: 58: 64) M re, die nächsten 11 M nach R 1 des Zählmusters, mit Fbe B 82 (89: 97: 104: 112) M re.

R 2: Mit Fbe B 82 (89: 97: 104: 112) M li, die nächsten 11 M nach R 2 des Zählmusters, mit Fbe B 38 (45: 51: 58: 64) M li.

Die beiden R platzieren das Muster, mit R 3 des Musters in folg Streifenmuster weiterstr:

R 3 und 4: Mit Fbe B.
R 5-8: Mit Fbe A.
R 9-12: Mit Fbe B.
R 13-16: Mit Fbe A
R 17-20: Mit Fbe B.
R 21-26: Mit Fbe A.

Diese 26 R beenden das Streifenmuster und das Zickzackmuster.

Fbe B abschneiden und mit Fbe A glatt re weiterstr so, wie beim Rückenteil ab ★★ angegeben bis 20 (20: 22: 22: 24) R unterhalb des Beg Schulterschrägen, enden mit einer Rückr.

Vord Halsausschnitt

Nächste R (Hinr): 32 (36: 40: 44: 48) M re, Arbeit wenden, die restl M auf einer Hilfsndl stilllegen, beide Seiten getrennt beenden. Am Halsausschnitt in den nächsten 8 R je 1 M abn, danach 2 (2: 3: 3: 4) x in jeder folg 2. R und 1 x in der folg 4. R je 1 M abn = 21 (25: 28: 32: 35) M.

Nach 3 R enden mit einer Rückr.

Schulterschräge

Am Anf der nächsten R und 3 (3: 1: 2: 3) x in jeder folg 2. R je 4 (5: 5: 6: 7) M abk, danach – (–: 2: 1: –) x in jeder folg 2. R je – (–: 6: 7: –) M abk.

Nach 1 R die restl 5 (5: 6: 7: 7) M abk.

Die stillgelegten M aufn, die mittl 33 M auf einer Hilfsndl stilllegen, mit neuem Fd in einer Hinr re bis zum Ende.

Die 2. Seite gegengleich beenden.

ÄRMEL

53 (55: 57: 59: 61) M mit Ndl Nr. 2 ¼ und Fbe A anschl.

Nach 10 R in kraus re wechseln zur Ndl Nr. 3.

Mit einer Rechtsr beg und 4 R glatt re str, enden mit einer Rückr.

Das Muster und die Farben wie folgt einteilen:

R 1 (Hinr): Mit Fbe B in der 1. M 1 M zun, 20 (21: 22: 23: 24) M re, die nächsten 11 M nach R 1 des Zählmusters, mit Fbe B 20 (21: 22: 23: 24) M re, in der letzten M 1 M zun = 55 (57: 59: 61: 63) M.

R 2: Mit Fbe B 22 (23: 24: 25: 26) M li, die nächsten 11 M nach R 2 des Zählmusters, mit Fbe B 22 (23: 24: 25: 26) M li.

R 3: Mit Fbe B 22 (23: 24: 25: 26) M re, die nächsten 11 M nach R 3 des Zählmusters, mit Fbe B 22 (23: 24: 25: 26) M re.

R 4: Mit Fbe B 22 (23: 24: 25: 26) M li, die nächsten 11 M nach R 4 des Zählmusters, mit Fbe B 22 (23: 24: 25: 26) M li.

R 5: Mit Fbe A 0 (1: 1: 1: 1) x (in der 1. M 1 M zun), 22 (23: 24: 25: 26) M re, die nächsten 11 M nach R 5 des Zählmusters, mit Fbe A 22 (23: 24: 25: 26) M re, 0 (1: 1: 1: 1) x (in der letzten M 1 M zun) = 55 (59: 61: 63: 65) M.

R 6: Mit Fbe A 22 (24: 25: 26: 27) M li, die nächsten 11 M nach R 6 des Zählmusters, mit Fbe A 22 (24: 25: 26: 27) M li.

R 7: Mit Fbe A 1 (0: 0: 0: 0) x (in der 1. M 1 M zun), 21 (24: 25: 26: 27) M re, die nächsten 11 M nach R 7 des Zählmusters, mit Fbe A 21 (24: 25: 26: 27) M re, 1 (0: 0: 0: 0) x (in der letzten M 1 M zun) = 57 (59: 61: 63: 65) M.

R 8: Mit Fbe A 23 (24: 25: 26: 27) M li, die nächsten 11 M nach R 8 des Zählmusters, mit Fbe A 23 (24: 25: 26: 27) M li.

R 9: Mit Fbe A 0 (1: 1: 1: 1) x (in der 1. M 1 M zun), 23 (23: 24: 25: 26) M re, die nächsten 11 M nach R 9 des Zählmusters, mit Fbe A 23 (23: 24: 25: 26) M re, 0 (1: 1: 1: 1) x in der letzten M 1 M zun = 57 (61: 63: 65: 67) M.

R 10: Mit Fbe A 23 (25: 26: 27: 28) M li, die nächsten 11 M nach R 10 des Zählmusters, mit Fbe A 23 (25: 26: 27: 28) M li.

Diese 10 R beenden das Streifenmuster und das Zickzackmuster, Fbe B abschneiden und nur noch mit Fbe A glatt re str wie folgt:

In der 3. R und in jeder folg 6. (4.: 4.: 4.: 4.) R bds je 1 M zun bis 83 (65: 71: 85: 99) M erreicht sind, danach in jeder folg 8. (6.: 6.: 6.: 6.) R bds je 1 M zun bis 87 (93: 97: 103: 109) M erreicht sind.

Nach einer Länge von 35 (35: 36: 36: 36) cm enden mit einer Rückr.

Armkugel

89: 93) M.

In den nächsten 5 R bds je 1 M abn, danach 5 x in jeder folg 2. R und 2 (3: 5: 5: 6) x in jeder folg 4. R bds je 1 M abn = 55 (57: 55: 59: 61) M.

1 R str.

In der nächsten R und in jeder folg 2. R bds je 1 M abn bis 37 M übrig sind, und in den folg 7 R bds je 1 M abn, enden mit einer Rückr.

Die restl 23 M abk.

FERTIGSTELLUNG

Alle Teile dämpfen, siehe Informationsseite.

Die re Schulternaht schließen.

Halsblende

Von re mit Ndl Nr. 2 ¼ und Fbe A aus der li vord Halsausschnittkante 22 (22: 24: 24: 26) M aufn und re str, die 33 M auf der Hilfsndl in der vord Mitte re str, aus der re vord Halsausschnittkante 22 (22: 24: 24: 26) M aufn und re str, aus der re rückw Halsausschnittkante 7 M aufn und re str, die 45 (45: 47: 47: 49) M auf der Hilfsndl im Rückenteil re str und aus der li rückw Halsausschnittkante 7 M aufn und re str = 136 (136: 142: 142: 148) M.

Nach 10 R in kraus re in der folg Rückr alle M re abk.

Die li Schulternaht und die seitl Blendennaht schließen.

Die Seiten- und Unterarmnähte schließen, die Ärmel in die Armausschnitte nähen.

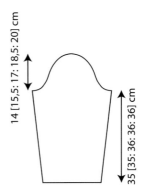

Rücken- und Vorderteil

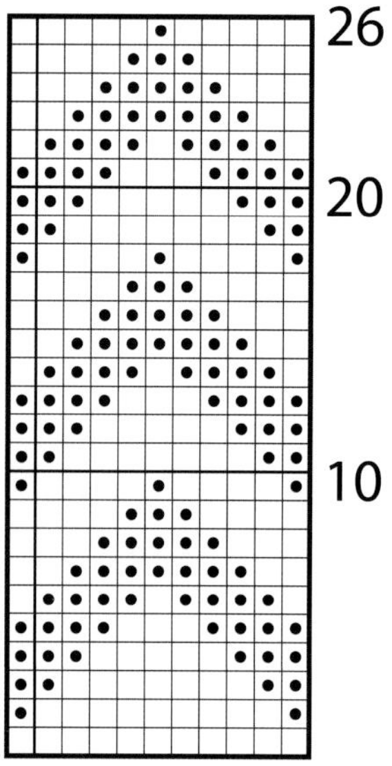

26

20

10

Ärmel

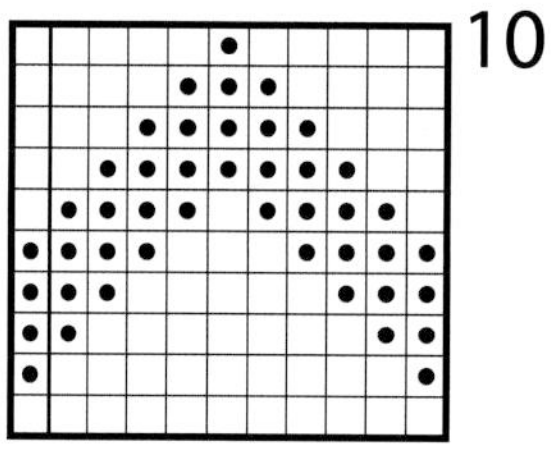

10

Legende

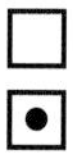

☐
⊡

Wenn Sie ein Rowan Modell stricken und tragen wollen, wünschen wir, dass es gut aussieht und Sie sich darin wohl fühlen. Das alles beginnt mit der Wahl der richtigen Größe. Wir helfen Ihnen, eine erfahrene Stricker/in zu werden, weswegen wir uns die im Heft angegebenen Größen der Damen- und Herrenmodelle angesehen haben. Im Resultat sehen Sie unten eine Einführung in unsere neue Maßtabelle mit speziellen Hinweisen.

Unsere Größen beruhen auf den Standardgrößen der Fertigkonfektionen. Wenn Sie Konfektionsgröße 38 tragen, dann ist in der Anleitung die Größe M richtig.

Die Herrengrößen sind jetzt angegeben von XS bis 2 XL, das entspricht einem Brustumfang von 97 – 127 cm.

Außerdem haben wir jetzt noch eine UNISEX Größe angegeben. Es sind die gleichen Größen wie bei den Herren Standardgrößen angegeben, hinzu kommt noch XXS.

Die in den untenstehenden Listen angegebenen Größen sind immer Körpergrößen, und nicht die gestrickten Größen, so sollen Ihnen die Maßtabellen dabei behilflich sein, die richtige Größe zu finden.

STANDARD DAMENGRÖSSEN

Zusätzlich zu den Standardgrößen sind die einzelnen Konfektionsgrößen angegeben d.h. Größe M entspricht Größe 38.

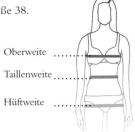

UK SIZE	S	M	L	XL	XXL	
EUR Größe	36-38	38-40	40-42	42-44	44-46	
Oberweite	81 – 86	91 - 97	102 – 107	112 – 117	122 – 127	cm
Taillenweite	61 – 66	71 – 76	81 – 86	91 – 97	102 – 107	cm
Hüftwweite	86 – 91	97 – 102	107 – 112	117 – 122	127 – 132	cm

Oberweite ....

Taillenweite ....

Hüftweite ....

RICHTIGES MASSNEHMEN

Für maximalen Tragekomfort und korrekte Passform beachten Sie bitte folgende Tipps.
Messen Sie Ihre Größen eng am Körper über der Unterwäsche, das Maßband dabei nicht zu fest ziehen.

Oberweite: Die Oberweite wird über der breitesten Stelle der Brust gemessen und den Schulterblättern gemessen.
Taille: Die Taille wird direkt über dem Hüftknochen in der natürlich verlaufenden Taille gemessen.
Hüfte: Die Hüfte wird über der breitesten Stelle der Hüfte gemrssen.

Wenn Sie selbst nicht Maß nehmen können, dann nehmen Sie Ihren Lieblingspullover. Unsere Maße entsprechen der handelsüblichen Konfektionen, wenn also Ihr Lieblingspullover die Größe 38 hat, müsste Größe M ungefähr die gleichen Maße haben.

Um sicher zu gehen, dass Ihr Lieblinspullover und die angegebenen Größen in der Rowan Maßtabelle übereinstimmen, vergleichen Sie die Zahlen mit den individuellen Anleitungen.

Schließlich, wenn Sie die richtige Größe gefunden haben, empfehlen wir Ihnen, eine Maschenprobe für jedes Modell anzufertigen, das Sie stricken möchten.
Sollte die Maschenprobe zu locker sein, wird das Strickstück größer und die angegebene Wollmenge reicht nicht aus, ist sie zu fest, wird das Strickstück zu eng und es bleibt Wolle übrig.

Hinzu kommt, dass, wenn die Maschenprobe nicht korrekt ist, das Strickstück entweder zu fest oder zu locker wird. Es ist wirklich wichtig, vor dem Beginn eines Projektes eine exakte Maschenprobe anzufertigen.

GRÖSSEN UND HINWEIS ZU DEN DIAGRAMMEN

Die Anleitungen werden immer für die kleinste Größe geschrieben. Wenn die Zahlen abweichen, stehen die Zahlen für die nächsten Größen in Klammern hinter der kleinsten Größe. Steht nur eine Zahl da, bezieht sie sich auf alle Größen. Zu allen Anleitungen finden Sie unten rechts ein Schnittdiagramm, es zeigt die Maße für das fertige Modell an. Die Zahlen am unteren Rand beziehen sich auf die Breite 2,5 cm unterhalb der

Armausschnitte. Um ihre richtige Größe zu finden, sollten Sie erst in der Maßtabelle Ihre Maße mit den angegebenen Zahlen vergleichen. Generell ist der untere Rand eines Modells genauso breit wie die Oberweite. Allerdings haben manche Designs eine A-Form oder einen abgerundeten Rand, dann kann der Rand breiter sein als die angegebene Oberweite.

Armausschnitttiefe

Unterarm gemessen vom unteren rand des Bündchens bis zum Beginn der Armkugel

Länge gemessen von der seitlichen Halsausschnittkante bis zum unteren Rand des Büündchens

Brustumfang gemessen 2,5 cm unterhalb des Beginn der Armausschnittkante

Maschenprobe

Die Einhaltung der richtigen Maschenprobe ist wahrscheinlich der wichtigste Faktor, der den Unterschied zwischen einem gelungenen Meisterwerk und einem verpatzten Kleidungsstück ausmacht. Form und Größe, aber auch Fall und Sitz des Gestrickten hängen von ihr ab, daher können bereits kleinste Abweichungen die Gesamtwirkung zerstören.

Am Anfang jeder Anleitung steht die tatsächliche Maschenprobe des Designers und diese müssen Sie einhalten. Es kann sogar sein, daß für ein Strickstück mehrere Maschenproben genannt werden, wenn Teile der Arbeit in Intarsientechnik, andere Teile glatt rechts und wieder andere in Jacquard-Technik gestrickt sind. Wir raten Ihnen dringend eine Strickprobe im jeweiligen Muster zu stricken, die 5-10 Maschen breiter und 5-10 Reihen länger ist als in der Maschenprobe angegeben. Legen Sie diese Strickprobe flach auf den Tisch und messen Sie sie in ihrer Mitte ab. Wenn Sie zu viele Maschen auf 10 cm zählen, stricken Sie eine neue Maschenprobe, bei der Sie dickere Nadeln verwenden. Zählen Sie weniger Maschen auf 10 cm, versuchen Sie es noch einmal mit dünneren Nadeln. Die Angaben über Nadelstärken in den Anleitungen sind nur sehr ungenaue Orientierungshilfen, da jeder eine andere Fadenspannung hat und die Maschen dadurch von Person zu Person unterschiedlich groß werden.

Größen

Bei vielen Anleitungen sind mehrere Größen angegeben. Steht nur eine Zahl da, gilt sie für alle Größen, sind mehrere Zahlen hintereinander angegeben, gilt die erste für die kleinste Größe und die restlichen in Klammern jeweils für die dann folgenden größeren Größen. Die kleine Schnittzeichnung am Ende jeder Anleitung zeigt die fertig gestrickten Maße, außerdem finden Sie eine genaue Größentabelle auf der vorherigen Seite.

Zählmuster

Einige der Modelle in diesem Heft werden nach einem Zählmuster gearbeitet. Darin steht jedes Kästchen für eine Masche und jede Kästchenreihe für eine Strickreihe. Beim Stricken nach den Zählmustern werden die Hinreihen von rechts nach links gelesen und gestrickt, die Rückreihen von links nach rechts, falls nicht anders angegeben. Jede verwendete Farbe ist durch ein eigenes Symbol oder einen eigenen Buchstaben gekennzeichnet. Zur Erleichterung der Arbeit können Sie das Diagramm vergrößert fotokopieren und die benötigte Größe, auch im Text, farbig markieren.

Lochmuster

Beim Lochmuster müssen immer ebenso viele Umschläge gestrickt werden, wie Maschen zusammen gestrickt werden. Sollten, bedingt durch die seitlichen Ab- oder Zunahmen für die Formgebung an den Rändern nicht mehr genügend Maschen für eine vollständige Musterfolge vorhanden sein, werden die restlichen Maschen solange glatt rechts gestrickt, bis wieder genug Maschen für eine Musterfolge vorhanden sind. Eine Hilfe ist es, links und rechts des vollständigen Musters je einen Markierungsring einzuhängen.

Stricken mit Farben

Für das Arbeiten mit Fraben gibt es zwei Haupttechniken: Intarsientechnik und Norweger- oder Fair-Isle Technik. Mit der ersten Technik erhalten Sie einen einlagigen Stoff und sie wird meist nur dann verwendet, wenn Farbe an einer bestimmten Stelle gestrickt wird. Die Norweger- oder Fair-Isle Technik hingegen produziert einen dickeren Stoff, da mehr als eine Farbe durchgehend über die ganze Reihe gestrickt wird.

Intarsientechnik

Am einfachsten geht es, wenn man für jedes Motiv oder für jedes Farbfeld kürzere Fäden der benötigten Farben abschneidet (je nach Größe des Motivs 50 cm bis 3 m lange Fäden, die auf der Rückseite hängen bleiben, wenn sie nicht benötigt werden), – so verhindert man, dass sich die Knäuel verknoten. Bei jedem Farbwechsel innerhalb der Reihe werden die Fäden miteinander verkreuzt, damit keine Löcher entstehen. Die Enden der Fäden können am Schluss entlang der Farbwechsel vernäht oder beim Stricken "eingewebt" werden. Das Einweben erfolgt nach dem gleichen Prinzip wie das Einweben bei der Norwegertechnik, und erspart das zeitraubende Vernähen der Fäden. Bei der Intarsientechnik ist zu beachten, dass die Maschenprobe von einer glatt rechts gestrickten einfarbigen Maschenprobe abweichen kann.

Norweger- oder Fair-Isle Technik

Wenn zwei oder drei Farben im Laufe einer Reihe ständig wiederholt werden, nehmen Sie den oder die gerade nicht benötigten Fäden locker gespannt auf der Rückseite der Arbeit mit. Wenn Sie mit mehr als zwei Farben arbeiten, behandeln Sie die mitgeführten Fäden wie einen einzigen Faden und dehnen Sie die Maschen immer wieder auf ihre richtige Weite aus, damit die Fäden locker genug, aber nicht zu locker hängen. Spannen Sie die mitgeführten Fäden nie über mehr als drei Maschen, sondern geben Sie den Spannfäden Halt, indem Sie sie bei jeder 2. oder 3. Masche einweben, d. h. umfassen Sie sie abwechselnd unter und über dem Arbeitsfaden. Dadurch werden sie auf der Rückseite der Arbeit festgehalten.

Fertigstellung

Nachdem so viele Stunden an einem Strickstück gestrickt wurde, ist es schade, dass so viele Modelle durch die falsche Behandlung beim Bügeln verdorben werden. Hier einige Tipps für eine wirklich perfekte Konfektionierung.

Dämpfen

Nach Abschluss der Arbeit werden alle Fäden vernäht und alle Strickteile einzeln auf einer weichen Unterlage mit rostfreien Stecknadeln aufgesteckt (oberhalb der eventuellen Rippenmusterbereiche) und mit einem feuchten Tuch bedeckt. Wenn das Tuch trocken ist, ist die Arbeit auf sanfte Art in Form gebracht, ohne dabei ihr Volumen und ihre lebendige Struktur zu verlieren, wie das beim vielfach empfohlenen Bügeln unter einem feuchten Tuch leicht der Fall ist. Beachten Sie auch immer die Hinweise auf der Banderole.

Zusammennähen

Beim Zusammennähen der Teile achten Sie auf genaue Übereinstimmung der Farben. Sie können die Teile sehr sorgfältig von links mit Steppstichen (besonders Armkugel und schräge Schulternähte) verbinden oder von rechts im Matratzenstich zusammennähen. Dieser empfiehlt sich besonders bei geraden Nähten, Bündchen und feinteiligen Farbmustern. Für die Befestigung von Blenden und Taschenbeuteln auf der Innenseite eines Strickstücks ist vielfach der Maschenstich die unauffälligste Lösung.

Für die Ärmel gibt es verschiedene Methoden des Einsetzens.

Beim **Ärmel ohne Armkugel** wird der Ärmel mit der Mitte der oberen Ärmelkante auf die Schulternaht geheftet und in der angegebenen Armausschnitthöhe am Vorder- und Rückenteil eingenäht, danach werden die Ärmel- und Seitennähte geschlossen.

Beim **Ärmel mit L-Ausschnitt** wird die Mitte der oberen Ärmelkante auf die Schulternaht geheftet und der Ärmel bis zum Beginn der Abnahmen für die Armausschnitte in die Armausschnittkante eingenäht. Anschließend werden die letzten geraden Reihen des Ärmels mit den Abnahmen der Armausschnittkante verbunden.

Beim **Ärmel mit Armkugel** werden zuerst die Seitennähte von Vorder- und Rückenteil geschlossen. Die Mitte der Armkugel wird auf die Schulternaht geheftet, danach wird der Ärmel mit eingehaltener Weite in den Armausschnitt genäht.

Die Seiten- und Unterarmnähte schließen.
Die Taschenblenden und Taschenbeutel festnähen.
Die Knöpfe in Höhe der Knopflöcher festnähen. Gerippte Bündchen oder Halsblenden sowie kraus rechts gestrickte Abschnitte dürfen nicht gedämpft werden.

Abkürzungen

Abk	abketten
abn	abnehmen
Anf	Anfang
anschl	anschlagen
arb	arbeiten
bds	beidseitig
Fbe	Farbe
Hinr	Hinreihe
li	links
M	Masche
mark	markieren
Ndl	Nadel
Nr.	Nummer
R	Reihe
Rde	Runde
re	rechts
Rückr	Rückreihe
seitl	seitlich
str	stricken
U	Umschlag
verschr	verschränkt
vord	vordere
wdhl	wiederholen
ZN	Zopfnadel
zun	zunehmen
zus-str	zusammenstricken

Abkürzungen in den Häkelanleitungen

Wlm	Eine Lm die nach dem Wenden der Arbeit oder am Anf einer R gehäkelt wird, diese Lm zählt nicht als M;
Lm	Luftmasche
Fm	Feste Masche
Km	Kettmasche
St	einfaches Stäbchen
DST	ein doppeltes Stäbchen.
Lm-Zw	Luftmaschenzwischenraum

Experience Bewertungen

• = Für Anfänger
Für Anfänger mit Grundkenntnissen geeignet, gerade Passform mit unkomplizierter Maschentechnik.

• • = Einfache Technik
Einfache, unkomplizierte Stricktechnik mit einer
Einweisung in verschiedene Schnitttechniken bei
der Fertigung von Strickstücken.

• • • = Schwierige Techniken
Für erfahrenere Stricker, die gerne anspruchsvollere Techniken mit mehrfarbigen Mustern verwenden.

• • • • = Für Fortgeschrittene
Für Stricker, die gerne nach Schnitten mit herausfordernden Techniken und Mustern arbeiten.

Alle im Magazin angegebenen Knöpfe und Bänder sind erhältlich bei

Groves & Banks
Eastern Bypass
Thame
Oxfordshire
OX9 3FU
www.grovesltd.co.uk
groves@stockistenquiries.co.uk

Bedecked Haberdashery
Bedecked Haberdashery
The Coach House
Barningham Park
RICHMOND
DL11 7DW
Tel: +44 (0)1833 621 451
eMail:Judith.lewis@bedecked.co.uk
www.bedecked.co.uk

Hinweise zur Pflege

Sie haben sicher bemerkt, dass sich in der letzten Saison die Symbole zur Pflege auf den Banderolen und Farbkarten geändert haben. Wir haben die Symbole aktualisiert, sie sollen Ihnen eine Hilfe sein zur weiteren Pflege für Ihre gestrickten oder gehäkelten Modelle. Unten sehen Sie die Symbole mit einer kurzen Erklärung.

Symbole für die Waschmaschine

Symbole für die Handwäsche

Symbole für chemisches Reinigen

Symbole zum Bügeln

Symbol für das Verwenden von Bleichmitteln

Symbole für den Trockner

AUSTRALIA: Australian Country Spinners, Pty Ltd, Level 7, 409 St. Kilda Road, Melbourne Vic 3004.
Tel: 03 9380 3888   Fax: 03 9820 0989   Email: customerservice@auspinners.com.au

Morris and Sons 50 York Street, Sydney NSW 2000
Tel: 02 92998588

Morris and Sons Level 1, 234 Collins Street, Melbourne Vic 3000
Tel: 03 9654 0888

AUSTRIA: MEZ Harlander GmbH, Schulhof 6, 1. Stock, 1010 Wien, Austria
Tel: + 00800 26 27 28 00   Fax: (00) 49 7644 802-133
Email: verkauf.harlander@mezcrafts.com

BELGIUM: MEZ crafts Belgium NV, c/o MEZ GmbH, Haupstasse, Herbolzheim 79336, Germany
Tel: 0032 (0) 800 77 89 2   Fax: 00 49 7644 802 133
Email: sales.be-nl@mezcrafts.com

BULGARIA: MEZ Crafts Bulgaria EOOD, 25A Rozhen Blvd, 1220 Sofia, Bulgaria
Tel: (+359 2) 439 24 24   Fax: (+359 2) 976 77 20   Email: office.bg@mezcrafts.com

CANADA: Sirdar USA Inc. 406 20th Street SE, Hickory, North Carolina, USA 28602
Tel: 828 404 3705   Fax: 828 404 3707   Email: sirdarusa@sirdar.co.uk

CHINA: Commercial agent Mr Victor Li, c/o MEZ GmbH, Haupstrasse 78, 79336 Herbolzheim, Germany
Tel: (+86-21) 13816681825   Email: victor.li@mezcrafts.com

CHINA: Shanghai Yujun CO.LTD., Room 701 Wangjiao Plaza, No.175 Yan'an (E), 200002 Shanghai, China
Tel: (+86-21) 63739785   Email: jessechang@vip.163.com

CYPRUS: MEZ Crafts Bulgaria EOOD, 7 Magnaurska Shkola Str., BG-1784 Sofia, Bulgaria
Tel: (+359 2) 439 34 24   Fax: (+359 2) 976 77 20   Email: office.bg@mezcrafts.com

CZECH REPUBLIC: MEZ Crafts Czech Republic s.r.o.. Na poříčí 1079/3a, Praha,110 00
Tel: (420) 461 616 633   Email: info@mezcrafts-cz.cz

DENMARK: Carl J. Permin A/S Egegaardsvej 28 DK-2610 Rødovre
Tel: (45) 36 36 89 89   Email: permin@permin.dk

ESTONIA: MEZ Crafts Estonia OÜ, Helgi tee 2, Peetri alevik, 75312 Harjumaa, Talinn
Tel: +372 630 6759   Email: info.ee@mezcrafts.com

FINLAND: Prym Consumer Finland Oy, Huhtimontie 6, FI-04200 Kerava
Tel: +358 9 274871

FRANCE: 3bcom, 35 avenue de Larrieu, 31094 Toulouse, France
Tel: 0033 (0) 562 202 096   Email: Commercial@3b-com.com

GERMANY: MEZ GmbH, Haupstrasse 78, 79336 Herbolzheim, Germany
Tel: +49 (0) 7643 33 30 288   Email: endverbraucherservice@mezcrafts.com
Fax: 0049 7644 802 300

GREECE: MEZ Crafts Bulgaria EOOD, 7 Magnaurska Shkola Str., BG-1784 Sofia, Bulgaria
Tel: (+359 2) 439 24 24   Fax: (+359 2) 976 77 20   Email: office.bg@mezcrafts.com

HOLLAND: G. Brouwer & Zn B.V., Oudhuijzerweg 69, 3648 AB Wilnis
Tel: 0031 (0) 297-281 557   Email: info@gbrouwer.nl

HONG KONG: East Unity Company Ltd, Unit B2, 7/F., Block B, Kailey Industrial Centre, 12 Fung Yip Street, Chai Wan
Tel: (852)2869 7110   Email: eastunityco@yahoo.com.hk

ICELAND: Carl J. Permin A/S Egegaardsvej 28, DK-2610 Rødovre
Tel: (45) 36 36 89 89   Email: permin@permin.dk

ITALY: Mez Cucirini Italy Srl, Via Milanese 20, Sesto San Giovanni - Milano 20099
Tel: 0039 0264109080   Email: servizio.clienti@mezcrafts.com   Fax: 02 64109080

JAPAN: Hobbyra Hobbyre Corporation, 23-37, 5-Chome, Higashi-Ohi, Shinagawa-Ku, 1400011 Tokyo.   Tel: +81334721104

KOREA: My Knit Studio, 3F, 144 Gwanhun-Dong, 110-300 Jongno-Gu, Seoul
Tel: 82-2-722-0006   Email: myknit@myknit.com

LATVIA: Latvian Crafts, 12-2, Jurğu street, LV-2011
Tel: +371 37 126326825   Email: vjelkins@latviancrafts.lv

LEBANON: y.knot, Saifi Village, Mkhalissiya Street 162, Beirut
Tel: (961) 1 992211   Fax: (961) 1 315553   Email: y.knot@cyberia.net.lb

LITHUANIA: MEZ Crafts Lithuania UAB, A. Juozapaviciaus str. 6/2, LT-09310 Vilnius
Tel: +370 5207 2002   Fax: +370 527 2305   Email: info.lt@mezcrafts.com

LUXEMBOURG: MEZ GmbH, Haupstrasse 78, 79336 Herbolzheim, Germany
Tel: +49 (0) 7643 33 30 288   Email: endverbraucherservice@mezcrafts.com

MEXICO: Estambres Crochet SA de CV, Calle 1° de Mayo # 230 Interior 8, Col. Trabajadores, 64650 Santa Catarina
Tel: +52 (81) 8335-3870   Email: abremer@redmundial.com.mx

NEW ZEALAND: ACS New Zealand, P.O Box 76199, Northwood, Christchurch, New Zealand
Tel: 64 3 323 6665   Fax: 64 3 323 6660   Email: lynn@impactmg.co.nz

NORWAY: Carl J. Permin A/S Selma Ellefsensvei 6, 2610, Rødovre
Tel: (45) 36 36 89 89   E-mail: permin@permin.dk

PORTUGAL: Mez Crafts Portugal, Lda, Av. Vasco da Gama, 774 - 4431-059 V.N, Gaia, Portugal
Tel: 00 351 223 770700   Email: sales.iberia@mezcrafts.com

RUSSIA: Family Hobby, Zelenograd, Haus 1505, Raum III, 124683, Moskau
Tel.: 007 (499) 270-32-47 Handtel. 007 916 213 74 04 Email: tv@fhobby.ru
Web: www.family-hobby.ru

SINGAPORE: Golden Dragon Store, 101 Upper Cross St. #02-51, People's Park Centre
Tel: (65) 65358454 /65358234   Email: gdscraft@hotmail.com

SLOVAKIA: MEZ Crafts Slovakia, s.r.o. Seberíniho 1, 821 03 Bratislava, Slovakia
Tel: +421 2 32 30 31 19   Email: info@mezcrafts-sk.sk

SOUTH AFRICA: Arthur Bales LTD, 62 4th Avenue, Linden 2195
Tel: (27) 11 888 2401   Fax: (27) 11 782 6137   Email: arthurb@new.co.za

SPAIN: MEZ Fabra Spain S.A, Avda Meridiana 354, pta 4B, 08027 Barcelona
Tel: +34 932908400   Fax: +34 932908400   Email: atencion.clientes@mezcrafts.com

SWEDEN: Carl J. Permin A/S Skaraborgsvägen 35C, 3tr, 50 630, Rødovre
Tel: (45) 36 36 89 89   E-mail: permin@permin.dk

SWITZERLAND: MEZ Crafts Switzerland GmbH, c/o Puplicitas AG, Mürtenstrasse 39, 8048, Zürich Switzerland www.mezcrafts.com

TAIWAN: Cactus Quality Co Ltd, 7FL-2, No. 140, Sec.2 Roosevelt Rd, Taipei, 10084 Taiwan, R.O.C.
Tel: 00886-2-23656527   Fax: 886-2-23656503   Email: cqcl@ms17.hinet.net

THAILAND: Global Wide Trading, 10 Lad Prao Soi 88, Bangkok 10310
Tel: 00 662 933 9019   Fax: 00 662 933 9110   Email: global.wide@yahoo.com

U.S.A.: Sirdar USA Inc. 406 20th Street SE, Hickory, North Carolina, USA 28602
Tel: 001 828 404 3705   Fax: 828 404 3707   Email: sirdarusa@sirdar.co.uk

U.K: Mez Crafts U.K, 17F Brooke's Mill, Armitage Bridge, Huddersfield, HD4 7NR
Tel: 01484 950630   Web: www.mezcrafts.com

For more stockists in all countries please logon to www.knitrowan.com